HIS HIDING PLACE
IS DARKNESS

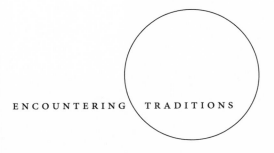

ENCOUNTERING TRADITIONS

Stanley Hauerwas, Peter Ochs, Randi Rashkover, and Maria Dakake

EDITORS

HIS HIDING PLACE IS DARKNESS

A Hindu-Catholic Theopoetics
of Divine Absence

FRANCIS X. CLOONEY, S.J.

STANFORD UNIVERSITY PRESS
STANFORD, CALIFORNIA

Stanford University Press
Stanford, California

Printed in the United States of America on acid-free, archival-quality paper

Library of Congress Cataloging-in-Publication Data

Clooney, Francis X. (Francis Xavier), 1950– author.
  His hiding place is darkness : a Hindu-Catholic theopoetics of divine absence /
Francis X. Clooney, S.J.
     pages cm -- (Encountering traditions)
  Includes bibliographical references and index.
   ISBN 978-0-8047-7680-6 (cloth : alk. paper) --
   ISBN 978-0-8047-7681-3 (pbk. : alk. paper)
  1. Hidden God--Comparative studies. 2. Namma_lvar. Tiruvaymo_li. 3. Bible. Song
of Solomon--Criticism, interpretation, etc. 4. Vaishnavism--Hymns--History and
criticism. 5. Christianity and other religions--Hinduism. 6. Hinduism--Relations--
Christianity. I. Title. II. Series: Encountering traditions.
   BT180.H54C56 2013
   261.2'45--dc23
                              2013026233
Typeset by Bruce Lundquist in 10/14 Minion

When Nampillai was teaching the *Holy Word*, there was a man who listened attentively to his lectures on the first three songs. But the fourth song was about a woman bereft of her beloved, sending messengers from her garden. Hearing this, the man walked away, complaining, "This is nothing but romance." Nampillai commented, "That man is unfortunate. This is the song that shows what the Upanishad means where it says, "One must meditate."

Nampillai

I feel the Lord visits me all the more often as He realizes I need visitations of this kind more frequently. If between these visitations, anyone asks me, still numb from the feelings of devotion experienced a few days past, and complaining of my Lord's delay, where He has gone or turned aside, the only ready answer I can find is: "He has made darkness His hiding place" (Psalm 18.11). A cloud, not of light but of darkness, has taken Him from my eyes, and now that my love has grown so cold again, I feel I have good reason to fear that perhaps, after all, He has turned away from His servant in anger.

John of Ford

God's absence is something tricky, perhaps impossible, to tell. This writer will have to invoke a God who arrives bringing her own absence with her—a God whose Farness is the more Near. It is an impossible motion possible only in writing.

Anne Carson

It's the old idea that the only way to experience faith is through active doubt. You have to undertake the encounter with the "monument," and it has to remain essentially unknowable. The desire to apprehend it, the act or attempt at apprehension, description—and the failure of that attempt—is the beginning, as she says, of imagination, of art.

Jorie Graham

CONTENTS

PROLOGUE

Love and the absence of the beloved matter most, but *His Hiding Place Is Darkness: A Hindu-Catholic Theopoetics of Divine Absence* is first of all a reading of the biblical *Song of Songs* (*Shir ha-Shirim*) and the Hindu *Holy Word of Mouth* (*Tiruvaymoli*).[1] All that follows is entirely in the debt of this biblical and Hindu poetry, and proceeds as reflection more particularly on the experience of a woman whose beloved has not returned and seems nowhere to be found. It is this experience of love and absence that in more than one culture has been taken to manifest what loving God is all about. It is a drama of love and loss that has been written about abundantly, over and again.[2] In this reading, therefore, I attend especially to the absence of the beloved as this has been imagined, suffered, and turned back into presence in several strands of Hindu and Christian tradition. I do so in order to write about the real God who can be absent, a real beloved whose real absence makes life impossible. But it is also true that this absence is a particularly powerful site for encounter with God.

To encounter (or not) the God who at times hides from us may be first of all recognized as an intimate event, personal to the seeker, even private. But the absence of God is also a matter of public concern and interest, in an age when a multitude of religious possibilities abound and when any particular religious love stands near to religious and secular alternatives. As such, the particularity of God and the possibility that God is real enough to be absent are also matters of public import, if we are still to think and talk about God in an intelligent way.

Quite apart from arguments about the existence or importance of God, there is room here the work of the imagination: for the individual and for society, God may be most real when it is uncomfortably noticed—felt—that the beloved has gone away, as if into hiding, no longer to be found in familiar places, no longer responsive to ways of speaking and acting that worked in the past. It is a more passionate love of God that cares about this beloved's coming and going. In this sense, *His Hiding Place Is Darkness* speaks to the matter of a deep love for a real beloved, noticed most vividly when suffered in absence. In the pages that follow I also argue—by way of a single extended example—that more particular and specific faith commitments enable rather than deter our learning from the images and words, events and surprises, of other religious loves, in religious traditions other than our own, and in the gaps no tradition can quite manage.

To love deeply and affirm deep truths in a world where many loves flourish in the particular, we need first of all to be grounded in the specificity and particularity in our own enduring love—for this author, in Jesus Christ. This is particularly in an age when the centrality of this beloved, or any, is by no means evident. Confident rhetoric about God and God's presence will be to many of us unconvincing, particularly if a true love is supposed to exclude all others. Love has its own reasons, but at our moment in history it does not translate into a truth that rules out every exception, every alternative. It is better, then, to honor the fragility of this passionate and particular truth about Jesus—or Krishna, or the beloved known by still other names—while admitting that this claim "speaks for itself" only in particular places and times. No matter how universal the truth, what we say is still the tale of the comings and goings of a beloved whose presence cannot be conceptualized as simply universal. To speak to the truth and love central to our faith bears with it an acute awareness of the failures and gaps that make claims to faith more fragile, vulnerable—and only in that way more convincing. The more evident and difficult the failing of our words, the deeper their truth. This book is not an elegy about the end of theology, but rather a plea that we leave room for the silence that comes upon us when we stretch our words beyond their capacity, mindful that we are speaking of just one love.

Ours is an era that both celebrates and tames religious diversity. It privatizes religion and shifts the deepest experiences to the realm of the inner life. It is difficult now for a Christian to speak and write openly of the intense, singular fact of Jesus, the concrete and universal Reality at the heart of the Christian faith, without also giving the impression that she does not really understand or have room for passions aflame in other traditions too. A Hindu in a devotional tradition likewise faces a challenge nearly the same as that of the Christian: one love surrounded, impinged upon, by many loves, in a world that might well be satisfied with less of such loves. It is good then that committed members of faith traditions insist upon the concrete, universally significant particularities of their faith, provided we view honestly and without amnesia the myriad intense and concrete religious possibilities so evident around us. The challenge is to find a way to speak of and from the specificity of our faith—our faiths— even as our religious imagination wanders uncertainly across myriad religious possibilities. As we read carefully back and forth, sensitive to the literary possibilities and not just to the ideas, this practice accentuates the problem of particular, passionate engagements. We learn and remember multiple commitments, while yet learning our way beyond the dichotomy of too much and too little religious belonging.

But this is difficult. Our way forward lies not in stepping back and theorizing the other, but in greater particularity and more refined, carefully considered instances. Reading is a wonderful way to do this, so in these pages we will be reading of the absence of the beloved in the *Song* and the *Holy Word*. *That* we read and *how* we read therefore become inseparable questions. In *His Hiding Place Is Darkness* I will be reading the *Song of Songs* guided by a single medieval Christian tradition of good reading, that Bernard of Clairvaux and Gilbert of Hoyland and John of Ford, three monks who over many years produced a complete series of sermons on the *Song*, each beginning where the previous had left off. One could spend a very long time learning from these sermons, but I pay particular attention to the situation of the woman at those moments when her beloved is absent. Along with the *Song*, I read also the songs of another woman in love, similarly bereft of her beloved in the *Holy Word of Mouth*, and here too I am guided by its medieval interpreters, particularly the revered teachers Nanjiyar and Nampillai. Each tradition of reading opens up poetic and spiritual possibilities in an unanticipated yet deeply engaging way, and all the more so by the double reading itself, as the songs cohere in a still greater Text.[3] Not that any of this will be easily achieved. The *Song* and the *Holy Word* are similarly intense in their love and love's particularity, and both care about the problem of divine absence, but in the distinctiveness of their poetry and the intensity of the love driving them, they are not easily susceptible to the work of comparison. Yet, as poetry, they also cannot resist the play of imagination—so in the end these utterly distinct works yield a shared reading.

In this shared reading, there is more at stake than either text provides on its own. To negotiate the possibilities and gaps arising in this sacred poetry with respect to this beloved who hides from us—we need to imagine ourselves falling, mostly by choice, into the somewhat obscure and unstable space lying between traditions. For the beloved hides from us in each text, in both, and at the point where they meet but neither has the final word. If we find ourselves reading and writing of a love that is both intensely focused yet laced with ambiguity, we do well not to retreat to the ready answers of relativism or exclusivism. Instead, we find ways to suffer the adventures of our imagination, moving to theological judgments only when we have found the right words, words arising in the midst of today's mix of uncertainty and longing.

In its conviction that depth and particularity are the means to greater openness and that love can be a matter of improbable, ill-advised excesses, *His Hiding Place Is Darkness* is the last act in a project I began implicitly in *Seeing Through Texts: Doing Theology Among the Śrīvaiṣṇavas of South India* (1996). In that book, I first explored the lyric and dramatic dimensions of divine-human love, sought and suffered, so richly evident in the Hindu text central to this book as well: the *Holy Word*. In terms of the intensity of focus and care for the poetic, *Divine Mother, Blessed Mother: Hindu Goddesses and the Virgin Mary* (2005) manifests the same energy, clearing the way for Christian readers to take seriously and learn from Hindu goddess traditions, even when there is no place for goddesses in Christian theology. The immediate predecessor of the current book is *Beyond Compare: St. Francis de Sales and Śrī Vedānta Deśika on Loving Surrender to God* (2008), where I explored the narratives of loving surrender proposed and cultivated by two prominent medieval theologians, the Srivaishnava Hindu Vedanta Deshika (fourteenth century) and the Catholic Christian Francis de Sales (seventeenth century). There I once more argued that engaging multiple traditions of loving surrender increases rather than attenuates the uncompromising devotion deeply rooted within a particular tradition. *Beyond Compare* highlighted the choices before the individual seeking God, and so too the aesthetics of love intensified by acts of interreligious reading. *His Hiding Place Is Darkness* goes a step farther in focusing on the holy uncertainty afflicting those who love God most intensely. In pondering the God of absences, my writing is not an innocent bystander, since the double reading essential to comparative study most often accentuates a sense that the beloved is present somewhere but not here, ever remembered even if never known in some definitive way. *His Hiding Place Is Darkness* thus pushes to a still greater extreme the necessary risk of interreligious reading that lies at the heart of the practice of comparative theology. It is dangerous work, love's burden, for we are now implicated in the dilemma arising when one finds that the texts studied— such as these songs of loss in love—deepen the reader's own loss in love, not by less concreteness and intensity, but by more than we can handle. There is a holy abundance in the beloved's departure. Yet when his absence is acutely, painfully noticed, the prospects of his return become all the more intense.[4]

I close this prologue with a word of thanks to the many friends, colleagues and students, who have helped me think through this project and at long last bring it to conclusion. My Harvard colleagues Kimberley Patton and Luis Girón Negrón kindly read the manuscript. I was greatly encouraged by my conversations and shared teaching with Stephanie Paulsell, as she was finishing her own beautiful commentary on the *Song*, and likewise I am indebted to the recent theological commentary by Paul J. Griffiths, which, though so very different from mine, has to no surprise been an instigation and inspiration. Gloria Hernandez, West Chester University, went through the manuscript in detail as well, enriching it with insights drawn from her own brilliant reading of John of the Cross's *Spiritual Canticle* and Jayadeva's *Gita Govinda*. While the translations from the *Holy Word of Mouth* are my own, I benefited greatly from working together with John Carman, Vasudha Narayanan, and A. K. Ramanujan on the songs many years ago, and more recently with Archana Venkatesan, in a new collaboration that moves slowly but surely toward a full translation of the songs. I am grateful also to my students at Harvard University for their comments, especially Brad Bannon, Jim Robinson, Shoshana Razel, Axel Takacs, Ben Williams, and, with reference to the poetry of Jorie Graham, Kythe Heller. Lee Spriggs, a recent graduate of Harvard Divinity School, took on the added work of proofreading the manuscript and preparing the bibliography and the index. Finally, I appreciate the never-failing support of my faculty assistant, Lori Holter, and my staff at the Center for the Study of World Religions—Charles Anderson, Jane Anna Chapman, Alicia Clemente, Alexis Gewertz, and most recently Corey O'Brien—who patiently helped me to balance the work of the Center with precious moments eked out for the tasks of writing and then revising every word of this book.

I have been fortunate to have had opportunities to present parts of this project in a variety of settings: the Translating God(s) seminar at the Irish School of Ecumenics, Dublin (June 2010); the Hanley Memorial Lectures at St. Paul's College of the University of Manitoba (October 2010); the New England–Mid-Atlantic Region of the American Academy of Religion (New Brunswick, March 2010); the Bishop Jonas Thaliath, CMI Endowment Lectures at Dharmaram College, Bangalore, India (August 2011); the Advent Mission, Memorial Church, Harvard University (November 28–December 3, 2011); the Loyola Lecture at Le Moyne College (March 2012); a presentation at the Hans

Urs von Balthasar Consultation at the Catholic Theological Society of America (St. Louis, June 2012), where I was helped in particular by the comments of Martin Bieler, Barbara Sain, and Edward Ulrich. I had occasion to discuss my project several times during my stay in Melbourne, Australia, as Visiting Research Scholar at the Australian Catholic University in the summer of 2012. Last of all, I benefited from discussing the book as a whole in my presentation at the conference, "The Song of Songs: Translation, Reception, Reconfiguration," held at the Center for the Study of World Religions, Harvard University, April 13–15, 2013. I wish also to acknowledge that part of Act Two appeared in an earlier form in the journal *Exchange: A Journal of Missiological and Ecumenical Research*, with the title "By the Power of Her Word: Absence, Memory, and Speech in the *Song of Songs* and a Hindu Mystical Text."

I thank the editors of the new Encountering Traditions series with Stanford University Press for their interest in my work and invitation to include this book in this most interesting and timely series. I wish also to thank the renowned Indian artist Jyoti Sahi for his kind permission to adorn the cover of this book with his "Mountain of Meeting." Finally, I am very much in the debt of the Association of Theological Schools, which awarded me a faculty research fellowship for 2010–11 to write this book, for giving me the occasion to present a draft at the annual meeting in Pittsburgh in November 2011, where I could benefit from the feedback of those in attendance, particularly the kind and insightful response offered by Denise Hanusek of Emory University. While duties at Harvard prevented me from actually taking a sabbatical for the project, I am grateful to Stephen R. Graham, Director of Faculty Development and Initiatives in Theological Education, for his patience with the vagaries of my academic life.

I put the final touches on this manuscript in the days just after the bombs exploded at the Boston Marathon on April 15, 2013. While my book is thematically unconnected to the topic of such violence, the sad events of that day and its aftermath have darkened this final writing, how I read my own work and weigh it against greater things. I therefore dedicate this book to the victims of that day, those who died and those who lost their loved ones; and by extension, to the still larger group of lovers everywhere who have lost, for a time, those they have loved most dearly.

Center for the Study of World Religions, Cambridge, Massachusetts

January 13, 2013

A NOTE ON EDITIONS
AND TRANSLATIONS

I have consulted the Latin Vulgate of the *Song of Songs* and used throughout the Douay-Rheims translation of the Vulgate.

For Bernard of Clairvaux's Sermons, I have found useful the Cistercian Fathers Series volume 4 (1971; sermons 1–20, translated by Kilian Walsh); Cistercian Fathers Series 7 (1976; sermons 21–46, translated by Kilian Walsh); Cistercian Fathers Series 31 (1979; sermons 47–66, translated by Kilian Walsh and Irene M. Edmonds); and Cistercian Fathers Series 40 (1980; sermons 67–86, translated by Irene M. Edmonds); but for quotations in the text, I have preferred the Mount Melleray translations (1920; volume 1, sermons 1–43; volume 2, sermons 44–86). For Bernard's Latin, I have consulted both the *Sermones in Cantica canticorum* (1888) and the critical edition, *Sermones super Cantica canticorum*, in *Bernardi opera*, volumes 1–2, edited by J. Leclercq, C. H. Talbot, and H. M. Rochais (1957–58).

For Gilbert of Hoyland, I have used the Cistercian Fathers Series translations (translated by Lawrence Braceland), volumes 14 (1978; sermons 1–15), 20 (1979; sermons 21–32), and 26 (1979; sermons 33-48). For his Latin, I have consulted the Jean Mabillon edition (1852 and reprints).

For John of Ford, I have used the Cistercian Fathers Series translations (by Wendy Mary Beckett), 29 (1977; sermons 1–14), 39 (1982; sermons 15–28), 43 (1982; sermons 29–46), 44 (1983; sermons 47–61), 45 (1983; sermons 62–82), 46 (1984; sermons 83–100), 47 (1984; sermons 101–20). For his Latin, I have consulted the critical edition, Corpus Christianorum, Continuatio Mediaevalis 17 and 18 (1980).

With respect to all of the preceding, I have occasionally made (only) small changes in the translations, in accordance with my reading of the Latin. But I remain exceedingly grateful for and indebted to the published translations.

All translations of the Tamil *Holy Word of Mouth* and the Tamil-Sanskrit commentaries on it (the *Bhagavat Vishayam*) are my own. I have used the standard available edition, the *Bhagavat Vishayam* edition of the five classical commentaries (with subcommentaries), published by S. Krishnamachariyar (Madras: Nobel Press, 1924–30), except with regard to the first three Hundreds of *Tiruvyāmoḷi*, where I have used the four volumes of the newer edition by Krishnaswami Ayyangar: volume 1 (1975; *Tiruvaymoli* 1.1–2), volume 2 (1977; *Tiruvaymoli* 1.3–10), volume 3 (1979; *Tiruvaymoli* 2) and volume 4 (1987; *Tiruvaymoli* 3). The Bhagatvat Vishayam includes all the medieval commentaries—including those by by Nanjiyar, Periyavacchan Pillai, and Nampillai—used throughout this book. In notes I refer to the Krishnamachariyar edition simply by 1, 2, and so on, and to the Ayyangar volumes as A 1, A 2, and so on.

HIS HIDING PLACE IS DARKNESS

ACT ONE
MISSING HIM

[1] Let him kiss me with the kiss of his mouth!
For thy breasts are better than wine,
[2] Smelling sweet of the best ointments.
Thy name is as oil poured out;
Therefore young maidens have loved thee.
[3] Draw me; we will run after thee to the odour of thy ointments.
The king hath brought me into his storerooms.
We will be glad and rejoice in thee,
Remembering thy breasts more than wine.
The righteous love thee.
[4] I am black but beautiful,
O ye daughters of Jerusalem, as the tents of Kedar,
As the curtains of Solomon.
[5] Do not consider me that I am brown,
Because the sun hath altered my colour.
The sons of my mother have fought against me,
They have made me the keeper in the vineyards:
My vineyard I have not kept.
[6] Shew me, O thou whom my soul loveth,
Where thou feedest, where thou liest in the midday,
Lest I begin to wander after the flocks of thy companions.
[7] If thou know not thyself, O fairest among women,
Go forth, and follow after the steps of the flocks,
And feed thy kids beside the tents of the shepherds.

(*Song* 1.1–7)

¹ O innocent crane with lovely wings, be
    kind,
You and your mate with lovely wings, cry
    "Alas!" and give me your grace.
Be my messengers to the one who rides
    the eagle with fearsome wings—
But if you go and if He should cage you—
    if that is your lot, what can be done?

² Be messengers to my Lord whose eyes
    are like red lotuses.
What harm can come from speaking on
    my behalf?
O cuckoos, nestled together, won't you
    do this?
Because of everything I have done before,
I made no effort to serve humbly at His
    feet:
So shall I just leave now and go away?
    Such is my fate.

³ Your fortune is to be with your mates,
    graceful swans,
He came as a small dwarf, and by His
    wits that trickster begged the earth,
And because of Him I've lost my wits.
Will I ever be done with my stubborn
    deeds?
I am alone, my wits in disarray, I am
    bewildered—so will you speak for me?

⁴ He should notice my condition, pity me,
    and say, "This is not right,"
But He says nothing.
So what shall I say to my Lord dark as a
    rain cloud?
Tell Him this one thing, "Her gentle
    nature will not survive in this state."
Good dark love birds, will you help?
    won't you help?

⁵ He helps, protects, nourishes the seven
    worlds:
Then why doesn't He help me even
    despite my deeds?
If you see that Narayana—

O lovely little heron stalking your prey in
    the garden
Where streams rush like the tears
    streaming from my eyes—
Grace me by just a word from Him.

⁶ "You are not gracious, but show her
    Your grace before her life dries up,
Come to her street on Your eagle, that
    ocean of grace, even for just a day":
If you see the Lord, that ocean of grace,
    by such words remind Him of that
    grace.
No? O striped bee? Is it something I've
    done?

⁷ Like a needle this cool breeze pierces
    me to the bone.
He considers only my faults, and shows
    me no grace.
So at least ask Tirumal, "How did she
    offend Your majesty?"
Will you also pierce me through, tender
    parrot? didn't I raise you?

⁸ Aren't you my little myna? As my
    messenger to the tall Lord
You were supposed to tell Him of my
    sickness,
But you didn't say a thing, you just stayed
    here.
I've lost my looks and jewel-like luster.
From now on, find someone else to put
    sweet rice in your beak.

⁹ Narayana's feet are like never fading
    flowers, and
Daily we seek rare flowers to place upon
    them.
That is what I am made for.
But sunk deep in His absence, I deserve
    nothing, what can I do?
Ask Him that, cold breeze wafting back
    and forth between us,
Then pierce right through me.

[10] He is freedom from the body's wheel of births,
Life's breath and everything else.
He appears in the ocean's depth too, and there He sleeps.

If you see that Lord whose weapon is a discus, tell Him all this.
But don't leave me, deep simple heart, until despite my deeds I am one with Him.

(*Holy Word* 1.4.1–10)

WE BEGIN IN THE MIDDLE OF THINGS, however disconcerting this may be. If we do not begin here, at the start, no amount of explanation will help us to notice the first inklings of uncertainty that unsettle the love of these women for their unpredictable lovers.

A HINT OF ABSENCE

From the start she speaks passionately and directly to her beloved, manifesting their intimacy even as she yearns for more:

> Let him kiss me with the kiss of his mouth!
> For thy breasts are better than wine,
> Smelling sweet of the best ointments.
> Thy name is as oil poured out;
> Therefore young maidens have loved thee.
> Draw me; we will run after thee to the odour of thy ointments.
> The king hath brought me into his storerooms.
> We will be glad and rejoice in thee, remembering thy breasts more than wine.
> The righteous love thee. (1.1–3)

Yet now a hint of trouble appears, even when things have been going well and love has seemed intense, even settled. All at once, she has to justify herself before the women and her brothers:

> I am black but beautiful,
> O ye daughters of Jerusalem, as the tents of Kedar,
> As the curtains of Solomon.
> Do not consider me that I am brown,
> Because the sun hath altered my colour.
> The sons of my mother have fought against me,

They have made me the keeper in the vineyards:

My vineyard I have not kept. (1.4–5)[1]

Amid this uneasiness, she admits a still more difficult uncertainty regarding her own beloved:

Shew me, O thou whom my soul loveth,

Where thou feedest, where thou liest in the midday,

Lest I begin to wander after the flocks of thy companions. (1.6)[2]

She wants to find him; not finding him means also to settle for less, to be entangled in other relationships that can be put aside only in the face of a greater love.

He may actually be nearby; perhaps it is he who speaks to her in 1.7, not drawing her close, but giving her a task:

If thou know not thyself, O fairest among women,

Go forth, and follow after the steps of the flocks,

And feed thy kids beside the tents of the shepherds. (1.7)

If this is her beloved, right here, at the start of the *Song*, then the trouble between them is a sign of things to come—the mix of nearness and absence that makes searching necessary even while calling its usefulness into question. Perhaps he is somewhere else, and she wants to go there, in the noontime.[3] If so, then it is the response that is more ambiguous.[4]

For millennia readers have entered this uncertain space hoping to ground more deeply their understanding of the love binding God and the soul. Bernard of Clairvaux, meditating on the Latin of the *Song* in the twelfth century, ponders with interest and intensity her uncertainty in *Song* 1. Working with a Christian language of love, and a deep interest in the spiritual lessons to be learned from lovers' exchanges, he reads the scene as expressive of the soul who searches for the beloved, for a God who, though known and beloved, has gone away and needs to be sought after.[5] Though ever-present, God presents himself in various guises to those seeking him. He cannot yet be seen as he is; he comes in various forms, appearing differently at diverse times, in every case in a way still hiding himself: "Now, indeed, He appears to whom He pleases and as He pleases, but not as He is."[6] Those who have eyes to see may find God anywhere and everywhere, but few gain the immediate and more vivid experience a lover seeks.

The yearning for a still more interior visit is evident in *Song* 1.7, where "God vouchsafes to visit in person the soul that seeks Him, provided, however, that she devotes herself with all desire and love to this holy quest."[7] The soul desirous of

God is a soul on fire, and it is in that fire that the soul shall know "that 'the Lord is nigh,' when she feels herself inflamed with that fire."[8] This soul then quietly receives a still more subtle interior visit that cannot be seen, even if it is felt. She prays that he descend "into her from the height of heaven so that she may embrace Him with her tenderest and strongest affections, and in the very centre of her heart." She yearns to be "intimately united to the Divine Object of her heart's desire," but such a meeting comes not "in bodily form" but "by a spiritual dwelling," not "as beheld in vision" but as "clasped and clasping in a close embrace of mutual love." It is tactile, close-up, and intimate. The more subtle and interior such visitations are, the more delightful they will be.[9] This Word that penetrates her is a silent word: "For the Word of God is not a sounding but a 'piercing' Word, not eloquent but effective, not sensible to the ear, but fascinating to the affections. His Face does not possess beauty of form, but forms it all. It is not visible to the eyes of the body, but gladdens the face of the heart. And it is pleasing by the work of love and not by colour."[10] So she must seek her beloved even when he is very near, because ordinary means of recognition always fall short.

Whoever "desires this ardently, thirsts for it eagerly, and meditates on it assiduously," will certainly "meet the Word not otherwise than in the guise of a Bridegroom, at the time of His visitation."[11] Yet recognizing the beloved succeeds only imperfectly and occasionally: "I would not venture to say that He shows Himself as He is," even if it is also true that "He does not appear in this kind of vision altogether different from Himself as He is. For He does not constantly manifest Himself thus, even to the most fervent minds, nor yet in the same way to all."[12] Though she knows and loves him, she can never hold onto him with assurance; every arrival and lingering presence ends in a departure: "For 'his heart's desire' has been given to him, whilst still sojourning in the body. Yet only in part, and that but for a time, and a short time." These abrupt turns, arriving and disappearing, are true to the nature of this most faithful beloved: "After having been sought and found with so many watchings, so many supplications, such floods of tears," suddenly "when we are supposing that we still hold Him fast, He slips away." But then he returns and "unexpectedly confronts us as, weeping, we pursue Him." For a moment he allows himself to be held, "but not to be detained, for He once more flies suddenly away from our hands."[13] The devout soul in this way acts out the drama of intense desiring "with prayers and tears," expecting that the beloved "will come back soon to her and will not withhold from her the will of her lips." But "very soon again He disappears, and is no longer seen, unless He be followed with the fullness of desire," with a resignation to the fact that although "the visitation brings us gladness" after that moment of love "the sudden change causes pain."[14] Love teaches patient waiting, which in turn excites still more intense desire.

And so she yearns for God even while still caught up in this world, unable to find her way back to the beloved. As if by a rule, those who love are chastised by the lord; to be cured, they must first be denied the "kisses and embraces" for which they long: "Has this not been our own experience in prayer, still daily afflicted as we are by our present excesses, and tortured by things past?"[15] Prayer in absence is punctuated by brief moments of the overwhelming nearness of the beloved. The best efforts to find and respond to God's arrival always fall short, while the brief moments of recognition occur at his initiative: "Our meditations on our Bridegroom, the Word, on His Glory, His Beauty, His Power, His Majesty, may be considered as His conversations with us. . . . For there is, in some respects, the closest resemblance between the thoughts of our mind and the words of Truth speaking within us."[16] Indeed, the work of the Spirit is never easily distinguished from the movements of our own spirits; we are a mystery unto ourselves, says Bernard, and so we must read ourselves through and beyond ourselves. Searching for the beloved is a search for self, a careful decipherment and reading of a person given over to love.

When she asks where her beloved pastures at midday, Bernard recognizes that she is seeking a place of secure rest with him: "With good reason does she yearn for that place of pasture and peace, tranquility and security, of exultation, of wonder, and ecstatic bliss."[17] Here Bernard speaks of himself: "For during the whole period of my mortal career, I have been accustomed, under Thy care, to feed myself and others upon Thee as Thou art wont to be found in the law and in the prophets and in the psalms," and in "evangelical pastures and in the writings of the apostles."[18] But such moments of safety are not meant to become ordinary, predictable. By his delays and departures, the bridegroom rebuffs the presumption that finding him will be easy; holding on to him is impossible.[19] Bernard admits that his own teachings on patience and humility were suggested by "the Bridegroom's reply, wherewith He thought it proper to rebuke the presumption of His Spouse, asking things too far above her. This He did, not with the intention of confounding her, but in order to give her an occasion for greater and better tried humility, whereby she would become more deserving of the higher gifts and more qualified to receive the graces she solicited."[20] In his absences, the beloved puts her off, that in her more desperate love she might desire him all the more. In Sermon 35 Bernard delves deeper into the ignorance of self that is hinted in the words, "If thou know not thyself, O fairest among women, go forth." Much needs to be done if one is to be ready to see the beloved; those who do not know themselves are very much unprepared. That she goes forth, even if in the wrong direction, is an erring that does her good, for she has been chastened by her previous passing over "from the spirit to the flesh, from the goods of the soul to earthly desires, from interior peace and joy of heart to worldly tumult and the distractions of worldly cares."[21] Now this soul has "learned from the Lord and obtained the grace to enter into herself, and within herself to 'seek His Face at all times.'"[22] She grows closer to the beloved even during the absence that had led her astray.[23]

Since she is already advanced in love, Bernard says, the beloved's rebuff readies her for the still greater knowledge that arises as she faces this imperfect world. She learns that drawing near to her beloved is almost impossible, for he is ever a little at a distance. This distance—dramatized as his rebuff—deters her from seeking beyond what is possible in this life even for a person of her great love: "'The vision, O my spouse,' the Bridegroom seems to speak, 'which thou desirest to be shown to thee is entirely above thy capacity. Thou hast not the strength to gaze upon that marvelous and meridian brightness wherein I dwell. . . . To be drawn up into the clouds, to penetrate into the plenitude of glory, to plunge into the abyss of splendour, and to dwell in light inaccessible—this neither suits this time nor this body.'"[24] Yet there will be a time when she will see him face to face, "and on that day thou shalt be wholly beautiful, just as I am wholly beautiful; and being thus made most like unto Me, thou shalt see Me as I am. Then shalt thou hear it said to thee, 'Thou art all fair, O my beloved, and there is not a spot in thee.'"[25] But until then, her drama plays out in a drearier world of distances and dissimilarities: "Meantime, although thou art like to Me in part, yet, because thou art also in part dissimilar, thou must be content to know in part. Attend to thyself, and 'seek not the things that are too high for thee, and search not into harder things.'"[26] All that follows in the search scenes of the *Song* appears in condensed form here: God's fidelity is reaffirmed, but so too her human condition, her extraordinary love and her grief at her beloved's absence.

TELL HIM FOR ME

We meet another woman in the *Holy Word*. She is presumably a South Indian, Srivaishnava Hindu, though she too is distinguished primarily by her extraordinary love, even in the face of absences. For reasons never stated, her beloved is elsewhere and unresponsive, his return in doubt.[27] Suffering his absence, she wanders her garden and ends up addressing the birds:

> O innocent crane with lovely wings, be kind,
> You and your mate with lovely wings, cry "Alas!" and give me your grace.

Complimenting their plumage is not just a gentle courtesy but a practical matter, for she knows what she needs. Just as an infant is intent on her mother's breasts and the nourishment they promise, Periyavacchan Pillai observes,[28] she is intent upon the wings by which these cranes can fly to her beloved. So too, by the great Garuda eagle with its powerful wings, her beloved could easily come to her, yet he seems not to move at all. This the cranes should point out to him, when they fly there:

> Be my messengers to the one who rides the eagle with fearsome wings—

But the verse ends curiously, when she warns the cranes that he might cage them, even without listening to their message at all:

> But if you go and if He should cage you—if that is your lot, what can be done? (1)

The beloved might never turn toward the birds or even listen to them; he might simply catch them and cage them. They would then be kept for his pleasure, receiving little in return beyond knowing that they do exist for him. To be kept with him, prevented from leaving: perhaps this is a risk she would love to take. By implication, she herself desires this captivity, precisely now as he ignores her; to be kept with him, prevented from leaving: this is the danger she is ready to risk.[29]

Like *Song 1, Holy Word* 1.4 is puzzling, unexpected after a preceding song that praises divine accessibility: he is always nearby. Shatakopan himself gives no explanation for the shift in mood from praise to anxiety, intimacy to absence. The Srivaishnava teachers weave such abrupt transitions into their narrative of the saint's long journey to the lord, as if each of his hundred songs marks another moment, consolation or desolation, in that journey.[30] The early commentator Nanjiyar detects in the gap between songs a deliberate withdrawal on the beloved's part: "In order to bring to birth in the saint that healthy state of devotion suitable to participating in Himself, just as a physician will forbid a sick person to eat anything, the Lord resists for a while the saint's desire to experience Him." In the persona of this woman, the saint becomes the ideal patient for this divine cure: "The desperate saint cannot endure this separation. He exists only as part of the Lord and nothing else."[31] Fevered with love, he takes no other nourishment, since only the beloved can satisfy him.

Nanjiyar explains why the saint takes on the persona of the young woman:

> Should he unite with the Lord in experiencing this total dependence, there will arise in him that experience which a young woman has for her lover;[32] for such union is his only pleasure, and he cannot bear separation. So the saint becomes just like a young woman who suffers greatly when, after union with her beloved, now she is separated from Him and cannot bear it. In her voice he makes known to the Lord his condition.[33]

He is this woman, and sings in her voice. Because her friend seems to have fallen asleep, or into a trance, she is also a woman alone in her grief. He does not come, "and she laments, 'He just won't come, just because He notices our faults. So we must point out to Him how He is renowned for forbearance toward sins.'" Accordingly, "she sends as messengers to her Lord birds living in the garden, disregarding the fact that they will not understand what she is saying."[34]

Nampillai, a disciple of Nanjiyar and the greatest of the old commentators, similarly traces her distress to the intensity of her love. If the previous song arose from the poet's pleasure at how near the lord can be, the poet's shift to the woman's voice here occurs due to the frustrations of an elusive love: "The song he sang previously arose from a delight now gone. This next song arises from her inability to bear this separation."[35] Unable to appropriate the wisdom the lord had given him, the poet no longer speaks in his own voice, but as a woman desperate in love, for he shares her state of utter dependence on the beloved: "He belongs to no one else, takes refuge with no one else, but survives through union and is unable to endure separation. The Lord alone is his perfect joy. The Lord supports, he is the one supported."[36] Such features characterize the young woman yearning for her beloved, says Nampillai, so it is only fitting that he take on her persona and sing in her voice.[37] Here he can imagine and express more daringly the problem of the beloved's absence, unhampered by a general consensus in so devout a community that the beloved is always present, always faithful, and so on.

The necessity and futility of sending messengers are evident in this first verse, but here, as in every song in the *Holy Word*, subsequent verses provide variations on the theme. Her sins may be the reason for the lord's absence; she alludes to them over and again in the next verses. But she also makes those sins, real or imagined, the pretext for reminding her beloved that he is renowned precisely as one who overlooks sins: "She does not give up after scrutinizing her own flaws. Since tolerating faults is a quality defining the Lord, she sends messengers with the goal of making known His willingness to bear faults."[38] She blames herself, but implicitly accuses him of hardness of heart and of not living up to his reputation. By sending messengers she seeks to gain his attention by any effective means. Moreover, in addressing the birds, she is really also talking to herself, even as she still hopes that He overhears. But his incomprehension mimics theirs.

In verse 2 she presses her case, this time addressing cuckoos. The absent lord is not just a lover, but also a ruler, a man of power who should be able to travel wherever he wants. That his eyes are bright and red suggests power, or anger, or passion. As Nanjiyar observes, it is precisely when she cannot see them that his eyes have greater power to enthrall her:

> Be messengers to my Lord whose eyes are like red lotuses.
> What harm can come from speaking on my behalf?
> O cuckoos, nestled together, won't you do this?

That the cuckoos sit cozily together only accentuates her loneliness. Agitated, once again she blames herself:

> Because of everything I have done before,
> I made no effort to serve humbly at His feet:
> So shall I just leave now and go away? Such is my fate. (2)

Constrained first by what she has done in the past, she is also a woman who cannot do what she wants. What she has done and what she cannot do both undercut her goals.

In verse 3 she turns to the swans, implicitly contrasting their happiness with her lonely fate:

> Your fortune is to be with your mates,[39] graceful swans,

but I am left entirely alone. Yet neither is her beloved entirely absent, given that she is very much captivated by him. He still catches her unawares, like that divine dwarf who in ancient times crossed earth and heaven in three steps, gaining much more than the demon king thought he was offering:

> He came as a small dwarf, and by His wits that trickster begged the earth,
> And because of Him I've lost my wits.

But again, the nagging idea returns: no matter how close he came before, now he is gone, and this may be due to her own graceless deeds:

> Will I ever be done with my stubborn deeds?
> I am alone, my wits in disarray, I am bewildered—so will you speak for me? (3)

Frustrated by his silence and theirs, she complains still more sharply,

> He should notice my condition, pity me, and say, "This is not right,"
> But He says nothing.
> So what shall I say to my Lord dark as a rain cloud?
> Tell Him this one thing, "Her gentle nature will not survive in this state."

Next, she states her case to the love birds, as dark and fickle as her beloved:

> Good dark love birds, will you help? won't you help? (4)

She doubts their good will: they too are dark, they too may share his unpredictable nature. Nor is she consoled in seeking the grace of the heron, that sharp-eyed bird who could very well detect the lord and perhaps help her even by just some small word of his:

> He helps, protects, nourishes the seven worlds:
> Then why doesn't He help me even despite my deeds?
> If you see that Narayana—
> O lovely little heron stalking your prey in the garden
> Where streams rush like the tears streaming from my eyes—
> Grace me by just a word from Him. (5)

she invokes that lord by his sacred name, as Narayana, thereby reminding him that he has always been a safe refuge of humans.[40] Right now, though, he is failing to live up to that name. But this heron too does nothing, and so she suffers all the more.

Perhaps more than a little annoyed, next she turns to the bees—associated with flowers, beauty, pleasing sweetness, all that she does not have for herself—and gives them an urgent message for her supposedly gracious beloved:

> "You are not gracious, but show her Your grace before her life dries up,
> Come to her street on Your eagle, that ocean of grace, even for just a day":
> If you see the Lord, that ocean of grace,[41] by such words remind Him of that
>   grace.

But when the bees too ignore her, again doubt intrudes—perhaps she herself is the problem:

> No? O striped bee?[42] Is it something I've done? (6)

In so graceless a world, now even nature's benevolent elements, such as cool breezes in a hot climate, torment rather than soothe her:

> Like a needle this cool breeze pierces me to the bone.
> He considers only my faults, and shows me no grace.
> So at least ask Tirumal,[43] "How did she offend Your majesty?"[44]

She expects kindness at least from her pet parrot, yet its bright colors and smooth words seem merely to betray her kindness in ever feeding it:

> Will you also pierce me through, tender parrot? didn't I raise you? (7)

Even the normally loquacious myna is silent:

> Aren't you my little myna? As my messenger to the tall Lord
> You were supposed to tell Him of my sickness,
> But you didn't say a thing, you just stayed here.

Uncared for herself, soon she will be unable to care for her pets:

> I've lost my looks and jewel-like luster.
> From now on, find someone else to put sweet rice in your beak. (8)

And so, despite all her messages, her condition worsens, verse by verse. Yet the implication is that by such verses he will come to know of her condition. Talking about him and herself is her way of talking to him; eventually he will have to act.

Since no bird will carry her messages or speak on her behalf, she thinks instead about those simple, devotional acts she might manage even by herself:

> Narayana's feet are like never fading flowers, and
> Daily we seek rare flowers to place upon them.
> That is what I am made for.
> But sunk deep in His absence, I deserve nothing,[45] what can I do?

With this thought in mind she turns outward again, hoping that the wind might end her misery as swiftly as it cuts through her. But in the end, she makes no further effort to resolve matters, and offers only simple words that mingle praise and plea:

> Ask Him that, cold breeze wafting back and forth between us,
> Then pierce right through me. (9)

> He is freedom from the body's wheel of births,
> Life's breath and everything else.
> He appears in the ocean's depth too, and there He sleeps.
> If you see that Lord whose weapon is a discus, tell Him all this.

At this point, she is speaking to no one but her own heart, which surely must not give up on her:

> But don't leave me,[46] deep simple heart, until despite my deeds I am one with
>   Him. (10)

It torments her by its disordinate passion, and yet it remains, in that untoward love, her only sure link to the absent beloved. As we shall see, many of her songs include this turn to her heart.

The drama of separation and yearning, dialogue with the birds, the sending of messengers—all matter simply in proportion to her desperate need for him. Later, as we shall see, her problem is compounded, when her own heart will be lost to her, gone over to him and refusing to return, just as he refuses to come. But this is all she has, her inner resolve, her heart.[47]

INTERLUDE: *Where Then We Find Ourselves at the Start*

Both women's difficult, pained songs manifest their uncertainty about the beloved: Why is he not here? Why does he not return? They are vulnerable, they love and cannot forget the one whom they cannot control, this lover who does not return and whose whereabouts are uncertain. Nowhere nearby, he is still palpably present in their inability to forget him.

Few of us can imagine slipping into the persona of such a woman, so desperate and helpless in love. It may be impossible to place ourselves in either scene in any straightforward manner. Perhaps we cannot even make sense of loving God in so intense, material, and fragile a way. But reading each text, and the the two together, should affect us, informing us, then unsettling how we see either side of this reading, either woman and her love. This deeper learning sends an uncertain message, introducing doubt at the start of our own reflection, about what we have read and what we are supposed to do with it. The more we know, the less likely it is that we will be able to say with certainty if either story is our own, if this beloved, absent twice over, really belongs to us.

If we enter upon the uncertainty of one woman and share her sorrow and by extension are taken up in her song, it is still the case that the words and sentiments of the other woman stay with us too. We remember her and begin to share her love and loss. Even as we live out most deeply the words and images and events of our own tradition—the woman of the *Song*, read with Bernard and his heirs, or the woman of the *Holy Word*, read with Nanjiyar and his heirs—the other story lingers, attracting and disturbing us: perhaps the beloved is there (too) or (only) there.

To accentuate such possibilities this Act One has deliberately and abruptly plunged us into the middle of things, without providing sufficient background and preparation. Such is love, and such too is our experience amid today's diversity: grounded in one tradition—it is Jesus alone, for me as a Christian, perhaps for the reader Krishna, or another—and unwilling to surrender so particular an intensity and deep a commitment, over and again we still see other such particularities that we cannot banish from our memories. We never start out in a pure and simple situation where one love is managed first and then later on we learn something about another. From the start we are implicated in this double exposure, and more too. We are already involved, our first love along with other loves. And so we draw this dynamic into our theological reflection. We patiently await the return of Jesus, not quite sure where to find him; perhaps uncomfortably, we learn also to sorrow with this other woman who pines for her beloved Krishna. It is in this cultivated uncertainty, the beloved lost twice over, that we are to imagine and find our way; more than spectators, we now share their loss and confusion. The beloved is more of a mystery than we had imagined. What is lost, and gained, now lies also in the denial of the comfortable adequacy of my own tradition's singular account of divine absence and presence.

All of this is but an opening word. Like these women we will not be finished for quite some time. Other scenes will tell us of their lonely vigils, their search and its failures, until we glimpse redemption in adherence to the very memories that so deeply disturb and arouse them. But before going deeper into their story, we need to clear the theological—and theopoetic, theodramatic—ground on which this project stands.

ENTR'ACTE ONE
LOVE IN-BETWEEN

ACT ONE RIGHT AWAY PUT US IN THE MIDDLE OF THINGS. There was no other way to get there, and delay would be fatal, since the problem of this book lies in deep loves disturbed in the presence of other such loves. But now we must step back and consider how actually we are going to learn amid the increasingly intense uncertainties with which the *Song* and *Holy Word* confront us. There is no reason to make our task more difficult merely by neglect and carelessness.

Finding our way forward requires striking a delicate balance. If we want to honor these acts of intimate reading but still care for what we already love and know to be true, we need to sort out the moments of our project—with texts and methods in mind—and then put them back together for the sake of a single, singular way of reading that is the practice of this book, most particularly in Act Two. I map the project as follows.[1]

First, I introduce the *Song of Songs* and its most poignant current, the suffering of this young woman when her beloved has just left her, has not returned. To orient our reading, at every step I draw on two modern commentators, Cheryl Exum and Elie Assis, and primarily for guidance on one lineage of medieval Christian commentary, that of Bernard of Clairvaux, Gilbert of Hoyland, and John of Ford. Second, to explain why I begin with a religious reading of the *Song* as poetry and drama rather than its history or the theologies that have grown up around it, I turn to the theology of Hans Urs von Balthasar. His expansive theological vision shows why and how a theologian can appreciate the beautiful and the good—the poetic and dramatic—that come into play before the work of theory, system, and doctrine (including theorizing about world religions) can bear fruit. Third, holding at bay for now the dilemma that arises when one moves from the poetic and dramatic realm to thinking theologically (in the narrower sense) about religions in relation to one another, I extend and risk and, I hope, deepen this meditation on the absent beloved by a turn to a body of Hindu poetry, the Tamil language *Holy Word of Mouth* (*Tiruvaymoli*). Here we find a theme similar to that of the *Song*, as the woman suffers through an unpredictable relationship with a lover who, though divine, is absent more often than not. Fourth, I ask how my project of reading back and forth between the *Song* and the *Holy Word* can be conceived of as a reading project that can be written up in an accessible and fruitful manner without a retreat to summations that would sacrifice the rich ambiguities of the *Song* and *Holy Word* for the sake of mere clarity and mere ease in reading. For this, I turn to the contemporary poet Jorie Graham, to learn from her deep and material mode of poetic attentiveness, her manner of reading religiously in a complicated and nonhomogeneous manner, and the necessarily "broken-style" writing that catches in words the stuff of our lives, including the complexities of love and loss. Fifth, with the preceding points in mind, I indicate what to expect in Act Two, where our close reading plays out more amply as we move back and forth between the *Song* and *Holy Word*. A concluding section looks still farther ahead, to Entr'acte Two, wherein I will estimate the writing theology after this reading.

THE *SONG OF SONGS* IN THIS PROJECT

The biblical *Shir ha-Shirim* is a Hebrew text of eight chapters containing 117 verses.[2] It is comprised of a set of smaller songs with fragmentary or only partially told narratives and rich descriptions of a man and a woman in love. They describe one another in passionate detail, share moments of separation and union, and experience joys and sorrows in a series of incomplete scenes. She in particular suffers moments of uncertainty and desolate loneliness, and more than once has to go looking for her beloved. It is not possible to identify an entirely certain structure for the *Song*, and however long we study it, we will remain puzzled by the abrupt shifts in what we read, scenes with no beginning or end. This poetry opens up multiple possibilities and makes us use our imaginations—as readers, as interpreters of religious texts—in order to understand what is going on.

I anchor my reading of the *Song* and its medieval interpreters in a basic appreciation of it as a Hebrew text, and for this I must rely on the assistance of contemporary scholars expert in the text. Out of the vast literature surrounding the *Song* I draw primarily on two recent commentaries.[3] For basic insights

regarding the verses in their original setting and as instances of Hebrew literature, Cheryl Exum's *Song of Songs* is a masterful guide that surveys the relevant
scholarship while remaining close to the poetry itself and the dynamics of our
reading. Her commentary is invaluable in situating and interpreting each passage in light of the major strands of contemporary scholarship, particularly
given her patience in staying with and not hastily resolving ambiguities in the
text. I have also drawn on Elie Assis's *Flashes of Fire*, another full commentary
that gives priority to the human dynamic of the *Song*—love and its frailties—
and for this reason fits this project particularly well. Assis's sense of the text
serves aptly to catch the dynamics of the *Song* as a story of real but flawed,
imperfect love. Although I am greatly indebted to Exum and Assis, given the
primarily comparative dynamics of this project I have largely placed my notice
of their insights in the endnotes of this book.

Assis helps us by identifying five major sections of the *Song*: 1.1–8, 1.9–2.17,
3.1–5.1, 5.2–6.3, and 6.4–8.14, each unit containing "the words of the lovers, the
description, the adoration and the desire, and all of which end with an attempt
to make a rendezvous."[4] Every scene ends in a climax, most of which leave us
uncertain, compelled to speculate on what comes next:

1.7–8 The woman's attempt to make a rendezvous with the man, and the
man's refusal

2.8–17, 3.1–5 The man's attempt to make a rendezvous and the woman's
refusal; and the woman's poem of yearning in a dream[5]

4.8–5.1 A rendezvous poem, followed by an abrupt shift into a scenario of
absence and search in 5.2

6.1–3 A poem in which, after a failed search, the daughters of Jerusalem
again tease the woman about the man's absence, and the woman's
response[6]

8.13–14 The man's attempt to make a rendezvous and the woman's refusal[7]

The *Song*, though eloquent in celebrating union, time and again arrives at the
edge of disappointment and despair, love achieved and then abruptly, inexplicably lost hold of, as once again the lovers are separated. Assis takes this to
mark the human tendency to back away from permanent intimacy; the lovers
repeatedly fail to match their desires and extend over time a precious and
fragile moment of love. While it is not necessary to psychoanalyze the couple,
the fragility of love and the permanent incompleteness of any love story are
always in play.

It is in accord with this structure that my reading of the *Song* proceeds. The first moment was already taken up in Act One, and the last occupies our Act Three. The three middle scenes will receive attention in Act Two:

Alone in the Night

In my bed by night I sought him whom my soul loveth; I sought him, and found him not. (*Song* 3.1)

In the Night, I Found Him

I will rise, and will go about the city: in the streets and the broad ways I will seek him whom my soul loveth. I sought him, and I found him not. The watchmen who keep the city, found me, "Have you seen him, whom my soul loveth?" When I had a little passed by them, I found him whom my soul loveth. I held him, and I will not let him go, till I bring him into my mother's house, and into the chamber of her that bore me. (3.2–4)

I opened the bolt of my door to my beloved, but he had turned aside and was gone. My soul melted when he spoke. I sought him, and found him not. I called, and he did not answer me. (5.6)

Deep in Her Memory

What is your beloved more than another beloved, O fairest among women? ?
What is your beloved more than another beloved, that you thus adjure us?
"My beloved is all radiant and ruddy, distinguished among ten thousand.
His head is the finest gold; his locks are wavy, black as a raven." (5.9–11)

The *Song* speaks most powerfully when intense love falls short and for a time goes astray, dissipating its energies; and this it does five times over in the course of the *Song*. With reference to each of the scenes I have chosen, I am indebted to Cheryl Exum and Elie Assis for illumining the uncertainties—textual, and pertaining to love—endemic to the *Song*, and that have for millennia generated spiritual and theological reflection. While my explicit attention to their work occurs almost exclusively in the notes, interested readers will share with me a deep appreciation for their guidance in our journey into the world of the *Song*.

A distinguishing feature of *His Hiding Place Is Darkness* is that I privilege the interpretations of three medieval and monastic readers. I draw simply on one continuous Christian narrative of the *Song*, such as we find in the sermons of Bernard of Clairvaux (1019–1153), Gilbert of Hoyland (died, 1172), and John of Ford (1140–1244). Together, they offer a complete explication of the *Song* in just over 250 sermons, Gilbert taking up where Bernard left off, and

John where Gilbert stopped.[8] However much we benefit from reading contemporary scholarship on the *Song*, we do well also to learn from the older wisdom of great readers in the past. The *Song* is rich in wisdom detected and enjoyed by centuries of readers who sought spiritual nourishment in it, and we benefit from their insights, particularly when the spiritual, transformative implications of the text are at stake. These traditional readers cherish the mysteries embedded in the *Song*, neither hurrying past them nor explaining them away. Committed to making sense of the *Song* in its parts and as a whole, they weave their still larger religious stories and teaching into the fabric of the *Song*, submitting to it as their guide in the ways of love.[9] Let us for a moment introduce Bernard, Gilbert, and John, each in turn.

M. Corneille Halflants offers an elegant summary of the theology and spiritual intentions underlying Bernard's eighty-six sermons.[10] He finds in Sermon 83 the core of Bernard's teaching: "What a great thing is love, provided always that it returns to its origin; . . . flowing back again into its source it acquires fresh strength to pour itself forth once again."[11] How this great movement of love works out in practice, in the relationship of God and the soul in this imperfect world, and in the words of the *Song*, is the substance of Bernard's eighty-six sermons. Bernard's spiritual theology presumes an anthropology in accord with which humans discover their true selves and, on that basis, turn from things and toward God: "To know God, man must know himself, and between these two extremes there must be some resemblance, since all knowledge supposes likeness: *iam in aliquo similis*.[12] Christ made himself known and loved by becoming like unto man. The tiny spark which always glows in the depths of the soul, the indelible image of God which lost so much of its likeness to him, is the ontological point of departure which opens to every human creature the possibility of a return to his Father's house."[13] Humans, ever conflicted, do themselves injury by plunging into the things that are not God and wandering ever farther away from their deepest happiness. By grace, the gift of the Word, humans are called back, returned to the Word, and so, little by little, recover the original and deep resemblance. By discipline and in obedience to the Word, erring humans move back toward God. Love reasserts its primordial hold on the soul, drawing it in the right direction, toward God. And so, at the beginning and in the end, love matters most: "It is sufficient, instead of describing all the virtues necessary for a soul in its return to God, to declare simply that it must seek God. The sincerity of this movement of love supposes all the virtues. Seeking after God unifies one's moral life; it engenders a continual spiritual activity, varied according to circumstances."[14] All of this is worked out in practice in Bernard's individual sermons, where he lingers attentively on every word and its every nuance and savors the *Song*'s many meanings, and in this way discloses the nature of God and the world, individuals and the community of the Church. The *Song* is richly dramatic and does not proceed in a predictable fashion; so it works well for Bernard to savor each word, engage and extend each moment of drama of its particularities, seeking to bridge the gap between the text and the life of the hearer.

In forty-eight sermons Gilbert of Hoyland extends Bernard's exposition, bringing to bear his own discernment of the dynamics of spiritual ascent and union. On occasion appealing to his own experience, Gilbert shows over and again what it means to say that the *Song* guides spiritual advancement.[15] As Jean Vuong-dinh-Lam notes, for Gilbert just as for Bernard and other medieval readers, this "treatise on love" occasions a wide range of teachings on matters related to doctrine, mystical union, and the spiritual life.[16] Yet the *Song* is not for everyone. Vuong-dinh-Lam points out that Gilbert's audience, like Bernard's, is comprised of monks, students and scholars enclosed deep within the Church.[17] This is an audience already removed from the world and its cares, already focused on the beloved. Marsha Dutton aptly notes Gilbert's emphasis on the perfection of knowledge in wisdom, nurtured in the monastery setting and actualized in the transformation of the monk.[18] While most of us today are not monastics, if we are to read well we must join Gilbert in submitting to the text and seeking that quiet, inner space where the beloved can both be noticed and missed in his absence. A major question shadowing all that follows is therefore the measure of our own commitment to this kind of intense, vulnerable learning.

In his 120 sermons on the last four chapters of the *Song*, John of Ford follows consciously in the footsteps of Bernard and Gilbert, and shares their concern for clues disclosive of the divine-human relationship, in the Church and for the individual. His goal, as Hilary Costello explains it, is above all "to arouse . . . 'that bold, wild eagerness of longing to desire the desire of Jesus' love, so desirable and lovable.'"[19] Both Church and individual are drawn into a way of prayer marked by "compassion, prayer, silence, the reading of Scripture and the pursuit of 'wisdom.'"[20] Silence is key, a best way to imitate "Jesus who gave no answer to those who accused him. . . . His silence was full of grace and truth."[21] In the quiet of that silence, one can enter upon the study of Scripture and discover the deep spiritual meanings therein. This silence opens into a deep contemplation, "in which the bride gazes long and steadily on the face of the Eternal Word."[22] In his distinctive manner, John carries on the work of his predecessors—the reading, the intensification—to its completion.

Bernard, Gilbert, and John traverse the *Song* with great agility, moving back and forth from literal meanings to deep insights into how the *Song* manifests the mystery of Jesus, and to its spiritual relevance for individuals within the larger life of the Church. They promote a particular kind of religious reading of the sermons, by a dazzling array of words that draw listeners into the great silence of the beloved's absence, presence.[23] They are most careful and reflective, yet rarely do they step back and describe the methods they employ in drawing out the spiritual meanings of the *Song*. Even if we readily admit that there are deep theological foundations to their expositions, it is also clear that Bernard, Gilbert, and John do not exhibit those foundations in their sermons systematically, but only indirectly, in the course of their readings of the *Song*. As the lovers sing, these monks preach, moving back and forth with agility across the range of possible meanings. Significance is detected from within, by those who learn to read from their vantage point: *solvitur legendo*, one might say; revisions in method following upon the requirements of an actual reading. Formal explanations and the elaboration of presuppositions in a systematic way may come later. Along this uncertain path, contemporary readers become participants in this unfinished story of loves human and divine, fashioning our own provisional tellings of the beloved present and in hiding. *His Hiding Place Is Darkness* is a contribution to this improvisation.

LEARNING FROM HANS URS VON BALTHASAR'S THEOPOETICS AND THEODRAMATICS

The poetry and drama of the *Song* and its sermons are works of the imagination, fragments uncertain in their progression, abrupt, and thus requiring attention at every turn. In the end, they leave us puzzled but deeply involved. Of course timing matters: the *Song* and these commentaries are ancient, but we are reading today, even if in the process we learn to see the presence and absence of God in accord with the *Song*'s ancient images and events.

From a certain vantage point, all this would be quite enough indeed. Few readers of the *Song* and Bernard and his heirs will be asking for explanations that connect the *Song* to any given ideas about gendered love or dramatic poetry or a high theology of God and the soul. But still, we not only read the text but also beyond it, and so we theologize, and if we are to manage a theology supple and deep enough to respond to the *Song* and to our contemporary religious situation and still stand on firm theological ground, we cannot put aside the work of a theology that teaches in prose while still speaking truth of poetry. To keep this project nearby to Christian and other theologies as an invitation and challenge, we need a richer sense of how the poetic and dramatic can be integral to a fuller theological discourse. For this I turn now to the influential Swiss Catholic theologian Hans Urs von Balthasar (1904–88), and in particular his plan to engage the beautiful, freedom and the good, and the true in three great, multivolume works: the *Glory of the Lord*, the *Theo-Drama*, and the *Theo-Logic* or what we may more briefly term his theopoetics, theodramatics, and theologic.

Theological reflection on the truth of the faith may diverge from or go beyond the simple contemplation of the beautiful and the good couched in living poetic terms, but for Balthasar a sound theologic is one that "forces us to face squarely the most vital questions of Christian faith and life. How, ontologically speaking, can God become man, or, to phrase the question differently: Does creaturely *logos* have the carrying capacity to harbor the divine Logos in itself?" Theologic cannot but be a reflection on the seemingly impossible prospect of limited images, words, and actions that still help us to know the glory, power, and truth that is the unlimited God. Theology, in its integral form, is nothing but the movement of "repeatedly circling around what is, in fact, always the same totality looked at from different angles."[24] Were we to imagine separating out the truth from the beautiful and the good, we would ultimately destroy theology as well. A theology indebted to the beautiful and the good moves from an implicit recognition that God is at work among human beings, toward express reflection on how "the infinite truth of God and his Logos can express itself, not just vaguely and approximately, but adequately, in the narrow vessel of human logic."[25] In the poetry that is the heart of this book, we see the hidden presence of God even in the fragile realities of today's passing images and provisional words, uncharted in their mingling and deep currents.

Each part of the trilogy exposes the limitations of theologizing, and the still greater possibilities of theology broadly and richly conceived. In the *Glory of the Lord*, the seven volumes of his theopoetics,[26] Balthasar draws on poetry and prose, narrative and theology, to discern in the works of imagination, with respect to the beautiful, the infusion of divine glory into human words. Apprehending the realm of this glory, divine beauty shining with human experience, is not in competition with theology more strictly understood, but rather a necessary practice of attention that precedes effort to apprehend and state the truth of Christian revelation and tradition.

In the five volumes of his *Theo-Drama*, Balthasar traces the dynamics of the theodramatic, which too is different from yet not contrary to the theological. God interacts in particular ways with the human race, in the great stories of the Bible and the overarching story that is salvation history. In the early sources and throughout history, the divine-human relationship remains an ongoing drama that must always, even now, be drawing ever closer to its own conclusion, even if unpredictably and at its own pace. The would-be spectator gets caught up in a drama that is in fact also her own story, her response to the beloved, who by an uncertain calendar is coming ever closer. We are drawn into the dark and radiant love that is improbably and deeply inscribed in the *Song*'s abundant drama.

He makes all of this clear in the introduction to the first of the five volumes of the *Theo-Drama*, highlighting the gracious encounter with God that stands at the core of the Christian faith, "for here the divine ground actually approaches us totally unexpectedly."[27] But a contemplative surrender to God is not of itself the real ending: even as we speak of this graciously revealed glory, it becomes increasingly clear that the "divine ground" withdraws "farther and farther away from any merely contemplative gaze . . ." Accordingly, it cannot "be translated into any neutral truth or wisdom that can be 'taught.'" In this glory we are confronted with a divine light that "cannot be bypassed and yet is invisible," "a word of incomparable precision" that nevertheless can be expressed "in the crying of a dying man, in the silence of death and in what is ineffable—in religious rebirth, for example, and in the sense of oneness with the universe."[28]

From the start, in the gaps between the aesthetic, the dramatic, and any later formulations, truth is already manifest, on the move; faith is never insulated against uncertainties about what comes next. The dramatic holds its place between aesthetics and theology, in a series of participations that recollect instances of beauty while yet too standing open to truth. The aesthetic itself is not static, but "must surrender itself and go in search of new categories." Similarly, even if theology may eventually conclude in settled terms, "this can only be justified if it has previously experienced the dynamism of the revelation-event and is reborn by it in a form that is always new, not a dead 'result.'"[29] One cannot move directly from the aesthetics (or theopoetic) to the theologic. Rather, in the in-between space of our in-between lives, there is still "the absolute com-mitment found in that drama into which the one and only God sets each of us to play our unique part. Death turns into life," as our hearts, "drawn into the action," learn to "look toward that center in which all things are transformed."[30] Enabled to reflect on the meaning of the drama, "we have been appointed to play our part, and thus we share responsibility for our own understanding and expression of it. So it is incumbent on us to create a network of related concepts and images that may serve to hold fast, in some fashion, in what we think and say, to the divine action."[31] This dynamic does not undercut the possibility of theological assertion or a community's desire for doctrinal certainty, but it does cast a harsher light on theologies that have become stagnant. It begs of us pa-tience with the slow learning that is poetry, commentary, and the play of the imagination.

If the human relationship with God remains still deeply open, this enduring incompleteness affects what we understand of the God we love, and the words we are to use in speaking of that love. It is important to nurture and not shut down that incompleteness; we need to resist the temptation to substitute a fin-ished, smooth retelling of the divine-human interplay, one far removed from a dramatic realm in which unpredicted events are still possible. There is truth in revelation, but for Balthasar it is found in movement, in "a continuous forward striving (*diastasis*)," which is "the truth of the *cor inquietum*,[32] of hope and love for what is absent."[33] Ben Quash nicely captures this dynamic:

> For Balthasar, that which is revealed to us about God in Christ is not "a lu-minous icon, crystallised into immobile perfection. It is the beauty of an action. It shows the dramatic movement within the Trinity to us." It is only because the Trinitarian life has such inescapably dramatic features that our relationship to that life is so singularly well-expressed in the terms which drama offers. Our active relation to God comes to be by God's action; that action is the "good" in which we, too, are permitted to share by our actions.[34]

There is no room here for mere spectators or for those who think they have mastered the drama and now own the truth. As Quash summarizes Balthasar's insight, "'The divine ground actually approaches us . . . and it challenges us to respond,' and yet it is increasingly clear also that it withdraws 'farther and farther away from any merely contemplative gaze and hence could not be trans-lated into any neutral truth or wisdom that can be taught.'"[35] This honest ad-mission of divine withdrawal leaves room for a richer, freer, and yet still more particular sense of Jesus, who is the Christ, who later on may still be conceptualized in technical Christological terms. So too, I suggest, the relationship among religions such as the Christian and the Hindu is played out as a *diastasis*, a "continuous forward striving" that will not be finished in any expected time period nor with any conclusive theological determinations.[36]

ADVICE FROM GERARD MANLEY HOPKINS ON HOW PROPERLY TO LOSE OUR WAY

I have selected just one example to show how Balthasar engages a poet carefully and in detail. His theopoetic, theodramatic, and theologic instincts come together in his reading of Gerard Manley Hopkins:[37] if "all natures and selves are fashioned and determined for Christ, who is both their ultimate inscape and instress,"[38] it is the duty of the Christian "to interpret all the forms of God's revelation in Christ throughout the universe, and this task is achieved by Hopkins the poet."[39] Reading the world properly and in light of its final unity in Christ yields insights clear only to the eyes of faith.[40] The whole is inscribed in the writing of the particular, and from there arise the challenges preoccupying Hopkins in his poetry: "Language must be revalued, at whatever price, it must be equipped anew so as to be able to express in a plausible and fine way the unique and extraordinary."[41] The mystery of God is inscribed in things, not merely behind them or beyond them. It is glimpsed not by the best of words or when words are abandoned, but in words that overflow the particularities to which they are forever indebted, words that get beyond themselves and no longer reduce to just one meaning. And so, "The mystery of Christ is, on the one hand, of infinite depth, penetrating all the levels of being from flesh to spirit and beyond into the abyss of the Trinity; on the other, it is an infinitely dramatic event that in the kenotic descent into man and matter exalts and changes them, redeems and deifies them."[42]

Hopkins writes from within that tension: "The language must reach out beyond its immanence because the mystery of God does not hold sway as something incomprehensible *behind* the forms of the world; rather, the divine Word was made flesh," in words speaking albeit imperfectly of that mystery. And so "the poet of the cosmic rapture will be, if he is a Christian, at the same time the poet too of the intimate dialogue between the lost sinner and the crucified Redeemer; as one who beholds he will also be the obedient believer."[43] Yet even as the encounter occurs, "he must always consider and express the reversal and the erasures."[44] Here the very possibility of imagining the Christ is pushed to the limit, failing even as it exceeds its potential. A particularity that "should interpret the mystery of Christ is, in itself as an image of nature, utterly overtaxed, but in so far as it is grounded in Christ as the presupposition of nature, it is allowed to say by grace of the archetype what it cannot say of itself."[45] This Christian imagining has its ground in the dark radiant failure of the cross of Christ, which is "not one historical fact among others to which a natural process can more or less arbitrarily be related: it is the fundamental, ontological presupposition of all natural processes that all, knowingly or not, intrinsically signify or intend by pointing beyond themselves."[46] And so there is no sure dividing line between "natural perception of God in the world" and "the supernatural, Christian perception," even if the latter presupposes "a dogmatic knowledge."[47] The intimate exchange of the man and woman in the *Song* already discloses what God is like. Crossing back and forth between the natural and the divine is therefore not only possible but, as a sacrament of interconnectedness, necessary too. This can be expressed doctrinally in more precise terms but the expression is first of all a language of rapture, words fracturing under the "overtaxing" that accompanies God's arrival in human minds, hearts, and words.

Hopkins offers us a deeply Christian language of beauty and God's—Christ's—work in the world, but this does not limit the imagination to images that are Christian, nor to the Christian story as if it were the only drama to be contemplated by those wanting to know God's work in the world. Hopkins—cherishes Christian specificity and a more abundant imagining and poetic utterance, in every natural thing. This is the way it must be:

> It is impossible to say where the natural perception of God in the world ceases and the supernatural, Christian perception begins, which presupposes a dogmatic knowledge. Faith is so deeply involved in flesh and blood (the Word has indeed become flesh), that the transfer of interpretation from sacramental signs to the indwelling grace of faith proceeds imperceptible, ultimately indeed because the christological-mariological has been understood as the inner condition of the possibility of the whole natural order.[48]

No matter how grand this claim may be in faith or doctrine, here it is ever on the verge of failure, albeit a properly, fruitfully poetic failure that stutters more than can be said: it is natural, yet it is supernatural; it is not the first, yet it cannot be the second. Hopkins the poet speaks to the experience of "foundering in

God," when one "finds nothing more to cling to, not his longing nor reward nor Heaven nor any of God's attributes, for beyond all that there is nothing but him alone: '*Ipse*, the only one'—the self beyond any nature."[49]

All that follows is indebted to Balthasar, but we must be diligent if we really are to step out into the realm of the interreligious imagination and not merely measure it from a safe distance. The poetics of the *Glory of the Lord* and the dramatics of the *Theo-Drama* might in the end still get frozen within conceptual structures that rule out the uncertain and unsettled. Were we to leave behind the poetic and dramatic, then the great and true story of God's engagement with us in Jesus may be reduced to a drama with an entirely familiar ending, and thus to a drama in name only.[50] As we listen to Balthasar, we need also to think about extending his insights into a realm that is all the more passionate, uncertain, and dangerous.

This unruly Hopkins can here too show us the way. Bernadette Waterman Ward pushes Balthasar's reading of Hopkins a few steps farther. On the one hand, Balthasar had "an unerring instinct for what is most important in the poetry of Gerard Manley Hopkins," for he "thoroughly understands the keen theological passion that permeates Hopkins's deeply individual and sensory aesthetic."[51] On the other, he circumscribes too narrowly Hopkins's sacramental spirituality, and in doing so underestimates Hopkins's appeal to a wider audience that includes even those not sharing his Christian faith.[52] Ward appeals to the intensity of observation required if one is to be attentive to nature, a necessary "yielding of self to the reality of the thing observed,"[53] in self-sacrifice and surrender. Characteristic of this is the particular "ineffable individuality . . . that [Duns] Scotus calls *haecceitas* and Hopkins called 'pitch.'"[54] The sheer *fact* that this Jesus is savior precedes any arguments in favor of Incarnation or admissions of human need for a savior.[55] Balthasar sees faith as key to a profoundly Christian sacramental aesthetics, and by his appeal to Hopkins he sheds light on this. In Ward's view, Hopkins's sense of the particular does not stay neatly within the margins of settled expectations about Christian faith. The claim that "the whole world is nothing but news, word of God" does not easily fit back into a narrowly Christian reading of the world, since "even the subject matter of poems that trumpet the active presence of Christ in the world can be understood with consistency from a thoroughly secular frame of mind." Though ever the faithful Christian, Hopkins "does no injustice to the coherency of visions of reality besides his own."[56] This is so, I add, because there is a difficult and errant "logic" even to a very Christian vision of the theopoetic and the theodramatic. This vision remains open to what is new, from somewhere else, and so endure a certain indeterminacy that eludes both relativism and an unthinking identification with any tradition's doctrines. Even if, for Hopkins, faith does in the end yield particular and more intense insights into Jesus and no one else—unsurprising, since Hopkins too sees the world in submission to the specific capacities of his faith—those insights can hardly be fixed: "Because of the multiple inscapes, the many realities, available in the individual things one encounters, it is possible to perceive the same world truly, albeit differently, with and without grace."[57] A theopoetic reading must hear all of this, and live in the indeterminacy of such unbounded grace.

Ward reminds us that Hopkins never steps beyond a necessary "fascination with the way language doubles back on itself."[58] This is a poet is not easily tamed, and words overflow the boundaries that Balthasar sets in appreciating him. As Hopkins himself puts it, words, even the theopoetic, are irreducible to their meanings: "Poetry is speech framed for contemplation of the mind by the way of hearing or speech framed to be heard for its own sake and interest even over and above its interest of meaning. Some matter and meaning is essential to it but only as an element necessary to support and employ the shape *which is contemplated for its own sake.*"[59] In a reversal of our usual expectations, meaning is a pretext for listening more closely, savoring how the words, heard or read, steep into every thought that afterward arises: "Hopkins spoke of 'bidding' the reader into new encounters with inscape. His poems constantly draw the reader from one aspect of meaning to another—not all at once . . . but 'so that lines and stanzas should be left in memory and superficial impressions deepened'" and always "'without exhausting all.'"[60] All of this is unruly and dangerous, deeply Christian but never slipping into a settled and systematic Christian theology. In the possibility and resistance of his poems Hopkins shows us how better to read the *Song* in its own passionate vitality and, as we shall see, even how to bring a grounded but open imagining to our reading of Hindu mystical poetry, neither harmful nor subservient to Christian theology.

Ward appreciates Balthasar's recognition that Hopkins, poet and priest, indeed finds Christ in his neighbors, but she also wonders if it is really necessary to insist, with Balthasar, that it is "the *Christian* neighbor" who is for Hopkins "a most transparent symbol of the Incarnate God," as if the mix of "obligation and inclination, ethical self-transcendence and aesthetic rapture" is rather more narrowly just a "Christian fashion."[61] Balthasar himself nearly admits this when, as cited above, he recognizes that the "Wreck of the Deutschland" offers a dizzying vision of how we are "foundering in God," finding "nothing more to cling to," neither "longing nor reward nor Heaven nor any of God's attributes." The reason is clear: "There is nothing but him alone: '*Ipse*, the only one'—the self beyond any nature."[62]

In his analysis of the "Wreck of the Deutschland" Quash shows how Hopkins is thinking through the interplay of image, event, and time, in order "to go *into* the events rather than to step *back* from them."[63] It is very much to the point—to that of this book too—to observe that this poet refuses to "think away the particulars into comprehensive explanatory systems," but is instead determined "to think the particularity of this [shipwreck] event with absolute seriousness and thoroughness *in relation to* Christ."[64] It is in such particular events, never to be merely generalized, that Jesus dwells. Timing too is crucial, lest too much be said too early, as if to preclude the importance of what comes next. Each reading is "unique to its own context which will not be shareable or transferable to new contexts without undergoing significant alteration."[65] Words hold specific imaginative and dramatic energies, and are irreducible to generalities removed from the immediate and the local. To make comparisons that respect the poetic and dramatic, like the poet we must intuit commonalities among particulars, even if those particulars by definition suffer gaps between them and even if ingenuity is required if they are to be held together. There are no rules to make this easy. What lives in the play of images and the rhythms of poetry gets retold as the story of God's action in the world, the inevitable and surprising human encounter with God, the infinite possibility played out in a very small time and space. Our ordinary ways of speaking are upset and broken open, if God is to be fruitfully evoked in human words, the beloved made known in presence but not only there, and thus too in absence, gaps, and silences. This necessary quandary leaves the reader—and speaker-writer—in jeopardy, wrecked, foundering in God. Theology after Hopkins (and after the *Song*) must be a dramatically charged and unsettled writing, irreducible to any tidy conclusions about the world or anything in it. *His Hiding Place Is Darkness* moves toward a similarly intense, Christic reading of our world, abundant and generous, yet ever aware that the object of speech is not something, someone we control. Love too is surely beyond settled, comfortable claims about it.

In this situation, our own writing can be appreciated as bereft of settled forms, for a time harder rather than easier. We are offered a richer and more daring imaginary that is neither predictable nor easily closed. Other religious traditions too require respectful reading, and their poetry and drama, as beautiful as our own, and unruly too, merit our unshielded gaze and imaginative play. The poetic and dramatic powers of good literature cannot be safely limited to the realm of "the natural," nor equated with the classics of European literature. In this way we make room even for things uncomfortable to a Christian worldview that would rule out new images and new stories. It is hard to travel in this direction without hurrying back too soon.

To make irreversible this excursion into love's poetic space, in addition to offering a reading of the *Song* and following after Balthasar (and Hopkins), *His Hiding Place Is Darkness* also tests what happens to text, and reader, and our sense of the beloved, when the same sensitivities of the poetic and dramatic are brought to bear on Hindu mystical poetry, similarly read with a tradition of medieval commentaries. In this new instance, we learn to learn without the safeguards of familiar interpretation and settled theological expectations, and so too without the comfort of any sure sense where things will end up.

COMPLICATING THE THEODRAMATICS: THE *HOLY WORD OF MOUTH* IN THIS PROJECT

To ensure that we escape with no easy discovery of the beloved, I have written a second layer into my work, reading also the South Indian Hindu *Holy Word* by the Tamil poet Shatakopan. The *Holy Word* is one in a canon of works attributed to twelve saints (*alvars*), who altogether composed nearly four thousand verses. It is a superlative instance of the proliferation of devotional poems (or songs) composed in the Tamil language in the sixth to ninth centuries c.e., mostly dedicated to either of two great deities, Shiva or Vishnu. The *Holy Word* praises Vishnu, invoked too as Narayana and by other names, and most often worshiped in the company of his consort, Sri Laksmi. It is a particularly large work, one hundred songs of eleven (mostly) four-line verses, 1,102 verses in all. The songs are diverse in content, some praising Vishnu as the transcendent lord of all, or in his *avatara* (divine descent) forms as the dwarf, boar, man-lion, Rama, or Krishna, or in his presence in the various holy temples in South India. Some songs chasten poets who praise other deities, some appeal to listeners to give up all things and focus on the lord alone. Many celebrate the presence of God as immediately recognized, even a God who seems too close, overwhelmingly near.

We also find here the theme of the beloved's absence, when the saint sings as a young woman longing for her absent lover. This is no minor theme, since Shatakopan shifts into the voice of this bereft young woman in twenty-seven of the one hundred songs.[66] Almost without exception, her songs depict separation, yearning, and near despair in the face of the beloved's unexplained absence. She cannot reach him even when she knows where he is. In the *Holy Word*, not so differently from the *Song*, intimate union is a real but momentary phenomenon, too often available only in the recollection of past encounters. Loss and longing stand in the foreground, even if absence never entirely stifles anticipation about a final union that will surely come; the God who is absent is a real and faithful beloved, not a notional being who might or might not also exist.

Though ever bereft, this young woman is eloquent in her lament. She sends messengers and speaks to the birds.[67] She yearns for her beloved's temples, hoping to find him in those famed precincts.[68] She argues with her mother, her friend, and the women of the town, who seem ready to settle for conventional, tame expectations about God.[69] Alone in the night, she sinks into despair, and cannot bring herself even to move.[70] She waits for dawn, then just as desperately for the evening.[71] Once she speaks directly to Krishna, as if she is one of the cowherd girls who dances with him. scolding him for being too playful,[72] and once she assumes his persona, as if she *is* him.[73] In her very last song, she faces him in the early morning, after a night together, and begs him to stay.[74] Although she seems never to move very far in these songs—she is in her home, the village, unable to go anywhere else—her mind and imagination travel far indeed, in and from the deep intimacies of their love, lost and imagined.

However steadily the poet speaks of divine presence, he—she—also finds it necessary to confess divine absence. That this most benevolent and faithful beloved keeps his distance and does not return is grievous particularly to those loving God most intensely. The songs in the woman's voice open up and unsettle what would otherwise be the *Holy Word*'s richly diverse but still rather straightforward insistence on divine goodness and supremacy. Without her songs, love would lack those darker, more painful and precious moments of absence and want that make love more than a fiction, an immaterial ideal.

I do not read the *Holy Word* on its own, by myself. Already in Act One I have been reading with the first great commentators of a Srivaishnava Hindu tradition that even today thrives in an unbroken lineage. I rely particularly on three of the most important medieval interpreters, Nanjiyar (1182–1287); Nampillai (thirteenth century to fourteenth century);[75] whose work was distilled into a more succinct commentary by one of his disciples, Periyavacchan Pillai (born 1228). While these commentaries are not sermons, they are the record of teachings. Each commentary, particularly that of Nampillai, retains the feel of teaching and exhortation, less than systematic and more than exegetical. As theologians, all these commentators stand in the tradition of Ramanuja (1017–1137), a most important theologian who wrote treatises and commentaries in Sanskrit and, through those writings and (as tradition has it) in his personal teaching, brought Shatakopan's poetry into dialogue with classical Sanskrit-language philosophy and theology. They enjoy the verses even as they discover in them rich theological insights.[76] By attending to every word of every verse, savoring every image and event, they open the way to a more richly voiced discourse on the beloved.

As theologians, the commentators hold fast to Srivaishnava Hindu orthodoxy regarding the goodness of God. They do not think that the lord really is derelict. But neither do they find the woman guilty. She is after all an inner voice of the saint, and she is the best of all lovers. The pain of her desperate love is a precious thing not to be explained away theologically or ethically. Her frustration is a holy thing. It is not directed at a vague higher deity, nor is she philosophizing about the ineffability of God. Rather, hers is a God who is intensely loveable but in hiding; he can be tantalizingly near, yet is ever just beyond her grasp. Theologians may defend his goodness and righteousness, but their doing so only accentuates for her the drama of the beloved's unexpected absence. The commentators protect their God from charges that he has somehow failed those who love him, but in hearkening to her lament they face the darker side of love, intensity of desire for an absent, hiding beloved. She sings for Shatakopan and for the commentators what they cannot say in their own voice.

While it would be worthwhile in another place to discuss at length their subtle and multileveled reading of scripture, these commentators are practical, caring for the detail more than a theory about it. In their explanations of each verse of the *Holy Word* they too, like Bernard and his heirs, simply defer formal expositions of presupposition and method, instead showing us how they read in the particular. But we may highlight one theological problematic that fires their curiosity and gives their readings its intensity, their conviction that, as Ramanuja taught, our sole and ultimate happiness is something we cannot achieve in this life. All living beings are most deeply oriented to God and exist in utter dependence on God. Humans are distinctive in that they can choose to live in accord with that dependence, choosing service of the lord and his community. Ramanuja drew on the Sanskrit Upanishadic tradition to argue that direct encounter—vision, realization of the lord—is the culmination of the spiritual journey that is human life; reality's true nature is fully realized only in direct encounter with the lord. But this encounter, though it be human destiny, is not possible in this life. The flesh and blood of that love yields in this life only passing moments of unity; vision and intimacy pass us by like flashes of lightning, memories long past. To be human, then, is to find oneself entangled in a theological impossibility: it is to exist entirely for God, seeking direct vision and intimate unity, while yet finding oneself unable ever to reach such goals while still in the body. Systematically, this is a matter of requiring what is impossible, what has no place; dramatically, of the lover's hiding; poetically, of a lover's distress. Among these interpreters too, there is no rush to replace her songs by a better theology. Indeed, Ramanuja's theological problematic—seeing God is the only thing that can satisfy a fully alive human being, yet there is no direct vision of God in this life—is what gives creative tension to the poetic and dramatic possibilities of the tradition. The drama of a beloved who hides from us is not explained by this account, but at least we have some ground to stand on when we contemplate the hiddenness of the beloved.

Shatakopan's songs of love in absence do not move forward coherently in telling a single, linear story. No song explicitly follows up on a prior one, though there are echoes and resonances everywhere. Most often a song ends with its drama simply unresolved, and the next song, in her voice or not, addressing a different issue. All that is certain is the beauty and power of her voice, her eloquent lament in the face of his absence. There is irony in the fact that she produces such fine songs, so expressive of what God is like, out of her singular distress at God's absence. Indeed, her solitary voice infuses the whole of the *Holy Word* with a sadder, darker yet more passionate hue. It is with her that I choose to read the *Holy Word*, and in that shadow also to reread the *Song*'s scenes of departure and searching.[77]

In Act One, we have already heard the first of the songs in her voice, her quixotic sending of the birds, the wind, and even her own heart as messengers to the distant, unresponsive Krishna.[78] After three songs,[79] which had expressed divine transcendence and immediacy and the need to focus intensely on God in and apart from the world, the fourth song abruptly presented us with a woman who finds herself urgently sending messengers to a lover inexplicably absent. We were never told why she is alone or where her beloved might be; the song ends in uncertainty, with no sign of his return. But Nampillai highlights the change in attitude that is required if one is to move from theology about the lord to a deep penetration of encounter with the beloved: "When Nampillai was teaching the *Holy Word*, there was a man who listened attentively to his lectures on the first three songs. But the fourth song was about a woman bereft of her beloved, sending messengers from her garden. Hearing this, the man walked away, complaining, "This is nothing but romance." Nampillai commented, "That man is unfortunate. This is the song that shows what the Upanishad means where it says, 'One must meditate.'"[80] In keeping with this meditative necessity, here too we continue to learn by a series of instances of close reading. In Act Two we take up four more of her songs:

In My Endless Night
He ate the whole earth,
Our Lord who is nearby the snake bed.

Near but Unreachable
You are lovely with those flowers in your hair,
But my grief-stricken self fades away.
There, where fine Vedic chanting resounds likes the waves of the sea
And the smoke of oblations wafts in every direction,
There in cool Tiruvallaval the tall Lord dwells.
So tell me, will I be able to gaze always upon His feet? (5.9.3)

Women, It Is Too Late to Thwart Me
¹With whirled white conch and *discus*
The lotus eyed Lord rides His eagle across my heart.
But you don't see it — so what can I say to you ladies? (7.3.1)

For a Moment, He Is Here
Oh, my heart is melting, overflowing the bounds of my life's breath, and
My desire grows large—
So what can this servant do now?
He dwells in holy Katkarai where the fragrance of kavi flowers perfumes the
    streets. (9.6.1)

We cannot become this woman, and as we shall see, we are not really invited to imitate her. Yet as we traverse these songs, with the *Song* and that other woman ever nearby, we may come to share her deep feeling. If we remember her words and make for them a place in our deeper understanding, we will begin to make our own the sorrows and rewards of her yearning, and in that way share this most particular instance of desperate love. But how we can integrate this learning with our similarly deep reflection on the *Song* as read by Bernard and his heirs, and then too still write theology in a way faithful to Balhasar's insights, is an issue that we must now address, though again indirectly.

BREAKING OUR STYLE:
ADVICE FROM JORIE GRAHAM

We have thus far listened to the woman in the *Song*, to Bernard and his medieval companions, and also to Balthasar. Alongside these we have read the *Holy Word* with its esteemed cohort of medieval expositors. All of this now belongs together, though the possibilities are so ample that no simple summary of meaning is possible. My hope is that in doing so I have also been creating a certain literary and spiritual indigestion. It is tempting simply to offer more of such holy confusions, moving quickly to Act Two and to further readings that crisscross the boundary between the two poetic universes, with the hope that we become better readers and lovers. To some extent, such is my plan. But still, we cannot escape too easily, since we still face the question of how we are productively to catch in words these two women, two loves that we read together. The challenge here is to write in a way enabling the reader to get entangled in these women's stories, seeing their truth from the inside, unable to step outside them again. The goal is a writing that shows the way, but then leaves little room for spectators unwilling to get involved.

As a guide to the chastened, constrained energies with which we must read and then write, I turn now to the poetic vision of Jorie Graham, to foreshadow what will happen more amply in Act Two, consequent upon the brief starting point of our Act One. At issue is how our reading (and first, my writing) properly succeeds and fails in speaking of God, and in particular of God named—as Jesus, for instance—in a world where calling upon the beloved seems inevitably to fall short or go too far, the bland or the overly earnest. We need to avoid both an unreflective multiplication of words and names, and an amnesia that would paper over the manifold with a language of sameness. Graham the poet helps us who write in prose to see how to "fail with difficulty, and productively" in our writing of this beloved, now across two traditions.

Graham is one of the most respected and challenging poets writing in the United States in recent years. She is intensely watchful over every detail of the ordinary realities around her, and nearly obsessed with using words in a way honest to that reality, in a materially palpable deference of the written to the observed. In the eleven volumes of her poetry from 1980 to 2012,[81] we observe her commitment to a thinking-in-writing, as this is pursued word by word, in side-tracks, in erring, and by way of revisions of word and line that accentuate the tension between images, intentions, and the words we improvise in our speaking.[82] It is poetry, and a personal journey:

> I think, in a way, the central impulse of each new book involves my wanting to go into a more moral terrain—a terrain in which one is more accountable, and therefore in which one has to become increasingly naked. For me, the stages of that unveiling require . . . Well, the motion we were talking about as eroding is really just writing poems up to the point where I can, and then admitting the failure, if you will.[83]

Graham wants to see so clearly that she will by design also fall short, over and again, in finding the right words for what she perceives. What she sees, must say, disturbs how she is to write; fidelity to the writing breaks up the linearity and narrative of what she is trying to think; all of this alters how she perceives, and in turn brings pressure to bear on how religious things are represented in a time when neither religious ideas nor religious words work as they did before. Hers is a poetry troubled and enlivened with religious sentiments, difficult and ambiguous questions, and the fragmentary, faltering evocations of the spiritual that recur from volume to volume. But in its brokenness and by a sacramental logic Hopkins would recognize, her poetry is deeply evocative of spiritual and even divine prospects, even when she is decomposing the traditional flow of words about God.

The patient reader is drawn into a Graham poem first by a confrontation with the difficulties of reading any such poem properly, for we are vexed by its long lines, breaks, hyphens, brackets, and parentheses—and then by trying to catch hold of some meaning/s for the tumble of words that conclude to no certain meaning. This is a path of frustration, to be sure, but also a way of coming to participate, as Helen Vendler says, "in making the sun come up, the birds awaken, and the churchbells ring . . . as the town turns from night to morning," and this is "a human, and therefore effortful, *Fiat lux.*"[84] This is an act of "biblical proportions" that nevertheless remains human and not divine in any ordinary sense, since "it cannot have the concision and effortlessness of the divine illumination of chaos, because it is made from a human sensing and concentrating body striving to comprehend a moment in one internalized physical and mental gestalt."[85] Unlike Hopkins, Graham finds in Christ no steady compass, no still point amid the chaos. The Christ too—and other such fundamental loves—are gone from us, absent from faith and word alike. Or perhaps she is simply making even that bare minimum of faith a more difficult thing too.

In this sort of writing thought and word, gaze and breath, contest one another, and the reader has to work at making sense of the poet's labor. Graham defers to her errant gaze and lets go of any hope for a complete account of what is to be gleaned in the field of vision: "The poet has to substitute, for the metaphysical divine will and the intellectual divine Logos, a frail human eye and an even frailer human will, which must concentrate fiercely to translate into internal kinesthetic sense-response 'the most loud invisible' of the light and 'the vapor of accreting inaudibles,' the silent flocking of birds."[86] Such fragile perceptions then find their way into words that produce a system of signs: "The poet must translate these first into a consciousness of her own internal physical mimicry of the external stimuli, and then, in turn, she must translate that internal kinesthetic mimicry into the visible and audible signs of English, a language with its own internal constraints on expression."[87] She frustrates the reader expecting to find in her poems a coherence and transparency lacking to the world around us; at the same time she gives us a poet's entrée into the condition of the woman of the *Song* and the *Holy Word* as she speaks of her real, vividly remembered, absent lover. Even if in its materiality this act of translation may be recognized as deeply incarnational, it provides no solace for the believer who would fix the meaning of the Incarnation. But as we read with an eye to the theopoetic and the theodramatic, we can travel in and out of this spare yet finely detailed, in its own way excessive poetry, where power lies in what is broken.

One volume of her poetry and one poem within that volume must suffice to show us Graham at work. *The Errancy*, a 1997 volume, begins with a question, "Shall I move the flowers again?" and ends with a dash, "eyeing the spot where the birds must eventually land—" These framing devices starkly and without eloquence give voice to Graham's disciplined indeterminacy, her "awareness of the problematics of closure, of eloquence, and of arrangement and rearrangement." She teeters on the verge of altogether abandoning readability due in part to those unusually long lines, broken and marked with an overflow of dashes and brackets. As Brian Henry puts it, she "recognizes the destructive possibility of this process of arrangement and rearrangement: as soon as something is gained, something else is lost." Graham, therefore, is often self-corrective in her arrangements, "refocusing her lens," "questioning her own perceptions," and "rewriting her own words." The "dynamic between abolishment and restoration"—loss and rediscovery—"establishes the tension of many of these poems."[88] Indeed, "if the 'hysteria' initiated by the absence of 'the sensation of direction' in *The Errancy* threatens to drag the poet into a deadening stasis, her hunger for such rearrangements allows her to avoid such languor."[89] It is timely here to note that *His Hiding Place Is Darkness* is best understood, not as setting a direction, but as a work of rearrangement. Here too, while the deconstructive move is "neither original nor particularly rare," it "becomes both when established by a poet committed to serious arrangements and rearrangements of language, perception, and the inner life."[90]

For Graham, this (de)construction of how we use words offers a powerful antidote for words merely static and without life: "One needs to be both—the questor in the poem, the protagonist, the sufferer, the one who's lost in the forest of language, and simultaneously (because we can't just write 'nothing'), the one who understands enough to guide and shape; though without overunderstanding so that you move too swiftly (automatically) (rationally) towards closure . . . or without creating a form that understands itself so thoroughly . . . that once you set out in that form, the form will simply take you *home*."[91] The challenge then is to speak close to the perceived surface of things in a world now in pieces, a "mess of conflicting notions," a "mass of shapes no longer masterable by the old dream."[92] Or as Balthasar's "poet of the cosmic rapture" might ask: how is one to speak passionately of God after pluralism has seeped deep inside even the most resolute and confident believer? The truth lies in the extremity of this tension. Thomas Gardner rightly notes that *The Errancy* "seems to be written from within the exhaustion or wreckage of what it calls the dream of reason, for incandescence must always be threatened with guttering out. . . . [Graham has an] almost desperate desire to renew herself by writing through her fatigue."[93] The rapture, this extreme and impossible love, exhausts yet renews our efforts to speak in time of absence.

Graham's disciplined attention to rearranging words, patterns of reading, and insights resonates well with the seemingly unrelated work—in my project, not hers—of postponing but then too preparing a return to theology by way of a Christian theopoetics and theodramatics irreversibly indebted to the *Holy Word* and its tradition, in works of the imagination that do not respect even real and necessary religious borders. And so, soon enough, we enter upon the several scenes comprising Act Two. There we study and come more deeply to own two sets of powerful and suggestive texts, and we will have much to say on their meaning. But we also leave unfinished any account of their significance, so as to not run too quickly away from the prospect of speaking of God after the disturbance of a double reading held together not by a logic that would govern religions, but by respect for the theopoetic and theodramatic possibilities.

The Errancy's "Le Manteau de Pascal" serves as a good example of Graham's poetic style and intent as it pertains to our project.[94] This long poem starkly manifests the fragile possibilities of the things—words, writing, notion—we rely on in catching hold of realities that seem to endure because we wish it to be so. The poem is a meditation on René Magritte's painting of the seventeenth-century philosopher Blaise Pascal's coat. Both painting and poem hearken back to how Pascal is said to have been buried wearing a coat into the hem of which, at his request, his best proof of God's existence had been sown. Later, however, nothing of this writing is to be found. For Graham, the empty and now tattered coat comes to represent a "world woven and shaped and put on by the observer. It is what we draw around ourselves and consider familiar and knowable. We weave it by reason; we secret proof inside it. Torn and floating against the dark city, then, the coat now seems useless, fit for the trash, but it is also, Graham is convinced, richly generative."[95] As it decays, we end up seeing through tears and holes that serve now to focus our attention on small glimpses of sky, narrowed and irregular windows of light. Those seeking answers about God receive instead the decaying garment of those expectations. This is for the sake of a God who cannot be proven, who is still missing everywhere we had expected to find him, yet who is at every step still unforgotten.

Willard Spiegelman captures the dynamic of this poem (and of The Errancy as a whole) by noting that "this is a sophisticated person's nostalgic wish for presence and reality, for an unmediated vision." That Graham looks so intently is due to "her double sense that, on the one hand, she may be saved by looking or at least learn something by it, but that, on the other, looking—like language—is restricted by human consciousness and thus can never be other than partial." In choosing elusive or disintegrating things for her poems—the sea, light, air, a frayed coat, a promised text nowhere to be found—Graham wagers the impossible (as if she knew Ramanuja's theology), "looking at what she cannot grasp."[96] Pascal's coat ultimately dashes any hope of security against the resisting facts of a life without such proofs and or any real hope for them.

We contemplate it against a background sky that accentuates its raggedness lifted up, and for that reason releases light in an unexpected way:

> But the night does not annul its belief in,
> the night preserves its love for, this one narrowing of infinity,
> that floats up into the royal starpocked blue its ripped, distracted
> > supervisor—

Yet in its disrepair the coat becomes a sacrament of things more enduring that while absent still cannot be forgotten:

> this coat awaiting recollection,
> this coat awaiting the fleeting moment, the true moment, the hill, the
> > vision of the hill,
> and so it endures in its uneasy way,
> and then the moment when the prize is lost, and the erotic tinglings
> > of the dream of reason
> are left to linger mildly in the weave of the fabric,
> the wool gabardine mix, with its grammatical weave,
> never never destined to lose its elasticity,
> its openness to abandonment,
> its willingness to be disturbed.

Graham sees right through not just the coat but also the old story of a proof hidden right in front of us. She is asking her readers to look closely, return to what we see, now with the intensity of the realization that there is no secure written word, no concealed proof, by which to cross over more certainly to what we cannot gain by seeing. She writes from and for the moments of that shedding and the hope it (still) does (not) retain, for hers is a writing riddled with memories of old hopes for certainty about God, and the erasure of such hopes. But *His Hiding Place Is Darkness* adds: even the erasure need not be final; the beloved might just be hiding for a time.

Catherine Sona Karagueuzian highlights what Graham gains by her hard-won failure: "It is significant, as well, that although her scrutiny of the visible is fraught with failure, Graham nonetheless returns to the visible world as both a metaphor for the possibility of spiritual consolation and as an avenue to that consolation." Karagueuzian insists on the quasi-religious power of Graham's project as written in "Le Manteau de Pascal:" "The poem's emphasis on a work of visual art, as well as the metaphoric notion that gaps in the coat enable us to see through to something of beauty and perhaps greater significance beyond it, reinforce Graham's old, essential notion that vision is an avenue to the revelation of truth,"[97] even when we can see through a thing only because it is in a state of decay, coming apart.[98]

Part way through "Le Manteau de Pascal," as her words search and see and come apart, Graham turns to Gerard Manley Hopkins—even if, unsurprisingly, she uses his writing in a way rather different than Balthasar and even Ward. She includes in the poem, by way of a composite,[99] a diary entry of Hopkins in which Hopkins is detailing the structure of an oak leaf but then notes down a sudden admission of a quite different order: "July 11 . . . Oaks differ much, and much turns on the broadness of the leaves, the narrower giving the crisped and starry and catherine-wheel forms, the broader the flat-pieced mailed or chard-covered ones, in wh. it is possible to see composition in dips, etc. But I shall study them further. It was this night I believe but possibly the next that I saw clearly the impossibility of staying in the Church of England." Paying close attention to discrete, visible detail,[100] Hopkins's scale of vision seems to shift, the observable now exerting an irresistible force on interior things he had not observed closely but assumed to be true. He realizes that he has lost his footing in that familiar albeit immaterial religious world where nothing concrete shows itself. Disoriented by the strain of unrelenting attention, he recognized all at once that the ground had already shifted beneath his feet; "staying" in the Church of England was no longer possible. It is as if he could no longer secure this settled spiritual realm over against the myriad small materialities of life. Truth, as Graham reads Hopkins, lingers in glimpses of where it used to be, as it were in fading memories of a beloved now gone away. That Hopkins conversely discovered the possibility of being a Roman Catholic is a turn Graham does not mention in her poem. What is no longer possible may sometimes show what *is* possible.

Graham returns to Hopkins's pronouncement twice in her final lines, now rewritten as her own, voiced in her own intense notice of detail and her struggle to find what (not) to hold onto, even as her poem, like Pascal's coat, is itself coming apart, unfinished, until suddenly there is no more to come and it just stops. The first time marks a moment of fullness that slips away, a dying:

> a neck like a vase awaiting its cut flower,
> filled with the sensation of being suddenly completed,
> the moment the prize is lost, the erotic tingling,

the wool-garbardine mix, its grammatical weave
—you understand, don't you, by looking?—
never never destined to lose its elasticity,
it was this night I believe but possibly the next
I saw clearly the impossibility of staying
filled with the sensation of being suddenly completed.[101]

Graham intensifies the feeling of completion as an ending that permits no staying on. Nothing endures, that one might rest upon it. But the words of this ending linger, as fragmentary and frail as Pascal's coat, still with their own power. Failed expectations become tears through which we come near to what we are (no longer) seeking:

I will vanish, others will come here, what is that,
never never to lose the sensation of suddenly being
completed in the wind—the first note of our quarrel—

Echoing, perhaps extending Hopkins's revelation—in the detail, the impossibility emerges—Graham finds in the quarrel of her own writing a sense of what it means to finish, be finished:

it was this night I believe or possibly the next
filled with the sensation of being suddenly completed,
I will vanish, others will come here, what is that now
floating in the air before us with stars a test case
that I saw clearly the impossibility of staying

Seeing is hard; finding and being done is still harder. Yet by the fragments of diminished expectations we do see something just beyond our grasp; this is why our words can outlive the fragility of our lives, and ourselves as well. That we cannot even be certain where it is that Graham cannot stay marks her condition as all the more acute, impossible, open. My hope is that the small-scale experiment of my own readings of the woman's words in the *Song* and the *Holy Word* also makes it impossible for us to stay put with words that hover safely above the realities of God and traditions.

Graham's project resists easy summation, and it is best to seize upon any clue she presents to us. She dedicated "Le Manteau de Pascal" to Anne Carson, poet and essayist, and so I close this section with some brief attention to Carson's essay "Decreation: How Women Like Sappho, Marguerite Porete and Simone Weil Tell God."[102] In this essay Carson explores the poverty permeating holy speech, the abnegation and denial of autonomy that opens into the divine. The "I" is what must be surrendered to God; in letting go of it, we speak most eloquently of God. Porete speaks of the mystery of the "true kernel of divine Love," which is "without creaturely matter and given by the creator to a creature *and takes away absolutely the practice of telling.*"[103] Resigning oneself to being far from the most intimately, intensely present God induces a most potent theopoetic utterance and theodramatic happening. In turn, this grounds a theology that speaks well of a God who is intensely present even while still hiding from us. God is the "longe propinquus," "the FarNear": "where the Soul remains after the work of the Ravishing FarNear, which we call a spark in the manner of an aperture and fast close, *no one could believe . . . nor would she have any truth who knew how to tell this.*"[104] Weil puts it most succinctly: "God can only be present in creation under the form of absence."[105] Carson herself, commenting on one of Sappho's fragmented poems,[106] elaborates: "God's absence is something tricky, perhaps impossible, to tell. This writer will have to invoke a God who arrives bringing her own absence with her—a God whose Farness is the more Near. It is an impossible motion possible only in writing."[107] The woman in the *Song* and the *Holy Word* knows this very well; in the end, as we shall see in Act Two, it is the word spoken in the time of absence that saves her.

It is in this difficult space of writing, traversed repeatedly by Graham and illumined by Carson, that *His Hiding Place Is Darkness* finds its home. Here I transpose Balthasar's primary theological insights to the indeterminate poetic and dramatic realm to be traversed particularly in Act Two. I read as a latter-day Balthasar might have read. My book is no work of poetry, but it devotes itself to the reading of poetry, the *Song* along with the *Holy Word*, each intensifying and unsettling the other. Because the beloved—beautiful, elusive, coming-and-going—is our single, singular, impossible topic, our goal is to enact a speaking across religious boundaries about that "which we cannot grasp," a beloved who is not ours for the holding—without letting go of the original love, in my case for Jesus, this beloved. We are seeking to understand and write how an uncompromised and deeply religious love can flourish even when we overhear and glimpse other such loves, and lose our beloved somewhere in between. There is no overarching theory that can entirely stabilize the intense poetic and dramatic particularities of traditions, as if to generalize them without killing them. And so our project must in some ways resemble Graham's, moving forward, if at all, only by an overtaxed writing that is more eloquent precisely in its despair of any sure, seamless conclusions.[108]

A THEODRAMATICS IMAGINED ACROSS TWO TRADITIONS: A KEY TO ACT TWO AND WHAT FOLLOWS

Accordingly, in Act Two we take up the work begun in Act One, entering upon the unwieldy space where the *Song* and *Holy Word* meet, a clearing rich to excess in poetic and dramatic meanings not ruled by one overarching narrative or single theory. Inspired by Balthasar's vision of the wholeness of the theopoetic, theodramatic, and theologic realms, we embrace with some intensity of our own the possibility of a hidden beloved, a prospect arising in the *Song* and the *Holy Word* and made intensely clear in the commentaries. We remain mindful too of Graham's errant reading of Hopkins and Pascal, so intensely specific and sensual a commitment to experience and the words arising from it. What more can be said after such reading will be the topic of Entr'acte Two. Vendler's words may, we hope, be extended to this situation: "While it is true that we are initially *drawn* to poems by their passions, their questions, and their tonal urgencies, we are *convinced* by them, finally, insofar as they can invent formal means for their impelling motives." When poets succeed in finding a way to write, "the world never seems the same again," since "the style of our own inner kinesthetic motions has, through them, been broken and remade; and as Yeats reminds us, in moments of the breaking of style it is ourselves that we remake."[109] My goal to write with this conviction, both the theology and the theologian remade after learning from both women in their encounters with the hidden beloved.

How can we manage to write this theology—still theopoetic, still theodramatic—across two traditions without too calmly forgetting or too blithely presuming to find the beloved? In light of such questions, it is possible to characterize Act Two, the heart of the real work of this book's close-up, unrelieved reading. It is comprised of the three pairs of scenes already mentioned, farther steps along the journey we embarked upon in Act One: *being alone, searching*, and, in the face of absence, *conjuring the beloved* in fierce remembrance. In these scenes we encounter over and again realities all too familiar from ordinary life: we are alone, we are searching, and even in our successes we fail to say what we mean. Such moments are first visualized distinctly, but afterward become episodes in a single story that grows vivid in our memories. And so too both stories together: despite the many differences in genre and speech that distinguish these women and their difficult loves, in our reading they become hard to keep apart, each love intensifying and upsetting the other.

Such reading is hard work. Assonances in tone and theme aside, the *Song* and *Holy Word* do not read smoothly together, the deeper one gets into each of them. Nor do they want to be read together. Each invites us to enter its world and stay only there; each shines inward, a world tolerating no other. Nor do Bernard and Gilbert, Nanjiyar and Nampillai, need anything more than what they find in the texts right in front of them.[110]

But in our double reading we resist this enclosure and do something else, seeking to intensify particular loves, while yet not forgetting just how far our imaginations can take us. By studying the *Song* along with its medieval Christian readers, a Christian may intensify her desire for Jesus, a Jesus real enough to come near, to hide, and later become manifest again. But if we are reading well, then even as we focus on this beloved, images and scenes from Hindu poetry flood our imaginations; taking to heart the *Holy Word* and its medieval Hindu readers, we wander off a straight Christian path only to find Krishna intimately, passionately nearby—not our beloved, but very close by. A Hindu reader given over to Krishna may find Jesus, the other beloved, likewise unpredictably nearby. In reading together the *Song* and the *Holy Word*, we multiply possibilities and accentuate the challenges facing readers who honor the theological and literary dimensions of both sacred texts and their traditions. We travel both ways, getting lost there and in the loves they express. Like the woman, we may find ourselves uncertain where to go next, our faith seeking to understand, but carried away by love and for the moment possessed of no sure, guiding words.

All this is worth the trouble. Working through the *Song* and the *Holy Word* in a carefully ambiguous reading across these uncertain boundaries is timely in a particular way. Today our religious seeing is more abundant and more varied than we can digest, and amid a torrent of details and perspectives we are becoming ever more vulnerable to the sheer multitude of nearby others, less secure in the simpler and sure commitments with which we started and to which we hope to return. The particular, uneven play of our reading of her words in the *Song* and the *Holy Word* mirrors the difficult interreligious terrain of today's world, where even the most passionate believers see too much, remember too much. In the exercises that constitute Act Two, therefore, we mirror and accentuate the crisis and gift of our time, writing at the difficult points of abundance and excess, absence and hiddenness. If we refuse to generalize and smooth away the most interesting and captivating images and words, the beloved known in just this way and no other way, we may for a time end up more and not less confused regarding how to think about the many religions we live among. This is inevitable, it is necessary. Aiming at an incomplete and destabilized theology, and delaying even a start on that theology until Entr'acte Two, leaves room for a real theodrama. This changes what we expect regarding how God may be imagined in a time when traditions intersect repeatedly in ways that cannot be anticipated.

In Entr'acte Two I will suggest that this latter-day absence is grounded not merely in the vacuum where words about God no longer work, but in excess too, in the surfeit of speech on divine love dramatized in the two traditions. For this purpose, in Entr'acte Two we retrace ground already covered. We return first to Jorie Graham, now traveling still deeper inside her exploration of un-certain spiritual realities by reading her "The Taken-Down God," a poem that marks a Holy Saturday when, in a small Italian church, she faces the prospect—the urge, the dread—of writing as a (inappropriate) material act and (uncer-tain) spiritual need, noisily scratching pen on paper, committing profane acts of writing in church, right near a lifeless Jesus taken down and now lying there at the foot of his cross. Here again she writes close up to spiritual energies and still urgent pieties, even when traditional religion—and the beloved himself—seem to have died, slipping from her grasp. Her writing an insistence forlorn and hopeless, yet too a manifestation of holy desire.

And then we turn back to Balthasar, in order to find our way on the path from theopoetics and theodramatics back to theology. Here I examine clues from the end of the *Theo-Drama* and in the volumes of the *Theo-Logic*, as he begins rewriting his theology after the theopoetic and theodramatic ventures of the preceding twelve volumes. He respects the space opened by the depar-ture of Jesus, required that the Spirit might be poured forth. At this point, even searching seems an unnecessary and impossible project: the beloved cannot be found except when he chooses—in his searching for us. Although Balthasar insists on a robust affirmation of the truth of the Christian faith, he does not neglect the speechlessness and silence endemic to the deeper testimonies of that faith. If we take his advice to heart, we will admit that the reader must speak beyond the images and events of the *Song* and the *Holy Word*, and even beyond our reading of them together. But this "speaking beyond" works only if it still bears resonances of those intensely particular images and events that prose cannot easily retain. I close Entr'acte Two by asking how those of us who are Christian might once again speak complexly but with care and desire about Jesus, the beloved, in a world that is going to remain religiously diverse. In the end, there is still reason to assert the truths in love, even if we cannot forget those other loves and other truths.

Act Three will leave us hanging, faced with the uncertainty still at play in the last words of each woman:

> Flee away, O my beloved, and be like to the roe, and to the young hart upon the mountains of aromatical spices. (*Song* 8.14)

> "Calamities will befall them and You too—mark my word—alas!
> By Kamsa's command brawny demons wander about, disturbing even ascetics.
> Yet being alone seems so important to You, You don't want even Your Balarama,
> Even with him You won't go about!"
> I keep saying this, yet inside me my soul burns:
> Herding cows pleases You more than heaven, but still—
> Your lips are so full and red, our smiling god of the cowherds. (*Holy Word*,
> 10.3.10)

Such texts mark an end point that is no ending.

But even this is merely prediction, until we have done the work of Act Two.

ACT TWO
SPIRITUAL EXERCISES
IN TIMES OF ABSENCE

ACT TWO PROCEEDS BY THREE STEPS. First, we visit these women in the depth of their abandonment in the night as they await in vain the return of a lover who does not come. Second, their paths diverge, and we must follow each in turn. The woman of the *Song* arises and goes out in search of her beloved in the night. Improbably, she finds him, even if later on she will lose him again. By contrast, the woman of the *Holy Word* knows where her beloved is—so very nearby—but still she cannot manage to travel the short distance to him. Hers is a yearning that turns out to be no search at all, only a more profound disorientation at the prospect of a beloved just out of reach, nearby, acting as if she were no one, nowhere. Third, in the depths of their inability to live apart from the beloved, these women become most eloquent in conjuring his presence by the power of their word, in desperate song overcoming the separation of these lovers.

FOR MEDITATION

[16] My beloved to me, and I to him who feedeth among the lilies,
[17] Till the day break, and the shadows retire.
Return: be like, my beloved, to a roe,
Or to a young hart upon the mountains of Bether.

[1] In my bed by night I sought him whom my soul loveth;
I sought him, and found him not.

(*Song* 2.16–3.1)

1 All the city sleeps, all the world is
    intensely black,
All the waters are calmed, and one long
    night stretches out.
He ate the whole earth,
Our Lord who is nearby on the snake bed,
But now He does not come.
Alas, who can save the life of this doer of
    stubborn deeds?

2 Who will protect my life now?
Finishing off the deep sea and earth and
    sky in one great move,
This stubborn night stretches on,
But my Krishna, the kavi-robed Lord,
    does not come—
O sinner's heart—even you are not on
    my side!

3 See, even you are not on my side, O
    heart! And so this long night
—When time does not pass—stretches
    on for ages.
My Kakuttan does not come with his
    furious biting bow,
Yet this sinner, born a woman, does not
    know how to die.

4 "I cannot look upon the great sorrow
    touching those born women,"
Says the radiant sun, and so it does not
    come, it hides.
This earth He spanned, my dark bull, His
    eyes wide and lips red, but now He
    does not come.
My mind is greatly disturbed:
Who will heal it?

5 Who thinks about me?
The women and my friend sleep through
    the long night and no one asks, "How
    are you?"
But even so my dark-cloud Krishna does
    not come.
My name does not let me fade away,
It stays on behind me, behind all the
    deeds I've done.

6 Right behind me, love's malady keeps
    smiting my heart, and
Right before me goes this night ages long,
    covering my eyes, blinding me,
But even so my marvelous one does not
    come bearing his steady discus.
My long-suffering spirit: who will be its
    protector in this situation?

7 Who will be my protector in this
    situation?
Within these walls of darkness and fine
    dew, night rolls along across endless
    ages,
But holding his discus and conch, pure
    and white, He does not appear.
My deeds are like fire—O gods, is there
    anything I can do?

8 O gods, is there anything I can do?
This night is seven ages long, on purpose
    it comes and wears down my spirit,
Yet my Krishna, discus in hand, does not
    come.
Winter's lovely south wind burns me
    worse than fire.

9 Worse than fire it burns, darkness
    swollen yet like a mist.
The tall adorned chariot of the radiant
    warm sun does not appear, and
My generous giver, his lotus eyes radiant
    bright, does not come:
So who now will end my heart's affliction?
I remain here, even as I dissolve.

10 I remain here, even as I dissolve, and
    just like that,
The lofty sky dissolves into fine dew, and
    night goes on.
"Once the Lord came and measured the
    earth, but now He does not come":
No one even once utters these words. The
    whole world sleeps.

(Holy Word 5.4.1–10)

ALONE IN THE NIGHT

In *Song* 3.1, this woman finds herself awake, alone in the dark and bereft of her beloved, uncertain whether he will come, whether she should go in search of him. Although she seems to have just sent him away, immediately she grieves his absence. After a moment of intense union, she is alone, and night after night, she yearns for him, unable to sleep. In *Holy Word* 5.4, this other woman remains alone as before, as she has been since lingering in the garden in 1.4. The intervening songs in her voice—and the voice of her mother—show only an increase in tension. As the situation worsens, here in *Holy Word* 5.4 the poet sings again in her voice, for only in that way can he find words for the beloved's absence. Let us now visit each of these women in their sleepless night.

The *Song* has not prepared us for the drama of this darkness. After all, *Song* 2 glowed with moments of intense intimacy, and beautiful words expressive of their love still echo around us. That chapter closed suddenly with her decision to send him away:

> My beloved to me, and I to him who feedeth among the lilies,
>
> Till the day break, and the shadows retire.
>
> Return: be like, my beloved, to a roe,
>
> Or to a young hart upon the mountains of Bether.

And yet—seemingly just a moment later—she lies unsleeping, anxious for his return:

> In my bed by night I sought him whom my soul loveth;
>
> I sought him, and found him not.[1]

Bernard, the first of our three guides, ponders this abrupt change in scene and mood. He traces it to the intensity of her love and her reckless neglect of self. In summoning her beloved just as he is leaving—at her behest—she shows how she no longer understands or controls what she wants. She cries out, "Return:[2] be like, my Beloved, to a roe, or to a young hart," but, "What is this? It only now He departed and does thou beg Him to return? What unexpected event can have happened in so short a time? Has the Spouse forgotten something? Aye, she has forgotten everything which is not her Bridegroom, forgotten even herself."[3] Surely she is "unsound in reason" and oblivious to the ordinary way of things: "This is all due to her intemperate love. For love is a power that conquers and renders captive to itself every sense of shame, every restriction of modesty, every counsel of deliberation, and induces a total disregard and neglect of all the rules of fittingness and decorum."[4]

But why has he gone away and not come back to her? The theologian might propose a clear reason: he is the Christ who must ascend whence he came. She cannot halt this great movement of salvation history, no matter no matter how passionate her pleas, or how vehemently she begs him to complete his work and come back to her. From her viewpoint, if he must ascend, then at least he should hasten to return as he had promised. This is why she begs him to hurry back like a roe or a hart, since their speed matches the intensity of her soul's longing: "By this she manifests the eager longing of her soul which reckons no swiftness enough. And does she not daily ask this when she says in the Lord's Prayer, 'Thy kingdom come'?"[5]

What the beloved himself intends by his departure is in Bernard's conjecture less clear. Perhaps he is testing her as he once tested his disciples on the road to Emmaus, when Jesus seemed as if to continue on his way, until the two disciples invited him to stay. Like them, she too is being tested, to see if she can bear to let him go: "When passing her by, He desires that she would lay hold of Him; and when going away, He wishes to be called back. For He is by no means an irrevocable Word. He goes away and He comes back according to His pleasure, visiting the soul 'in the early morning and suddenly testing' her."[6] He departs because he cares for her, and by that same love he will return.

She expects his return even at the moment she sends him away; this is simply the way of such love: "It is evident that He Whom she thus recalls is not now present, yet has been with her, and that but a short time ago. For she is calling Him back, as it seems, whilst He is still in the act of retiring. That He is in so untimely a way solicited to return is a proof both of the greatness of her love and of the attraction of His amiability."[7] But what does it mean to call God back? Theologically, one might insist that in reality the divine lover neither comes nor goes: "Shall we suppose that the Bridegroom is here acting with fickle inconstancy? He Whose immensity fills all space, whence can He be said to come, or whither to go or to return? Besides, He is a Spirit, and what manner of locomotion is a pure spirit capable of? Finally, how can He Who is God admit of any kind of motion, since God is absolutely and essentially immutable?"[8] But these certainties do nothing to alleviate her pain; she suffers real absence. Bernard, as it were, gives up seeking a middle ground between what theology allows and experience asserts: "He that can understand, let him understand these things."[9] The truth of what God intends lies still deeper; so great a mystery is disclosed only imperfectly in frail human words. Scripture "speaks of the wisdom hidden in the mystery, but does so in our own words."[10] Human speech serves its purpose, for this word, "even as it enlightens our human minds," also "roots our affections on God, and imparts to us the incomprehensible and invisible things of God by means of figures drawn from the likeness of things familiar to us, like precious draughts in vessels of cheap earthenware."[11] Diligent readers ought not consider themselves privy to a higher viewpoint whence they might look on the absence and presence of the beloved with dispassion; the best are caught up in the mystery of the beloved's coming and going about which they read.[12]

Yet thereafter Bernard again insists that this beloved does not really change, and here at least, experience does not translate directly into theology. While it is true that "the Word of God, as the Bridegroom of the soul, visits her and departs from her according to His good pleasure," in reality, "in all this there is question, not of any change or motion in the Word, but merely in the feelings of the soul herself."[13] If the beloved is not really going or really returning, then his "absence" is the drama of her inner disturbance. The Word's going and coming are "accomplished in the soul":[14]

> Therefore she cannot but seek Him when He is absent from her, and recall Him when He is going away. The Word, consequently, is recalled; He is recalled by the desire of the soul, yet only of that soul which He has once permitted to taste of His sweetness. Is not her desire a cry? Yea, and a strong cry. . . . Hence, when the Bridegroom withdraws, the soul, by her continuous desire of Him, keeps up one uninterrupted cry, as it were, one uninterrupted "Return, my Beloved," until He comes back to console her.[15]

He comes sooner than we deserve but not as soon as we desire, since "the haste which is sufficient for merit is not enough for desire." Indeed, "the loving soul is borne on by her feelings; she is drawn forward by her desires; she has no regard to merit; she closes her eyes to His majesty and opens them to His delights." This is why she calls him back and confidently asks again for his delights, in familiarity naming him "not as her Lord, but as her Beloved."[16]

His absence then is for her sake, "in order that her desire may increase, that her affection be tested, that the work of love be undertaken. This is no evidence of anger, but only dissimulation. It only remains, therefore, that He be sought, if perchance He may be found when sought, Who when called has not come. . . . On account of the reasons just given, He has not come back at her invitation.

This only makes her who loves the more desirous of His presence, and with all eagerness she begins at once to seek Him out."[17] Sleepless and discontented, she finally must leave her bed and go out searching for what she once had had but then lost hold of. Her love endures no separation, and the night of his absence simply makes the situation all the more intolerable: "Now the day makes manifest what the night conceals, so that what you sought in the night you discover in the day. It is therefore night so long as the Bridegroom is sought; because if it were day He would be evident and by no means would be sought."[18]

It is here that Gilbert of Hoyland takes up Bernard's unfinished work and begins his own sermons. Noting the gap between 2.17 and 3.1, Gilbert too traces the ups and downs of love, and with a certain equanimity: "The affections of lovers are subject to change, for their situations are subject to change," so it is not surprising that "the cries of the bride at times seem disjointed, for now according to her longing she enjoys her Beloved but again, contrary to her longing, she is bereft of Him."[19] This is why she tells him to go but immediately begs him to return: "In love affection blurts out, then checks its words, for affection does not always remain in one self-consistent mood. Even the Bridegroom himself is compared to a fawn, and rightly, because He misleads, and flees from His beloved." So the fluctuation in her moods "lacks neither sequence nor logic," given the mysterious reality it faithfully reflects.[20]

Indeed, if we attend to the undercurrent of her affections without fixing unduly on what she says at any given moment, we can see the coherence of her changes of mind and mood. This dramatic uncertainty gives body and form to her love.[21] Her words mark the grief of a lover who wants nothing more than to hold her beloved, when just seeing him is no longer sufficient to keep him close: she "longs not only to touch but also to enfold and embrace the Word of life" inside herself. To achieve this, like him she retreats and "shuns the public and seeks a secret place, the secrecy of her little bed at night."[22] These confines focus her meditation, "for in one's little bed and in the mind's secret retreat, He can be traced more freely, found more quickly, held more securely and perhaps even detained for a longer spell, if indeed any spell be long in delights which practically at their inception are wont to be interrupted."[23] That she is awake and desperate need not be counted merely as depression, unless perhaps it is "that grief which love begets for an absent spouse." The bride is where she needs to be, wishing "to be allured rather than to be cured and so to have sought a friend rather than a physician."[24] The night is "suited to the charm of charity," and so it "prompts the bride to seek more ardently."

That her sorrow be most intense at night is not unexpected, "for there, where she could enjoy Him with greater fruitfulness, she is bereft of her beloved with greater anguish."[25] Night is for lovers, and for the sleeplessness of those who are alone. Gilbert recognizes that nothing can be certain about such nights, since her beloved remains utterly free: "The Bridegroom is not always wont to meet the desires of the soul which seeks Him, either at the time or in the measure requested."[26] But this does not soften her complaint:

> Will it seem so delightful to You, O Lord, to torment a pitiful soul with such delay and to laugh at the torments of one who loves You and seeks You? If majesty sets You apart, let mercy make You stoop down. If You do not yield Yourself to Your beloved's affection, at least take pity on her affliction. . . . You feign not to hear, You put me off and turn Your face from me, and I am thrown into confusion. Therefore I complain, I lament and cry out, "I have not found Him."[27]

Theology is effective here because its expectations are thwarted: God is everywhere, it seems, except here; she is nowhere but here, yet it is her love that has no limits. He is nowhere to be seen, but she refuses to believe that he will hide forever; nothing will stop her, but nothing alleviates her pain: "I called Him, but He gave no answer."

IN MY ENDLESS NIGHT

She too is alone, in a very dark night:

> All the city sleeps, all the world is intensely black,
> All the waters are calmed, and one long night stretches on and on.
> He ate the whole earth,
> Our Lord who is nearby on the snake bed,[28]
> But now He does not come.
> Alas, who can save the life of this doer of stubborn deeds? (*Holy Word* 5.4.1)

Her beloved too is absent, and he shows no sign of returning. No one cares; she lies awake suffering his absence, and no one even hears her lonely cry. For this reason, she slips into still deeper darkness. At this point in the *Holy Word*, we have not been told of her previous union with him, perfect or even disrupted. There is no indication that they quarreled or that she has sent him away. All we have is her pure distress: he does not come. The only change is that she has been languishing for too long and is growing weaker, more anxious; this time, there are no messengers to send. She thought she knew him well, remembering how once he swallowed the whole world in order to protect it, and how even now he rests between heaven and earth on his serpent bed, near enough to help those in need. Perhaps she does know, but such knowledge does her no good, and even makes his absence all the more painful. So she falls into this endless night, cosmic calamity bereft of natural and divine light.

The early commentator Tirukurukai Piran Pillan explains her troubles against the background of the previous song, 5.3.[29] There she had threatened a public display, the culturally stylized protest of riding through the streets on a horse made of palmyra stems, that she might shame him into returning. She was exceedingly depressed at failing to manage even that public protest, and now, out of the public eye, she is entirely alone. As Nanjiyar puts it: "Night has come, and all beings that move or are unmoving sleep; all her relatives, unable to bear her anguish, are overcome and lie in a deep sleep; she is alone and agitated. This great blackness, lasting many eons, rolls along and gives no opportunity for escape."[30] Here too the thought crosses her mind that her own deeds are to blame. But she also knows he is famed for his compassion and readiness to help those in need, so if she is undeserving, that fact should motivate rather than put him off: "She describes the cruel karma causing her depression, but also that best of all males who should be helping her in her condition. She recalls his gallantry and other virtues, and recites them every day."[31] Nampillai observes that her longing is all the more painful since she does know very well the character of her beloved, how gracious he can be with other people at other times: "He came and helped the world in the time of catastrophe that was the cosmic dissolution, but He does not come and help me in this separation, as total as any such dissolution. Isn't my survival worth something?" And so "she gives up any hope regarding her own survival."[32] The refrain recurs in every verse: *now* he is not coming, *now* he is not doing anything for me, *now* my torment grows ever greater. Although this lover took the whole world inside himself during the dissolution in order to protect it, nothing like happens for her now, even if she is so small and could be swallowed so easily.

Her anguish is played out on a cosmic scale, as if matched only by the darkness and emptiness of a universe intensely devoid of light, as if already fallen into the cosmic dissolution where every world cycle terminates. It is not just a matter of darkness: every sound is silenced by the "calming of the waters." "She does not get to pass the time with anyone, because the whole city is asleep; she does not get to spend her time watching anything, because all the world is a great darkness; she has nothing to listen to, since all sound has been muffled as if beneath water. This is not like previous long nights; to this night one sees no end; compared to it, all previous nights are but a moment."[33] Lacking what she desires but without anything else to focus on, she is caught in a space of sensory deprivation, a naked experience of time itself: "If this had happened in daytime, the senses would like a lizard be clinging to all their proper objects, and so her unbearable suffering would have been cut in half. But at night, all the senses are without their individual objects, and so her unbearable suffering breaks all bounds."[34] Solitude itself is a problem, as "the whole city sleeps," so there is no one to console her, or even to notice her loss; her friend, faithful in past difficult times, is asleep, and so too her mother. Even words of mockery or rebuke would provide some human contact, but now no one says anything.

In her isolation she will not forget him, and she is tortured by memories of him; this torment is what keeps her from perishing:[35] "By knowledge of his qualities she endures."[36] Though he does not come and does not act, it is a consolation to remember what he is really like; she can still hope. Her desire for her beloved, frustrated at every turn, grows purer, to the point that she is entirely focused on him even when he is nowhere to be found. What the theologian might expect is reversed: this human woman is constant in her love, but her divine lover fails to live up to his reputed innate compassion: "She is pure by the intensity of her desire. Even if his activity is not in accord with his proper nature, she (in accord with hers) is intent on gaining him."[37]

The drama of this moment—lonely, unsleeping love, ever faithful in the face of a beloved who does not return—is captured in the first verse, but as in every song, the theme plays itself out in many variations in the verses that follow. In verse 2 she is worn down, dissolved by a night that never ends. It is all the darker because to no avail she awaits a Krishna whose kavi garment will be as rosy as the dawn:[38]

> Who will protect my life now?
> Finishing off the deep sea and earth and sky in one great move,
> This stubborn night stretches on,
> But my Krishna, the kavi-robed Lord, does not come—

To make matters worse, even her heart betrays her, preoccupied with him and of no help to her:[39]

> O sinner's heart—even you are not on my side! (2)

See, even you are not on my side, O heart! And so this long night
—When time does not pass—stretches on for ages.

In the same way she recollects the story of Rama,[40] who in the *Ramayana* is celebrated as coming into the world to protect the helpless; he is renowned for his bow, fierce against all those who would oppress those depending on him:

My Kakuttan does not come with his furious biting bow,

It should be easy, Nanjiyar suggests, for so fierce a warrior as Rama to banish her sorrow in a moment. Or, given her desperation, he could just as well kill her. But Rama does neither, and seems merely to ignore her. Like Sita in her captivity, she feels that suicide is her only option; but as a woman she is thwarted even in that, for she neither lives nor dies by her own choice:

Yet this sinner, born a woman, does not know how to die. (3)

Now death is no longer a worst fate, but rather her inability to hasten such an ending. In sympathy, the sun refuses to rise, but in that way inadvertently extends the darkness:

"I cannot look upon the great sorrow touching those born women,"
Says the radiant sun, and so it does not come, it hides.

He has betrayed his reputation as Krishna and Rama, and now her beloved also fails to live up to his reputation as the divine dwarf who grew large and stepped across the universe in three strides in order to set it free. That he can do, but toward her, he takes not a single step:

This earth He spanned, my dark bull, His eyes wide and lips red, but now He
    does not come.

Perhaps he is even taunting her with those wide eyes and full smile, now seared into her memory, even as he does nothing more for her. He just smiles. She languishes, her mind fevered with love:

My mind is greatly disturbed:
Who will heal it? (4)

But again, the fact that no one notices makes things worse:

Who thinks about me?

The women and my friend sleep through the long night and no one asks, "How
   are you?"[41]
But even so my dark-cloud Krishna does not come.

Nanjiyar observes that in this last line she once more returns to the image of
Krishna, by reputation ever loving and accessible; his refusal to help her is all
the more dismaying. In her despair she wants simply to disappear, so that even
her name is erased from memory, but even this is beyond her grasp. She lingers
as one blamed for her attachments, guilty of loving too much:

My name does not let me fade away,
It stays on behind me, behind all the deeds I've done. (5)

Right behind me, love's malady keeps smiting my heart, and
Right before me goes this night ages long, covering my eyes, blinding me

She evokes Krishna's discus, that weapon of war used to punish the evil and
protect the good:

But even so my marvelous one does not come bearing his steady discus.

It as if Krishna is showing it to her, even while neglecting to help her.[42] So again
she casts her question into the dark:

My long-suffering spirit: who will be its protector in this situation? (6)

Who will be my protector in this situation?

Nampillai comments at length on her question and emphasizes her daring: the
lord, the beloved, is known to be the protector par excellence, and she does not
hesitate to remind him of this. Knowing all about him, still she asks whether
there is anyone (else) who might protect her.[43] So too she knows that he is
superior to the gods, but knowing that divinities never sleep, she suggests that
therefore they might be able to console her now:

Within these walls of darkness and fine dew, night rolls along across endless ages,
But holding his discus and conch, pure and white, He does not appear.
My deeds are like fire—O gods, is there anything I can do? (7)

O gods, is there anything I can do?
This night is seven ages long, on purpose it comes and wears down my spirit,
Yet my Krishna, discus in hand, does not come.

But the gods too remain silent.

Oddly, in that dark and silent place she feels a gentle breeze; perversely, though cool it burns her, and the dark becomes now a kind of fiery mist:

Winter's lovely south wind burns me worse than fire. (8)[44]
Worse than fire it burns, invading her everywhere.

She can visualize her beloved astride the rising sun, but this only means that both he and the sun fail to rise:

The tall adorned chariot of the radiant warm sun does not appear, and
My generous giver, his lotus eyes radiant bright, does not come.

And so she is trapped, attached to her beloved and unable to let go of him, dying yet unable to fall into that oblivion:[45]

So who now will end my heart's affliction?
I remain here, even as I dissolve. (9)

I remain here, even as I dissolve, and just like that,
The lofty sky dissolves into fine dew, and night goes on.

All the more bitterly, she again notes that no one cares to speak a word on her behalf:

"Once the Lord came and measured the earth, but now He does not come":
No one even once utters these words. The whole world sleeps. (10)

As the verse ends, this lover is still alone in the night. By every expectation, he should come, and she settles on no explanation for his absence. Her song expresses this unresolved puzzle, and we are left hanging.

The commentators do not find her situation to be hopeless, even after such a bleak ending. After all, the next song, 5.5, presumes that she has survived, perhaps by visualizing her beloved in the temple town of Tirukurunkuti, evoked repeatedly in that song.[46] Moreover, the eleventh verse of 5.4 itself gives a different and not entirely unrelated clue: the beloved is not really absent or asleep; rather, he is in a state of utterly motionless yogic wakefulness, a waking sleep in which his senses, like hers, are in suspension even as he is totally aware:

He seemed asleep when He did his yoga, that Lord.

Periyavacchan Pillai comments that in this way the saint is commenting on the lord's nearby distance, removed presence: he "reflects on the Lord, on how He sleeps in the Milk Ocean to protect the world. 'Because He does not come now, for that reason we are angry. But He has not abandoned us. He lies there because from the beginning He has been thinking of our protection.'" With these thoughts, she endures. The beloved, ever awake and attentive, has simply drawn her into the dark light of his yoga, and it is of this phenomenon that the saint sings:

> About whom Shatakopan in Kurukur among beautiful gardens
> Composed these ten verses of this thousand threaded together in splendid melody.
> When you die, how could you not reach Vaikunta by these verses? (11)

To recite the qualities of the lord, even while lamenting the disjunction between those qualities and his absence from her life, has good effect.[47] Her song, possessed of an anguish possible only for those who love deeply, enables those who sing it to reach heaven. She does not cease grieving, yet her potent words become for others a transport beyond death:

> Those who meditate on these ten verses, upon separation from the body cannot but enter that highest place. She said, "My name does not let me fade away, It stays on behind me, behind all the deeds I've done" (5.4.5), and sought to die, but even that she could not manage. One need not experience what she suffered, but whoever hears this verse will not die. Whoever sees the anguish of this one intent entirely on the lord cannot but survive. Such is the reality behind all this. Even if you do not experience their relationship, as long as you meditate on her condition, your own experience will surely be to enter the highest place.[48]

INTERLUDE: *In Our Own Night*

I said earlier that the *Song* and the *Holy Word* are each sufficient unto itself. For centuries readers have taken their images and dramatic scenes to be complete and compelling bodies of poetry for reflection and for guidance along the spiritual path, without need of supplement from other religions. The larger theological meanings aligned with these texts, even if ever deferential to the poetry and the underlying mysteries of love, are taken to be more or less settled. The *Song* and the *Holy Word* and their communities do not need one other, and readers might well spend a lifetime with either of them, seeking no farther. But they certainly can be read together and in a certain harmony. In each case, the lover is exhausted by her love and she is longing for a beloved who has gone into hiding, and she lies sleepless in the night. In *Song* 3.1, she is unable to sleep, as if in that way to stop desiring that beloved who had so recently been with her. "Night after night" marks her habitual turbulence, as she lingers on the edge between learning to live with his absence—longing as a way of life—and finding that life without him is in fact intolerable. Her discontent soon drives her out into the streets. This unsleeping is not merely a lack, since her yearning is fueled by vivid memories of her beloved, so recently with her but no longer there. His absence at the center of her life is tangible, material. In *Holy Word* 5.4 she lies awake in total darkness, deprived of every object, no thing able to stand in for her beloved. This is a cruel emptiness.

If readers take all of this to heart—both poems, their dark nights, the stark and barely assimilated images, the dramatic uncertainties—and if we read attentively and vulnerably enough that we cannot forget either of them. We attain a certain empathy with each of them, and perhaps then a deeper affinity with both, the one in the presence of the other. It becomes harder to choose to follow one woman along her spiritual path without the longings and fears of the other infusing and perhaps confusing mind and heart. If we manage some empathy with each and both, we will not be able to finish off any neat comparison and then move on. In this poetic and dramatic realm, we find—to our pleasure or dismay—that our beloved is not only in hiding but that he is also more than we had imagined, he goes to places we do not visit, and may even be known by names we have not heard before. He has other lovers too. This admission need not make impossible a commitment to one true love or to one true colloquy in its specific concreteness, as if, because we now know so much more, we have to give up our one, particular, intense understanding of the beloved. This cooling of love is not necessary; this is about more love, not less. For this we tread no simple path, and it is all the harder to find our way through the now greater possibilities before us, if we have lost the innocence of expecting a single set of images, events, and answers to light our way. But as we plunge deeper into both women's deep loves, it is also the case that the abandonment of passionate deeper truths becomes less likely than ever: we are lost, but we are caught; we are lost, because we love more, not less. Where innocence used to be, instead we find a rich and holy bewilderment, lament at the hiddenness of the beloved.

The reader who remembers both poems no longer fits comfortably within the world of the *Song*, even as she cannot quite get a grasp on the *Holy Word*. Whatever the Christian or Hindu reader might think and believe, those who remember the beloved more capaciously can no longer *imagine* Krishna only as the beloved, nor Jesus alone as the one who might return but has delayed.

Each narrative takes ambiguity and loss to heart, but neither has anticipated it in quite this way: two women, not one, sleepless in the night. At this point we lose even the familiar contours of predictable love or familiar absences and conventional suffering, God present just this way or absent just that way. We too lie awake because the beloved really is acting in unexpected ways and faith no longer guarantees just one sorrow and just one consolation.

And so we end up in a rather lonely place, unlike readers who dwell at most in one tradition, or conflate traditions, or give up altogether on the very idea of loving God to excess. Yet this doubling also gathers a new community of readers, those curious at the woman's plight, twice over. At the start, the common point may be simply the very human dynamic of love and its fragilities, union and its abrupt intensifications and cessations. Whoever has loved and discovered the beloved to have slipped away may in the end share both women's passions and pleasures. But once we have managed to become unmoored and distressed, a rediscovery of this hidden beloved becomes a real, recovered possibility, because we are no longer comfortably settled in one canon, one body of interpretation, one set of theological meanings.

But we are by no means at the end of anything. These women find their way out of their dark nights; they get up and search. Since we too need to find a way out of our present situation, let us now see how they go about searching—in a kind of imperfect wandering, erring—for the beloved.

FOR MEDITATION

[2] I will rise, and will go about the city:
In the streets and the broad ways
I will seek him whom my soul loveth.
I sought him, and I found him not.
[3] The watchmen who keep the city, found me,
"Have you seen him, whom my soul loveth?"
[4] When I had a little passed by them,
I found him whom my soul loveth.
I held him, and I will not let him go,
Till I bring him into my mother's house,
And into the chamber of her that bore me.

(*Song* 3.2–4)

1 Good, doe-eyed women, day by day this
  sinner grows weaker.
There, where lovely areca palm fill the
  heavens
Where honey-rich jasmine wafts
  fragrance,
There amid honey-filled gardens is
  Tiruvallaval where the king dwells:
When will I, ever at his feet, reach those
  feet?

2 Friends, what do you get from afflicting
  me?
There, where the south wind carries the
  scent
Of the splendid flowering mastwood,
  apewood, and young white fig,
There in Tiruvallaval town the Lord
  dwells:
When will we, ever at His feet, wear the
  dust of those feet?

3 You are lovely with those flowers in
  your hair,
But my grief-stricken self fades away.
There, where fine Vedic chanting
  resounds like the waves of the sea
And the smoke of oblations wafts in
  every direction,
There in cool Tiruvallaval the tall Lord
  dwells.
So tell me, will I be able to gaze ever
  upon his feet?

4 Friends, you keep tormenting me, but
  why do this?
There, where tall young areca palms, jack
  trees, coconut palms, and mango
  trees
Rise above terraced houses,
There in cool Tiruvallaval He lies on his
  venomous serpent,
The Lord, our sole good.

5 My very good friends,
There the smoke of good brahmins'
  sacrifices
Conceals the lofty sky with a good
  darkness,
There, in cool Tiruvallaval, is that cane
  sugar, ripe fruit, sweet ambrosia,
That radiance who holds all my good:
When will my eyes get to see Him?

6 O gentle women with fine mouths, will
  this sinner ever get to see Him?
There, where fresh breezes carry the
  songs of bees
Amid the lofty branches of lush trees in
  luxuriant seashore groves,
There stands Tiruvallaval where that
  beautiful dwarf, the lovely Lord,
  resides.
Will this sinner ever get to see his lotus
  feet?

7 Will I get to worship even the flowers at
  his feet, O best of women?
There, where pools broad and deep hold
  tall lotuses and lilies
Bright like women's radiant faces and
  their eyes,
There, in Tiruvallaval dwells the ruler,
  the Lord who swallowed the earth.
Will I ever get to worship the flowers at
  his feet, all my days?

8 Will I get to worship without end, O
  fair-browed women?
There, where sweet sugar cane sways and
  paddy ripens on all sides
In fields everywhere adorned with
  flowering pools,
There in cool Tiruvallaval
Long has dwelled the Lord whose slender
  feet crossed the earth.
Will I ever get to worship Him?

⁹ Can we ever see Him and fill our
   slipping anklets and bracelets
And join our hands in worship?
There, where—as if with flute and harp—
Striped bees swarm in cool gardens,
   drink honey, hum and sing their
   songs.
Can we join our hands in worship there
   in Tiruvallaval
Where the Lord with the whirling discus
   shows his ancient grace?

¹⁰ Will we finally be able to recite his
   names?
By good deeds and their ancient grace,
   my lady friends,
This is the city where heaven and earth
   worship,
Tiruvallaval which supports the good of
   thousands of gracious good people.
There resides our Lord, our good grace.
Will we finally be able to recite the names
   of this Naranan?

(*Holy Word* 5.9.1–10)

IN THE NIGHT, I FOUND HIM

Neither woman is entirely helpless after the trauma of this night vigil. Both seek after a missing beloved who does not come as before.

In the *Song*, this woman rises from her bed and straightaway goes out in search of him. As we have seen, she seems to have sent him away in 2.16, but was confounded when he did not quickly return. As a result, now she cannot find him at all:[49]

I will rise, and will go about the city:
In the streets and the broad ways
I will seek him whom my soul loveth.
I sought him, and I found him not. (3.2)

She arises with some difficulty,[50] and runs from place to place throughout the town. When the verse goes on to specify that she will seek him in the streets and squares, this perhaps emphasizes how thorough her search is, but also its difficulty: "I sought him, but found him not."[51]

Mindful of salvation history, Bernard recognizes that in one sense searching is not really necessary, since by Christ's ascent the goal has already been attained, for him and for everyone else. Searching the city, with its distracting and dangerous alternatives, is in vain, simply because he is no longer there. But she understands none of this, for she has not studied the scriptures, and so she keeps on seeking him in places familiar to her: "Yet she supposes that He is to be sought 'in the streets and the broad ways'; for she eager to enjoy Him but ignorant of the mystery."[52] It is inevitable that at first she fails, but in doing so nonetheless participates in the deeper truth of the beloved: "Consequently she is once more disappointed, and compelled to say, 'I sought Him and I found Him not,' so that 'the word might be fulfilled which He said, 'A little while and you shall not see Me, because I go to the Father.'"[53] Christ is ever faithful but, gone off to heaven, he is no longer here as she was expecting. Those who know God to be faithful must endure this interim period, after ascension and before return, when the beloved's whereabouts remain uncertain.

The beloved has withdrawn, that she might deepen her patience: "Therefore, in order that He not empty faith of its value, He has withdrawn his visible presence, giving a place for virtue of faith. Besides the hour had come when He should return to His own place."[54] Yet—and this is the point—she cannot wait; her distress is not easily overcome, by virtue or theology. She might know that he only does what is best for her, but this recognition does not shield her from the pain of his absence: "But she can at present think of none of these things. As if inebriated with love, she runs hither and thither, seeking with her eyes Him Who the eye cannot touch, but only faith."[55] She forms her own opinion regarding how Christ should be present—for all, but for her in a special way: "For she believes that Christ ought not have entered into His glory without first manifesting to the world the glory of His resurrection, so that the impious might be confounded, the faithful might exult, the disciples glorified, the people converted, and He Himself finally honoured by all, when the resurrection had demonstrated to all the truth of His prediction."[56] If he can do all that, can he not come to her? But the time is not right, Bernard tells her: "Thou art mistaken, O Spouse. These things must indeed come to pass, but in their proper season."[57] If so, one can ask, "What then art thou doing, O Spouse? Dost thou think that thou canst follow Him thither? Hast thou the boldness and hast thou the power to intrude thyself into a mystery so sacred, into a sanctuary so secret, that thou mayst contemplate the Son in the Father and the Father in the Son? Surely not. Where He is thou can not come now, but thou shalt come hereafter."[58]

In the meantime, she is instructed to continue her searching: "Do not allow that inaccessible brightness, that unapproachable sublimity, to turn thee from thy quest or to make thee despair of finding. 'If thou canst believe, all things are possible to one who believeth.' 'The Word is nigh thee, even in thy mouth and in thy heart.'"[59] From yet another angle, she might realize that from the start her search has already succeeded: "Believe and thou has already found. For to believe is to have found. The faithful know that Christ dwelleth by faith in their hearts. What can be nearer? Seek Him therefore with security, seek Him with devotion. The Lord is good to the soul that seeketh Him. "Seek by desires, follow by actions, find by faith."[60] Where he is, she cannot go, but in faith she finds him, by not finding what she did not have, but in a search that is no search: "What is there that faith cannot find? It attains to the inaccessible, it discovers the unknown, it comprehends the immeasurable, it apprehends what is most new, it even includes eternity within the ample space of its own vast bosom. I make bold to say it: the Blessed and Everlasting Trinity, which I do not understand, I believe; and I hold by faith what I cannot grasp by my mind."[61] The beloved's (seeming) absence and her (seeming) search speak to the dynamics of the human situation before God.[62] Appearances matter and the drama must be enacted, that the story of divine-human love be told to its conclusion. Such is the theodrama.

And so the scene finally reaches its climax, as she asks advice, and in this way finds what she is looking for:

> The watchmen who keep the city, found me,
> "Have you seen him, whom my soul loveth?"

Her question receives no clear answer, indeed no reply at all, for they say nothing in return. Perhaps at this point her impetuous love, even as it fuels her question, has itself overcome all obstacles: "O love, so precipitate, so violent, so ardent, so impetuous, suffering the mind to entertain no thought but of thyself, spurning everything which is not thyself, content with thyself alone! Thou disturbest all order, disregardest all usage, ignorest all measure."[63] She is transformed, entirely captivated by her beloved, so completely has he "laid claim to her heart and her tongue."[64]

The more she is enthralled, the more halting her speech. Enraptured by love, she speaks to the watchmen in words that remain veiled to those not similarly caught up in love. This is why she forgets even to name the one she seeks; it is "as if she expects them to know what she was thinking of. Does thou enquire concerning Him Whom my soul loveth? And has He no other name except this? But who art thou thyself and who is He?"[65] Stepping back, Bernard is intrigued by "the strangeness of language and the remarkable disregard for the proprieties of speech which appear to distinguish the present Scripture from all the rest."[66] Mind and word lag far behind, since "holy love, which is manifestly the sole theme of the entire composition, can be measured 'not in word or in tongue, but in deed and in truth.'"[67] For this reason, as Bernard famously says, "it is useless for him who loves not to attempt to read or to listen to this Canticle of love, because a frozen heart can by no means bear this fiery word."[68] Rather, "should anyone desire to attain to an understanding of the things which he reads, let him love."[69] Rigorous theology—clear thinking and articulate words about the beloved—serves a purpose, but it cannot dissipate the dramatic uncertainty of his absence, as if reducing a real crisis to mere appearance. Love alone demonstrates how to read and understand properly. This fire of love can "obtain no lodging in a heart that is cold and frozen."[70]

The watchmen, whose advice we do not hear, have wordlessly instructed her on how to find the beloved. It is only when she has passed them by, that she suddenly, inexplicably, finds him:[71]

> When I had a little passed by them,
> I found him whom my soul loveth.
> I held him, and I will not let him go,
> Till I bring him into my mother's house,
> And into the chamber of her that bore me. (3.2–4)

They can somehow help her because they too are caught up in love, they have "received from the Spirit the gift of love, and so are able to comprehend what the same Spirit speaketh."[72] And so they are able to reply "in the same tongue, that is, by loving affections and offices of piety,"[73] and thereby set her on her way, so that immediately thereafter she encounters him: "How, indeed, could she have failed to find Him, seeing that, wither He has ascended in body, she has attained in mind?"[74] But if so, wandering turns out to be superfluous. In faith, one finds the beloved by an interior realization: the hidden one is always here, within. Yet even if this search is unnecessary, it expresses a desire that will never really be quenched: "The happy attainment does not extinguish this desire, but extends it."[75] The fullness of joy is rather like oil poured upon the flames; search is unnecessary (since he is here) and it is doomed to fail (since he is not here but in heaven). Yet in faith it will bear fruit (as the lovers are reunited).[76]

Gilbert of Hoyland takes up the story here, covering the same ground as Bernard, albeit in his own way. He too finds her search instructive regarding the absences and encounters suffered along the contemplative path. These unpredictable twists and turns more deeply unite her with the beloved. She suffers, he says, in part simply because she does not foresee why her beloved must be absent, neither in the place nor the time one expects. Yet her grief is also a grace: it is because she has loved that she suffers more than others. Her most acute suffering lies in the sudden loss of what she had held for a moment. For it is on the verge of true happiness that she is cheated: "How much more is she distressed who is pierced by a hunger for an interior sweetness once tasted and now lost?"[77] Depths of love and grief outrace one another inside her, and only she can say with full force, "I have not found Him." Because the promise is so great and so near, the waiting becomes all the more terrible: "All things have their proper time; there is a time for embracing and a time to be far away from the embrace. What time will be more suitable for embracing than night, or place than the little bed? In peace is your place and likewise your time of repose, and my little bed of peace I have prepared for you in my heart. Let my Beloved come, let my delight come and rest in His bed."[78] But he does not, and she suffers: "'I have sought Him' is a gracious statement, but 'I have not found Him' is grievous. How could it not be grievous and unbearable to one who seeks and loves as she does?"[79] Even if she knows at some level that the beloved's delay is for her own good, the pain of its slow fruition drives her to act: "I know that comfort is kept in store to be given me in due time but love argues against the slow pace of fleeting time. You keep me waiting; for my part I can bear it no longer but 'will arise and go about the city,'" but not by any measured plan of action: "I scorn my little bed and abandon the first half of my cry that I may be swept forward to what is more perfect."[80]

For Gilbert, too, good theology both diminishes and accentuates the drama of the moment: "Good Jesus, why is it that You are not found in some places, though You are believed to be everywhere? There are indeed many halls in Your Father's house, but do You abandon some when You pass on to others"— and when You do so unnecessarily, since You are 'infinite and unbounded by space?'"[81] Divine omnipresence does not satisfy this woman, since she wants a more intimate visitation: "All things then exhibit You to me for my knowledge, but not everything can move me inwardly to devotion. Everywhere I stumble upon You, but not everywhere am I touched to the heart! Everywhere the beauty, value and harmony of the universe thrust You upon my attention, but as the Word which is Wisdom, not as the Word which is Salvation."[82] She suffers even more than the prodigal son in the Gospel according to Luke: he arises and goes home, while she goes out alone in a dark night's search; his father comes to meet him, while her beloved withdraws from her.[83]

While it may seem pointless to search for this divine beloved who chooses to withdraw, her desire leaps across creation and even unto heaven; it cannot be resisted. She counters his majesty by her devotion, and in that way outdoes him: "One who loves falsely flees from Your sight, but a true bride endowed with the gift of charity pursues even one who is fleeing. Where will You go, good Jesus, from the face of such passionate desire? If You mount into heaven, it is there; if You go down to the depths, it is present. Everywhere, like an anxious sleuth, she follows You ranging throughout all Your creation step by step."[84]

Yet still this is necessarily a plodding search, as she goes looking where she had found him before, retracing familiar routes:"How much do you suppose it consoles her, brothers, to visit and repeatedly tread in the footprints where the feet of her Beloved used to stand?" This is no surprise, since "the places where we have experienced some blessing somehow imprint that blessing more vividly on our memory, paint it in detail before our mind's eye, and what we once experienced there we expect a second time."[85] He is there only in memory, and yet it works: "Whether she retraces what is already known and explored or probes into what is new, in all her inquiries she does but seek fresh kindling for her love."[86] By seeing the old in new ways, one finds the truth: "Good assuredly is going around, not only whenever new and more hidden truths are grasped but also when truths already grasped are unfolded with an affection ever new and ever fresh, not only when one covers new ground but also when frequently one retraces ground already covered."[87] Even as she searches outside herself, she also descends deep into those memories where once before she had encountered the beloved.

Driven by a great love that outstrips all lesser devotions, she bypasses every created thing: "The spirit which hungers and thirsts, finding itself unsatisfied by a few blessings, is always borne on towards the remainder. The spirit is whirled in a kind of roundabout, stretched on the wheel of its spinning desires, until hunger for love is sated with blessings and manages to stop its flight in the place where no limit is found."[88] To hold him in memory even while failing to catch him signals memory's power to find again what seems always to be lost in the past: "How am I not refreshed by what bears some pledge, shows some sign, recalls some memory, suggests some knowledge of my love?"[89] Yet such signs and memories are not enough: "How do I not suffer disappointment, as I reflect that I am being cozened with an image and delayed by a shadow, whereas I do not possess the naked and simple truth?"[90] Yet it is during this errant search that her beloved finds *her*: "No one loses his way or labors in vain on those narrow lanes. There, from every direction, the Bridegroom approaches, presents Himself, as it were, with glad countenance and pours Himself into the heart of

His beloved."[91] Those who quickly find what they seek or lose interest in what they do not have travel an easier yet ultimately fruitless path.[92]

Here in *Song* 3 she does find him, and the search seems over:

> When I had a little passed by them,
> I found him whom my soul loveth." (3.4)

Indeed, the sequel in *Song* 4 is a beautiful, intense portray of their pleasure:

> How beautiful art thou, my love, how beautiful art thou!
> Thy eyes are doves' eyes, besides what is hid within.
> Thy hair is as flocks of goats, which come up from mount Galaad . . .
> . . .
> Thou hast wounded my heart, my sister, my spouse,
> Thou hast wounded my heart with one of thy eyes, and with one hair of thy neck.
> How beautiful are thy breasts, my sister, my spouse!
> Thy breasts are more beautiful than wine,
> And the sweet smell of thy ointments above all aromatical spices. (*Song* 4.1, 9–10)

But nothing in *Song* 4 prepares us for what follows:

> I opened the bolt of my door to my beloved,
> But he had turned aside and was gone.
> My soul melted when he spoke.
> I sought him, and found him not.
> I called, and he did not answer me. (*Song* 5.6)

Later on, we will look into this second, seemingly vain search.

NEAR BUT UNREACHABLE

This other woman was alone too in the night, and her crisis too has remained unresolved. Escaping the dark of night, she tries in various ways to grapple with his absence: the women rebuke her for her stubborn and unseemly agitation (5.5); to fill the void of his absence, she imitates him, as if herself to become him (5.6); she wants to go to the Tirukutantai temple and make her case right in front of him, but fails to reach it (5.8); she wants to go to the Tiruvallaval temple, but she cannot get there either, although she is close enough to hear the sounds of the festival and smell the scents of flower and incense (5.9). Her search seems never to get started, as if it is both unnecessary and impossible.

Here we can consider only the last of these dramatic scenes (5.9), which accentuates the dilemma of a beloved nearby but out of reach. Now the challenge is not a dark night's search, but simply finding her way, in the light of day, to a lord who is famously nearby:

> Good, doe-eyed women, day by day this sinner grows weaker.
> There, where lovely areca palm fill the heavens
> Where honey-rich jasmine wafts fragrance,
> There amid honey-filled gardens is Tiruvallaval where the king dwells:
> When will I, ever at his feet, reach those feet? (5.9.1)

She never manages actually to get there. Close enough to desire nothing but him, she is unable to act upon that desire; in the end, her weakened state contrasts all the more sharply with the evident prosperity and vitality of a temple grown lush just by his presence.

Nanjiyar reminds us how it is that the poet falls deep enough into despair that he sings yet again in her voice: "The saint became very depressed when he did not gain what he desired even by entering Tirukutantai.[93] He endures for a while with the thought, 'The Lord's feet are refuge even in this condition.' Then he has a further idea, 'Going to Tiruvallaval will satisfy all my desires.' But he does not get all the way there, due to lack of strength, and so he is exceedingly depressed."[94] Again the saint expresses his distress in the voice of the young woman, thereby to speak more eloquently from and of his crisis:[95]

> She praises the gardens of Tiruvallaval, the fragrances there, the south wind carrying the fragrance, the sweet buzzing of bees dizzy by drinking the honey of those gardens there, the busy activity of the orthodox Vedic rites, the smoke of oblations, and everything else. But she grieves greatly, wasting away, because she cannot herself enter there.[96]

Building on Nanjiyar's narrative,[97] Nampillai assures us that she is not scolding her beloved, but only confessing her inability to live without him; the song should be taken as more revelatory of her nature than of his seeming disregard.

She argues with the more conventional women of the town, perhaps including her mother and her friend:

> Friends, what do you get from afflicting me?
> There, where the south wind carries the scent
> Of the splendid flowering mastwood, apewood, and young white fig,
> There in Tiruvallaval town the Lord dwells.

Not knowing their own true selves—that they too are made for nothing but love—they cannot understand the extremity of her desire, seeing it rather as evidence of her confusion. They think that in her haste to go to Tiruvallaval, she is neglecting her own dignity: "This agitation at not seeing Him come is not fitting to your nature."[98] They imply that she should calm down and behave herself. She seeks their help, but they simply rebuke her with their common sense.[99]

She ignores them, but in her desperation she is ready to settle for less. If she cannot reach his feet, then the dust on those feet suffices:

> When will we, ever at His feet, wear the dust of those feet? (2)

She also changes her tone toward the women: courteous and cool toward them at the beginning of verse 2, by its last line she gestures at solidarity: it is *we* who are ever at his feet. But right away her mood again shifts, and in verse 3 she sharply contrasts their good fortune and her woe, her solitude and the town's holy bustle:

> You are lovely with those flowers in your hair,
> But my grief-stricken self fades away.
> There, where fine Vedic chanting resounds like the waves of the sea
> And the smoke of oblations wafts in every direction,
> There in cool Tiruvallaval the tall Lord dwells.

Here too, she settles for less: if touching his feet or even the dust on them is beyond her, she will be content simply to contemplate them:

> So tell me, will I be able to gaze ever upon his feet? (3)

The women do not understand this deeply rooted desire, why she cannot settle for less, and so they hold her back. But there is no point to their interference:

> Friends, you keep tormenting me, but why do this?
> There, where tall young areca palms, jack trees, coconut palms, and mango trees
> Rise above terraced houses,
> There in cool Tiruvallaval He lies on his venomous serpent
> The Lord, our sole good. (4)[100]

Periyavacchan Pillai detects a triple parallel here: the city flourishes in dependence on the lord; as in the old mythology, the serpent Ananta serves forever as the lord's abode; the woman would flourish in the same way, were she able to get near to him.[101] All three have the lord as their only good, and life apart from him is unthinkable, but only she is denied the intimacy she craves; yet it is in her frustration and separation that she becomes the most faithful of those serving him, sustained only by the thought of him. By contrast, the neighboring women—her "friends"—seem to imagine a life in which the beloved plays only a modest part. They aim to dampen her desire, but she is determined to settle for nothing less than the beloved himself.[102]

Yet she concedes more ground, even as her desire grows more intimate:

> My very good friends,
> There the smoke of good brahmins' sacrifices conceals the lofty sky with a good
>   darkness,
> There, in cool Tiruvallaval, is that cane sugar, ripe fruit, sweet ambrosia,
> That radiance who holds all my good:

This more immediate sense of taste stands in for vision ironically obscured by the smoke of sacred fires. But then she abruptly wants for her eyes the pleasure of seeing him:

> When will my eyes get to see Him? (5)

Nampillai draws a parallel to a mother who cares nothing for her own suffering, hoping only that her child will survive. Similarly, this woman thinks, if I cannot reach him, as least my eyes might do so.[103] Yet then she again changes her mind and begs for that vision for her whole self:

> O gentle women with fine mouths,[104] will this sinner ever get to see Him?

Her deeds may keep her from him, but his deeds are troubling in a different way. He is so free, yet so selective: he was that dwarf who grew cosmic in size, spanning earth and heaven in three strides, overcoming every distance—except the small space between her and him:

> There, where fresh breezes carry the songs of bees
> Amid the lofty branches of lush trees in luxuriant seashore groves,
> There stands Tiruvallaval where that beautiful dwarf, the lovely Lord, resides.
> Will this sinner ever get to see his lotus feet? (6)[105]

Yet again she indicates she will settle for less: if she cannot see his feet, reverencing the flowers adorning them will suffice:

> Will I get to worship even the flowers at his feet, O best of women?[106]
> There, where pools broad and deep hold tall lotuses and lilies

Bright like women's radiant faces and their eyes,
There, in Tiruvallaval dwells the ruler, the Lord who swallowed the earth.
Will I ever get to worship the flowers at his feet, all my days? (7)[107]

Will I get to worship without end,[108]

Once again, she flatters the women and the loveliness of a temple she cannot reach:

O fair-browed women?[109]
There, where sweet sugar cane sways and paddy ripens on all sides
In fields everywhere adorned with flowering pools,
There in cool Tiruvallaval

Here too she cannot but remember that her beloved is the one who crossed the universe in just a few steps, and so should be able to come to her at any moment:

Long has dwelled the Lord whose slender feet crossed the earth.

But still her basic question remains unanswered:

Will I ever get to worship Him? (8)[110]

In her holy confusion, her desire grows still deeper. She grows weaker, and the only cure is to see him:

Can we ever see Him and fill our slipping anklets
And bracelets and join our hands in worship?
There, where—as if with flute and harp—
Striped bees swarm in cool gardens, drink honey, hum and sing their songs.
Can we join our hands in worship there in Tiruvallaval[111]
Where the Lord with the whirling discus shows his ancient grace? (9)

His grace is ancient, innate and natural to him,[112] an old truth that can be counted on; it is a grace everywhere in Tiruvallaval:

Will we finally be able to recite his names?[113]
By good deeds and their ancient grace, my lady friends,[114]
This is the city where heaven and earth worship,
Tiruvallaval which supports the good of thousands of gracious good people.
There resides our Lord, our good grace.

But as the verse and song end, she adds one more important insight: she names him. Until this point she has not called her beloved Narayana by his names, and now she survives in reciting them:

> Will we finally be able to recite the names of this Naranan? (10)

If she cannot see him or touch his feet, just chanting the names of Narayana—names recounting his qualities—might make his grace come to her. What she cannot achieve by crossing geographical distances, she might achieve by simple words of praise, desperate namings of the beloved, arising from her impossible love.[115]

We shall see that it is by the intensity of her love and her word that she is redeemed. But first, let us look a bit deeper into her crisis.

FOR MEDITATION

[2] I sleep, and my heart watcheth.
The voice of my beloved knocking:
"Open to me, my sister, my love, my dove, my undefiled:
For my head is full of dew, and my locks of the drops of the nights."
[3] I have put off my garment; how shall I put it on?
I have washed my feet; how shall I defile them?
[4] My beloved put his hand through the key hole,
And my inmost self was moved at his touch.
[5] I arose up to open to my beloved: my hands dripped with myrrh,
and my fingers were full of the choicest myrrh.
[6] I opened the bolt of my door to my beloved,
but he had turned aside and was gone.
My soul melted when he spoke.
I sought him, and found him not.
I called, and he did not answer me.
(*Song* 5.2–6)

[1] With whirled white conch and discus
The lotus eyed Lord rides His eagle
    across my heart.
But you don't see it—so what can I say to
    you ladies?
Flood of bliss, He reigns
Where unceasingly the Vedas and
    festivals and the games of children
    resound,
And there, to Tiruppereyil, I will go.

[2] Friends with fragrant dark hair,
    mothers, neighbors,
I cannot rule my unruly heart, it's out of
    my control.
Night and day, it's gone off to the fields of
    flowers filled with sweet honey and
To the cool paddy fields all around
    southern Tiruppereyil
Where the jewel-hued Lord of heaven
    rules.
To the radiant lips of that Krishna, my
    heart is captive.

3 My heart is captive to His berry red lips.
Bending low before His ravishing long
    hair,
Seeing His conch and discus and
    rejoicing,
Now it's done with everything but His
    lotus eyes:
Festivals never cease, month and day, in
    southern Tiruppereyil where resides
    our Lord.
Before Him, friend, my heart has lost
    both reserve and modesty.

4 My dear heart has run off after my lost
    radiance, and ended up staying there.
So now when I grieve, in whom can I
    confide?
Roaring like the thundering ocean
The Vedas resound throughout southern
    Tiruppereyil where He lives,
The resounding conch is in His hand, and
In that marvelous one I am immersed.
So women, what's the use of getting angry
    at me?

5 With anger He shattered the cart,
Sucked dry the deceiving demon's breast,
Passed between the trees,
Threw the demon calf at the demon
    woodapple tree.
He is my Lord Krishna,
And to Him I have surrendered my
    womanhood.
So what's the use of getting angry, women?
Long ago He came to dwell amid the
    flourishing gardens of Tiruppereyil,
So just show me how to seize the day, get
    myself there.

6 Show me how to seize the day,
For greater than the sea is my love for my
    dark cloud Lord.
He has come, stands before me but just
    beyond my finger's reach.
Long ago He came to dwell on earth
Where the sacrifices of men learned in
    the four Vedas never cease,
Where lovely ripe grain waves like the
    yak-tail fan,
Amid the abundant waters of
    Tiruppereyil:
So show me how to get there.

7 The Lord once came and destroyed
    southern Lanka surrounded by sea
    forts, and
Now in Pereyil He resides.
There my heart has gone in search of
    Him,
But now I cannot see it anywhere.
Friend, is there no one here who can
    summon back my heart?
So with whose help can I achieve my goal?
But really, what my heart has seen, I have
    seen.

8 All of them saw how it was between me
    and the Lord dark like the sea,
But together they spread gossip.
If you will speak of my love, friend,
Just tell them how it has become greater
    than the solid earth, seven seas, the
    lofty sky.
He resides there in Tiruppereyil
    surrounded by clear streams.
Just tell them that I'm going there, there I
    will reach.

9 I'm going there, there I will reach, my
    friend, ladies.
You need not comfort me: what good is
    your talking?
My heart is full, it is no longer here with
    me.
It has gone to Lord Krishna, the dark
    one who swallowed the earth and the
    dark sea.
He resides amid bright pools and fertile
    fields, in rich southern Tiruppereyil,
There, in that great town.

10 Town and country and everywhere else
    I have searched—
I have no shame, friends.
In the ancient city with tall towers,
    jeweled at its crown,
In lofty southern Tiruppereyil, there
    He dwells wearing long crocodile
    earrings.

He is amazing, He once destroyed the
    hundred warriors,
This peerless dark cloud bearer of the
    discus.
How many ages have passed since He
    seized my heart?

(Holy Word 7.3.1–10)

WOMEN, IT IS TOO LATE TO THWART ME

There is no permanence to love, and the beloved leaves and returns, or not, as he chooses. To make matters worse, even the search, undertaken over and again and not without some success, turns out to fail the next time, when more is at stake. Every search has its second scene, and in the *Song* and the *Holy Word*, these are scenes of growing desperation and acute loss.

The lover fails even in her modest goal of reaching Tiruvallaval. Yet her words grow more insistent because he is not there; his name is ever on her lips. In the next songs in the *Holy Word* she hangs between near despair and near realization of what she seeks. She dreams that she is one of the cowherd women who flirt with Krishna (6.2); to her mother's growing distress, she loses all sense of proportion, and seems near to death by love (6.5, 6, 7); she again sends bees and birds as messengers, hoping that they can get his attention (6.8). In 6.10, the poet surrenders entirely to the lord, but in 7.1, he—she—is again entirely abandoned.[116] And in 7.2, her mother watches as she meditates on her beloved in the Srirangam temple. She wants to go there, to see him face to face, but when she fails yet again, her mother looks on with alarm as her daughter recites the lord's holy names over and over:

"I do not know how this will end," she says,
"Master of the three worlds!" she says,
"Lord with fragrant red blossoms in Your hair!" she says,
"Four-faced one!" she says, "Leader of the radiant celestials!" she says,
"Handsome Lord of Srirangam!" she says.
Though she seemed like those not reaching His feet,
She did reach the feet of the cloud colored one. (7.2.10)[117]

A soul lost in love, it is in crying out his names that she finds him—in her own words. By word, her beloved is near even in his absence.[118] Or as Nampillai puts it, she reaches him not by going to him or by temple worship, but by increasingly clear inner vision whence passionate, holy words arise.[119]

But this is no happy ending. By the end of *Holy Word* 7.2 this woman was temporarily consoled by hearing of the divine beauty, yet in the same moment her longing to see him was again aroused.[120] Nanjiyar puts it this way: "Depressed, this woman has been crying out incoherently of the Lord's beauty, and other qualities. She has been reciting the entire array of His auspicious qualities, that He is the refuge for those with no refuge, and so forth. . . . When the sound of his holy names thus reaches her ears, this refreshment helps her to survive."[121] But her consolation vanishes in a moment, and again she is overwhelmed by distress as 7.3 begins. She has been dragged down again by her failure to reach him, and decides to seek him in yet another nearby temple, Tiruppereyil.[122] As this song unfolds again she argues with the women who once more refuse to go with her or let her go on her own. Her desire is unseemly; there is no place for a woman who would go it alone. But her resistance is her refusal to forget, voiced in her lament.[123]

By a powerful, violent metaphor, the beloved is the one who has ridden right across her heart:

> With whirled white conch and discus
> The lotus eyed Lord rides His eagle across my heart.
> But you don't see it—so what can I say to you ladies?

But her determination does not weaken:

> Flood of bliss, He reigns
> Where unceasingly the Vedas and festivals and the games of children resound,
> And there, to Tiruppereyil, I will go. (7.3.1)[124]

The lord is so close—in, on her heart—that actually reaching the temple might seem not to matter. Perhaps it is a question of timing, as she sees how brief are his visits; perhaps she hopes that at the temple she will find something that lasts.[125]

Here too, her argument with the women drives subsequent verses. Faced with the criticism that she is out of control, she diagnoses her problem as exactly that, a heart that bears no correction:

> Friends with fragrant dark hair, mothers, neighbors,
> I cannot rule my unruly heart, it's out of my control.

Yet this very heart goes exactly where needed:

> Night and day, it's gone off to the fields of flowers filled with sweet honey and
> To the cool paddy fields all around southern Tiruppereyil
> Where the jewel-hued Lord of heaven rules.
> To the radiant lips of that Krishna, my heart is captive. (2)[126]

Yearning for his elusive touch, she remembers fondly even his violence toward the demons who tried to kill him as a child:

> With anger He shattered the cart,
> Sucked dry the deceiving demon's breast,
> Passed between the trees,
> Threw the demon calf at the demon woodapple tree.[127]
> He is my Lord Krishna,

To this beloved, once powerfully present but now nowhere to be seen, she gives herself over:

> And to Him I have surrendered my womanhood.

In this extreme situation, the women's rebuke is to no avail. She is his, and all that is left is to go where he is:

> So what's the use of getting angry, women?
> Long ago He came to dwell
> Amid the flourishing gardens of Tiruppereyil.
> So just show me how to seize the day, get myself there. (5)
>
> Show me how to seize the day,
> For greater than the sea is my love for my dark cloud Lord.

Even as she makes this plea, the intensity of her imagining makes him become all the more vividly present, though just beyond reach:

> He has come, stands before me but just beyond my finger's reach.

The commentators take this experience seriously, a real vision conjured in her longing. Periyavacchan Pillai notes that it is both more real and more frustrating than a dream, since she expects actually to touch her beloved and to be touched. But this does not happen.[128]

But immediately, as if finding this close-up presence too intense, she changes the subject, pleading that they guide her to Tiruppereyil, that she might see him there instead:

> Long ago He came to dwell on earth
> Where the sacrifices of men learned in the four Vedas never cease,
> Where lovely ripe grain waves like the yak-tail fan,
> Amid the abundant waters of Tiruppereyil:
> So show me how to get there. (6)[129]

If it is not clear what motivates her desire to go there, neither is it clear what holds her back: does she not know where the temple is? But even as she asks, it is evident that her heart, run down then taken hostage, has already gone there and vanished inside him. There seems no way to get it back, and for herself no way forward:

> The Lord once came and destroyed southern Lanka surrounded by sea forts, and
> Now in Pereyil He resides.
> There my heart has gone in search of Him,
> But now I cannot see it anywhere.
> Friend, is there no one here who can summon back my heart?
> So with whose help can I achieve my goal?

But then, at this moment of stalemate she realizes that she *does* now see. Lost, her heart sees; recognizing her hopelessness, she sees.[130]

> But really, what my heart has seen, I have seen. (7)[131]

At the moment when she cannot be helped, in a way she no longer needs any help. All she has to do is run after her heart, already at its goal:

> I'm going there, there I will reach, my friend, ladies.
> You need not comfort me: what good is your talking?
> My heart is full, it is no longer here with me.
> It has gone to Lord Krishna, the dark one who swallowed the earth and the
>   dark sea.
> He resides amid bright pools and fertile fields, in rich southern Tiruppereyil,
> There, in that great town. (9)

Giving up, she wins. Such is the beloved's effect on people. In the *Mahabharata* war he destroyed the hundred cousins who warred against the favored five brothers, and in the same way he has conquered her heart. So she has nothing more to say to her neighbors:

> Town and country and everywhere else I have searched—
> I have no shame, friends.
> In the ancient city with tall towers, jeweled at its crown,
> In lofty southern Tiruppereyil, there He dwells wearing long crocodile earrings,
> He is amazing, He once destroyed the hundred warriors,
> This peerless dark cloud bearer of the discus:
> How many ages have passed since He seized my heart? (10)

Neither side has budged, and the song simply ends. The women have stymied her search and she never reaches Tiruppereyil. The beloved too is stubborn, holding her heart captive and not letting go of it, and so she becomes entirely his. In betrayal, her heart has saved her; while she has not found her beloved, he has entirely taken hold of her.[132]

BUT THEN SHE LOSES HIM

Even as she abandoned the very idea of searching and instead began to find her beloved Krishna deep within herself, this other woman, though successful in the past, now faces a similar crisis. He is gone, and in *Song* 5 her search fails. Yet in that failure she too truly finds her voice. Let us follow the next part of her story.

Previously she had found him, and as we have seen, *Song* 4 speaks to the joyful intensity of their union. Even *Song* 5 begins in a celebratory mood:

> Let my beloved come into his garden, and eat the fruit of his apple trees.
> I am come into my garden, O my sister, my spouse;
> I have gathered my myrrh, with my aromatical spices;
> I have eaten the honeycomb with my honey;
> I have drunk my wine with my milk.
> Eat, O friends, and drink, and be inebriated, my dearly beloved! (5.1)

The new night scene seems also to promise more of the intimacy:

> I sleep, and my heart watcheth.
> The voice of my beloved knocking:
> "Open to me, my sister, my love, my dove, my undefiled:
> For my head is full of dew, and my locks of the drops of the nights." (5.2)

But then, inexplicably, perhaps just in play, she hesitates:

> I have put off my garment; how shall I put it on?
> I have washed my feet; how shall I defile them?
> My beloved put his hand through the key hole,
> And my inmost self was moved at his touch. (5.3–4)

She is aroused, but waits too long:

> I arose up to open to my beloved: my hands dripped with myrrh,
> And my fingers were full of the choicest myrrh.
> I opened the bolt of my door to my beloved,
> But he had turned aside and was gone.
> My soul melted when he spoke.
> I sought him, and found him not.
> I called, and he did not answer me. (5.5–6)

He slips away, and she is once more alone.[133]

Gilbert, picking up on the dramatic shift between scenes, ascribes her delay not to ambivalence or lethargy, but to love's intoxicating power. Love inebriates her, but awakens her heart: "Love unites and love inebriates. Do you see how rightly one reply is made for all into whom the powerful draught of charity flows in common? Fierce surely is the power of love, inebriating and altering the lover."[134] Asleep to the world, in spirit she is awake, keeping vigil for the beloved: "A good slumber is transport of mind, a withdrawal both from sensations of the flesh and (if this also be mentioned) from the senses of the body."[135] And so her "sleep" can be read in either way, since both slumber and inebriation give "the appearance of withdrawal from oneself. . . . Each, so to speak, robs the soul itself of its pristine state and informs it with new affections."[136] This is why she can say, "I sleep *and* my heart watches."[137]

That *Song* 5 shifts abruptly should be no surprise, since the beloved's every move has its own style and character.[138] Yesterday, "the Lord Jesus was presented in flight from assaults; today let Him be presented as returning with joys. Yesterday He was presented as begging solace, today as bringing solace with Him. Yesterday He was full of insults, today full of graces."[139] Now she is invited to yield to the beloved's graces, for he is supremely delightful, like a light that in a dark place naturally attracts attention.[140] But Gilbert does wonder why the beloved is not bolder in getting his way:

> "Open to me, my sister." Why do You request, good Jesus, that the door be
> opened? . . . Your sudden appearance is an opening. Appear and no one closes

to You. When the glory of Your Majesty in its tiniest ray begins to flash upon the spirit, suddenly it swirls and sweeps the spirit toward itself. While it radiates, it allows no door to be shut upon it. The heart You penetrate, You open to Yourself; You hold it open, as long as You do not withdraw Yourself.[141]

Gentle though he be, still he steps away, that in his absence her ever increasing desire might surpass all limits: "The more affectionately you receive the embraces of the Beloved and strive with an open heart wholly as if to absorb and consume Him, so much the more quickly the fleeting presence of your Beloved fades away."[142] So intense is this experience that in this life it can be only momentary: "The joy of contemplation is indeed like a momentary flash. Swiftly it departs and in excellence it surpasses all the power of human capacity. While it goes, in our human flesh we cannot follow with matching strides. 'I said I shall become wise,' Solomon recalled, 'and wisdom withdrew further from me, much further than it was before.' . . . The more passionate it is, the more swiftly it passes."[143]

The instant of nearness overwhelms the soul that truly loves him; it pierces her through and dissolves her. This is why in desire she keeps seeking him, finding him, and then, upon every moment of union, immediately losing him again. Uncertainty about her beloved deepens her desire:[144] "When your Beloved has left you, He does not return to you when you will. This distress adds understanding to love and gives an increase to the affections. . . . When the Beloved has spoken, your soul melts. Melting, your soul faints, unable to endure, and your Beloved turns away. Your fainting prompts his flight. When your Beloved is present and speaks, you melt, faint and swoon."[145]

In a way, then, it is the woman herself who drives away her beloved, by the intensity of her desire. Gilbert reminds us of another passage where she is entirely too much for her beloved: "Later the Bridegroom says, 'Turn away thy eyes from me, for they have made me flee away' [*Song* 6.4].[146] How have they put your Beloved to flight except by fainting from excessive affection for Him? You know no moderation; therefore your Beloved is moderate and allots for you in due time the measure of his presence. So you seek but do not find; you call but He does not respond."[147] Such love neither tolerates the absence of the beloved nor guarantees his presence and so, in all this, it is grace that she suffers: "In His absence, love's longings labor for breath; in His presence, surfeited, they suffer a relapse. O happy love, which with endless ebb and flower either melts in Him or, in seeking, sighs for Him. . . . Yet the bride does not despair of finding Him, but complains of not having found Him. 'I sought Him, but found Him not. I called, and He did not answer me.'"[148]

It is not entirely surprising then that this second time the watchmen block her way with unexpected force:

> The keepers that go about the city found me:
> They struck me: and wounded me:
> The keepers of the walls took away my veil from me. (5.7)

To Gilbert they are like scrupulous physicians who "search out the various affections of spirits and discover the passions and the good qualities of each and the disease under which each labors: no one's thought escapes their search."[149] They probe beyond pretense, until she is left with nothing but her desire.[150]

This time she does not find him; what worked in *Song* 3 no longer does, old paths to union are not to be taken for granted. At a loss, she turns again to the audience, onlookers who are suddenly participants:

> I adjure you, O daughters of Jerusalem,
> If you find my beloved, that you tell him that I languish with love. (5.8)

As we shall see in a moment, when she responds to the women's request for more information about her beloved, it is by such words, her own, that she gains what searching had not given her.

INTERLUDE: *Searching Twice Over*

The more intense their love, the greater their anguish at his absence. Each scene ends at an impasse. Her frustration at not reaching Tiruvallaval is deepened when her neighbors adamantly refuse to assist her in reaching Tiruppereyil, when they give the impression that they do not even understand why she is so upset. More severely anguished, however, she becomes all the more stubborn, refusing to put aside the idea that she can find her way to him. The joy arising so vividly in *Song* 3 is undone, for soon this woman too loses sight of him again and cannot find her way back to him. The intensity of her love has not kept him close, no matter how tightly she held him. But as we shall see, neither searching nor unmet desire is the end of the story, since they finish with searching by their very words of lament and remembrance.

If we have continued to read well, these songs become all the harder to keep separate, particularly if we do not let an encompassing grand narrative divide them. But the more they mingle, the harder it is to know where we stand. Our own search must in part always be the work of sorting out how these songs and their dramas are alike and different, until an uneasy mix of the resonant and dissonant leaves us a little confused, unsettled, yet wanting more. The *Song*'s beloved comes near, departs, and hides, but he is not easily imagined also to reside just beyond our reach in Tiruvallaval. The *Holy Word*'s beloved remains distant even when nearby. He seems not the kind to come to her suddenly in the night, like a gazelle upon the high places.

At a loss, we are possessed of no neat resolution to the drama of a beloved who hides from us, no matter how deep our faith. It is not that tradition no longer matters; on the contrary, this problem is primarily for those who still find God in particular traditions and remain content where they have found love before. If we are Christians, it is our love for Jesus that makes it so unsettling to hear of her love for Krishna; it is because we love that our love risks losing its innocence and its purity. A Srivaishnava may still think that the woman of the *Holy Word* is the only one who really knows where to find the beloved, Krishna, and it will be this believer, firm in faith, who is most unsettled by that woman's search for him in the *Song*'s night. Familiar religious answers—the beloved is to be found just where he was found before, his absence is our fault, he is returning any day now—may seem pale assurances besides the rich testimonies of these women so stubborn in their longing.

But even if the flood of poetry and these troubled dramas are too much for us, we need not turn back or let go of the intense specificities of love. It is better that like these women we keep returning to desires that enflame just one particular love, over and again. If we have been reading well, their search will then be ours, the intensely present beloved who is at the same time the absent beloved—the singular beloved who is elsewhere too. We then have all the more to seek ways to draw on both traditions in order to write, in truth and in love's dark night, with a certain patience for the erring and imprecise determinations of love intensely imagined yet marked by the memory of other loves.

But neither woman's drama ends where we have left off, for they too are preoccupied with what to say. Each turns within and finds there some remedy, in the very words she speaks in her time of lament and longing. The word, her own word, saves her. Let us turn to these words beyond absence.

FOR MEDITATION

⁷ The keepers that go about the city found me,
They struck me and wounded me:
The keepers of the walls took away my veil from me.
⁸ I adjure you, O daughters of Jerusalem,
If you find my beloved, that you tell him that I languish with love.
⁹ What manner of one is thy beloved of the beloved,
O thou most beautiful among women?
What manner of one is thy beloved of the beloved
That thou hast so adjured us?
¹⁰ My beloved is white and ruddy, chosen out of thousands.
¹¹ His head is as the finest gold;
His locks as branches of palm trees, black as a raven.
¹² His eyes as doves upon brooks of waters,
Which are washed with milk and sit beside the plentiful streams.
¹³ His cheeks are as beds of aromatical spices set by the perfumers.
His lips are as lilies dropping choice myrrh.
¹⁴ His hands are turned and as of gold, full of hyacinths.
His belly as of ivory set with sapphires.
¹⁵ His legs as pillars of marble, that are set upon bases of gold,
His form as of Lebanon, excellent as the cedars,
¹⁶ His throat most sweet, and he is all lovely:
Such is my beloved, and he is my friend,
O ye daughters of Jerusalem.
¹⁷ Whither is thy beloved gone,
O thou most beautiful among women?
Whither is thy beloved turned aside, and we will seek him with thee?

¹ My beloved has descended to his garden, to the courtyard of aromatic plants,
In order to pasture in the gardens and gather the lilies.
² I am for my beloved, and my beloved is for me.
He pastures among the lilies.
³ Thou art beautiful,
O my love, sweet and comely as Jerusalem,
Terrible as an army set in array.
⁴ Turn away thy eyes from me,
For they have made me flee away.

(*Song* 5.7–6.4)

10 Now we too have upped and gone
And become one with Him whose home
   is heaven—
O flocks of fine cranes in pools, what's
   the use?
Little by little my lovely body is losing its
   radiance but still,
May this bliss spread, climax, and
   everywhere flourish.

1 Oh, my heart is melting, overflowing
   the bounds of my life's breath, and
My desire grows large—
So what can this servant do now?
He dwells in holy Katkarai where the
   fragrance of kavi flowers perfumes
   the streets.
Can I even imagine the wonders of that
   wondrous one?

2 In all it thinks, in all it says, my heart
   breaks down, it melts.
When I sing the excellence of Your deeds,
   my dear soul burns,
O my Lord in southern Katkarai with
   pools and flowering gardens, but still
I cannot imagine how to serve You.

3 True to character He misled my heart,
   He entered me,
He pierced through me, He became my
   life and consumed it too:
This Lord dwells in southern Katkarai
   amid flourishing gardens and
He is dark like a cloud:
I cannot understand his tricks.

4 I cannot understand it:
All the worlds are inside Him,
And in the proper way He himself abides
   within them, and
My Lord dwells in southern fragrant
   Katkarai too:
And yet He still consumes this small
   person's precious life.
Such is his grace.

5 As if simply gracious, He entered inside
   me but then
All at once He consumed my body, my
   whole dear life.
The Lord dwells in southern Katkarai
   where sacred gardens flourish,
His body dark and lovely, our Krishna:
Such are his tricks.

6 My Krishna's tricks are all that is good
   for me.
Nothing else is left of my dear life which
   lovely Krishna consumed.
In these straits what's left of me cries out
   day and night, "My Krishna!"
And in that way praises His Katkarai.

7 What's left of me praises Katkarai, it
   cries, "Krishna lives there!"
The disease of my desire climaxes, deep
   going, melting in a torrent.
It seemed He would just rule over me,
But instead He consumed my life, that
   amazing one, and
Just a little is left after He consumed my
   dear life.

8 I had not consented, but He came and
   consumed my life,
Day after day He came and consumed me
   altogether.
Except for serving my Lord in southern
   Katkarai with its dark rain clouds,
Is there anything else that my dear life
   could enjoy?

9 Whose life has enjoyed what my life has
   enjoyed?
His eyes are large blossoming lotuses, his
   lips red and full,
He dwells in the temple of southern
   Katkarai amid dark rain clouds,
His four shoulders are broad, fine, lovely,
This ocean of divinity.

¹⁰ In my desire I said, "I will swallow You
      completely when I see You,"
But He was too quick for me, He
      completely drank me up,
My Lord in dark cloud Katkarai.
How quick of Him.

¹ You've hunted in the marshes of our
      seashore grove and here you happily
      live,

O red legged cranes,
So be my messengers to Him who dwells
      in Tiru Mulikkalam.
Basil flowers brimming with honey
      adorn his hair, He is our pot-dancer.
So won't you and your consorts then
      place your feet on my head?

(*Holy Word* 9.5.10–7.1)

SHE IS ON THE BRINK OF RUIN, her searching uncertain, her purposes thwarted by well-meaning neighbors and watchmen. One temptation is simply to try harder, searching more often and more widely; another is to grow colder, caring no longer for the search. But the *Song* and the *Holy Word* turn rather more introspective. She finds power in remembrance—in the very fact that she cannot forget him—and in speaking from those past intensities. What she could not find by searching outside herself, she touches by words drawn from her memory. It is these that make the beloved vividly present, on the precipice of desperation: with nowhere to turn and her search unviable, he becomes present because in desperation she remembers. In the *Song* and in the *Holy Word* she lives out this dynamic in her own way, getting us to listen to her story, scene by scene. It is to this dynamic that we now turn, her words most effective as they arise from the depth of her penury.[151]

DEEP IN HER MEMORY

The watchmen had helped her before, but this time they rebuffed her with some force. Now even the little she has is taken away from her:

The keepers that go about the city found me:
They struck me: and wounded me:
The keepers of the walls took away my veil from me. (5.7)

And so she turns to the women of Jerusalem and speaks desperately, with power:

I adjure you, O daughters of Jerusalem,
If you find my beloved, that you tell him that I languish with love. (5.8)

In turn they pose two questions, repeating each of them. First,[152]

> What manner of one is thy beloved of the beloved,
> O thou most beautiful among women?
> What manner of one is thy beloved of the beloved
> That thou hast so adjured us? (5.9)[153]

Her description of him in response is stylized, recollected from past moments of encounter, yet on fire with love.[154]

Her languor now becomes also a grace to others, for now in her longing, she has become able to communicate even before words are spoken: "Aspirations in holy conferences, sighs emerging from the depths of the heart and frequent sobs, are these not emanations of the spirit and of grace conceived? Does the languor of love not betray itself by such evidence? Languor is not hidden when sobs are not concealed. Languor betrays itself when it produces such evidence."[155] The wearying decline brought on by her longing is evidence of a deeper grace: "This delay is a torture to me but it begets a wealth of consolation. When prayers are multiplied He will pour out more plentifully your long-awaited consolations. . . . Love does not languish but the lover languishes. Where love thrives, there languor thrives, if the object of love be absent. What is this languor but affection for the absent Beloved consuming the lover?"[156] These are verses that cut deep because they speak of nothing but the beloved; infectious, love's eloquent suffering infuses those not immune to love.

She then begs the women to speak on her behalf: "'Tell the Beloved I languish with love.' You tell Him, you who have familiar access to the Beloved. Tell Him you daughters who have experienced how great for a lover is the power of weakness, how 'love is as strong as death,' how 'jealousy is as hard as hell . . . '[157] Tell Him the news and He will listen to your cry, to give warmth to my desires. 'Tell Him I languish with love.'"[158] She begs them to do what she cannot, even if it is her words that will serve as theirs. Even if the beloved delays somewhere nearby, he must be told of her love and languor. By speaking to the women, she sends a message to him as well, challenging him "to repay her in kind, to rekindle the embers of one languishing in love." Theologically, this should not be surprising, Gilbert adds, since the beloved "has a store of consolations in His heart but He waits to be prompted by our prayers."[159]

Gilbert thinks that the women's first question is well-intentioned, not a taunt.[160] It is not surprising that her languor has overtaken them, inspiring them to question her: "How would they not be inspired to ask about his beauty, when they see the bride languishing and almost lifeless for love of Him?"[161] Seeing her, they can guess what he is like: "The languor of love detected in His bride prompted their curiosity in seeking Him," since when they see "that the love in His bride was passionate, they supposed that the causes and provocations of so much affection are in the Bridegroom."[162] The beloved was already described earlier in the *Song*,[163] but what the women now want is to hear of him again, described in her extremity: "It delights us to hear again what we have already heard about Him. Repeat for us what either must be believed or can be grasped about your Beloved. To hear both fills us with passionate delight, and what exceeds our capacity, captivates us nonetheless; we have been captivated with your own fervor of wonder and love, because we see you so captivated, so arrested, so inflamed."[164]

On fire, in turn they speak words that catch hold of the beloved: "If you report someone's plight to a compassionate person, are you not making Him a request? A modest hint is an effective petition. To point out the infirmities of the distressed, the misfortune of his lot, the arrogance of his foes, to whisper this in the ear of someone with power, I say, what else is this but to prompt his assistance by a respectful prayer?"[165] Unsurprisingly, readers too will be affected: "He surely feels the force of this verse, who languishes with a more passionate affection, overjoyed and distraught and consumed in meditation upon his God."[166]

Won over, eager to speak on her behalf, these women are ready also to walk with her, and so they pose their second question:

> Whither is thy beloved gone,
> O thou most beautiful among women?
> Whither is thy beloved turned aside, and we will seek him with thee? (5.17)[167]

In this way they make her realize that she knows where he is; otherwise, she could not be so eloquent in recollecting him.[168] Her response—he has gone down to his garden—in this light makes more sense: remembering where he was in the past, she intuits where he is now.

Gilbert's sermons break off at this point, and John of Ford commences his own meditative sermons,[169] and we can pick up where John turns to their second question.[170] Because they want to see for themselves, they ask their double question. Like Gilbert, John too recognizes why they are suddenly interested:

"It becomes clear that, while the bride was speaking, the very Spirit of love that possesses her has come down upon them too."[171] They are aroused most by her voice: "Sweetly conversing with the bride is found to have brought the daughters of Jerusalem to a high degree of love."[172] Now become "spiritual beings," they want to hear more,[173] but wisely she does not pretend to explain more than she can: "His ways are unsearchable, because, wherever his footsteps go, whether through the sea or the mighty waters or anywhere on earth, no one can ever recognize them."[174]

They also begin to share the work of interpreting his absence. By John's count, it is in four different ways that they gloss the beloved's departure:

> So He turned away but not far, nor to be away for long. He was delivered, to return and give himself to you. He turned away from you for an hour, so that, while He tarried, you might use the time to speak to us of Him, and "form Christ within us."[175] He turned away from you, but only so as to offer us, in you, a greater fullness of Himself, to let us enjoy his own self in this present life through you. He turned away, likewise, to visit His other little ones, "leaping upon the mountains, skipping over the hills" [*Song* 2.8], as the bride herself has said.[176]

But no matter how well-intentioned this lover may be, his sudden departure is a cause for desolation. To explain this now familiar point, in Sermon 43 John looks deeper into his own experience. Even when the Lord desires to visit him, he says, those arrivals are but the prelude to further moments of emptiness that only lovers can suffer: "From this throne, then, I feel the Lord visits me all the more often as he realizes I need visitations of this kind more frequently. If between these visitations, anyone asks me, still numb from the feelings of devotion experienced a few days past, and complaining of my Lord's delay, where he has gone or turned aside, the only ready answer I can find is: '*He has made darkness his hiding place.*'"[177] Love suffers a chill, a moment of dread: "A cloud, not of light but of darkness, has taken him from my eyes, and now that my love has grown so cold again, I feel I have good reason to fear that perhaps, after all, he has turned away from his servant in anger."[178] An instant of joy gives way quickly to intense desolation: "But, as far as I am concerned, this solemn celebration of the marriage feast comes very rarely, and even then, it is over in a brief minute. I am forced to return to my own poor cottage, while the spouse, as is only fitting, ceremoniously keeps the solemnity all the day, with his friends and companions. But I am desolate, lovingly turning over in my mind the crumbs and fragments that are left over from the marriage feast, and even those, within a very little, vanish from my mind."[179] Yet the absence of the beloved is seductive. It is to his bridal chamber that the beloved retreats, and "it is to there that He directs and invites my zeal and my love, and it is to there, where He so recently honored me by showing Himself, that I desire to follow and track Him down, as earnestly as I can."[180]

Even as the woman and her neighbors are conversing, the sorrow of absence occasions also an overflowing joy for which there are no words. She and the women grow quiet: "In the meantime it is permitted to experience this, but it is forbidden to speak about it."[181] They—and by extension John and his monks, and then too the reader—learn to remain wordless as they await his return: "For my beloved, this time is a time of silence, and for me and you, O Daughters of Jerusalem, it is a time of waiting."[182] An in-between space has now been opened up, presence in absence.

FOR A MOMENT, HE IS HERE

She is still apart from her beloved. Her situation continues to worsen as the *Holy Word* proceeds. Her songs continue to be only songs of separation, even if their power often lies in recollecting lost moments of union, in visualizing the presence of that absent beloved, or in simply singing of (hopeless) desire. By the middle and latter parts of the *Holy Word* 9, her beloved still eludes her, even if he is so nearby that she can feel his presence. The shifts in her mood become still more violent. She—and the poet who speaks in her voice—find the beloved nowhere around her and yet, as if by way of absence, still deeper inside.

All this becomes evident if we notice two such songs (9.5 and 9.7) and how there is placed between them a song of intense union (9.6) perhaps in her voice, or in the voice of the poet himself, now all the more deeply identified with her. And so we have:

9.5: a song of separation and lament

9.6: a song of the most intense, intimate union

9.7: a song of near despair

In *Holy Word* 9.5.1, again she laments, not merely the beloved's absence, but also the lingering, devastating effects of love. Despite his long absence, she cannot forget him and return to a sensible and moderate religious sensibility. Now her regrets are still deeper: forgetting him entirely would be wise, just as it might have been better never to have met him in the first place. Previously she had sent the birds as her messengers, but now she asks them no longer to bother her:

> Peahens, you and your mates—dear life to you—call to each another,
> But please stop afflicting my life with so much chatter.

She seems annoyed even that they might have tried to convey her message:

> Did you summon Lord Krishna, my life, to come here?
> But summoning my life, to give it to Him—is this really necessary? (9.5.1)

According to Nanjiyar, the poet has plummeted from the hopefulness of the previous song (9.4),[183] back into the stark reality of divine absence:

> In the previous song, the saint was filled with delight, for the Lord was directly manifest to Him. He set out then for external union. But unable to fulfill his desire, he was greatly depressed. He decides that he must not just tolerate this depression, but endure by making his heart intent on something else, that is, by reflection on ordinary things. He begins to reflect on them, but he is sorely grieved since even those things remind him of the Lord. And so he sings again in her voice.[184]

He, she, is still caught in the basic dilemma, unable to attain and unable to forget: "A young woman separated from the Lord is sorely afflicted. Like people who are very thirsty and suffer ever greater desire for water because they have been unable to drink, so too her great desire, born of their previous union, causes her great affliction."[185] Once again, she walks in her garden to pass some time, but its natural beauty reminds her of happier moments, pleasures other beings still enjoy and take for granted: "She ponders the lovely appearance of the birds who live there in pairs, and how in their enjoyment they incline toward one another. She reflects on how they look and act and talk to one another. She is greatly agitated because they remind her of the union between the Lord and herself."[186] The experience is killing her,[187] yet this is a precious suffering that happens only to a person who knows the joy of union. It is as if her beloved wants her to know the full force of separation, that she may glimpse the endlessness of their love; she recognizes "that separation is impossible without union," and so, "he joined intimately with me and then left me."[188]

But the first effect is that right now it seems that her beloved is killing her, first by their union, now by his absence, and the reminders of this lover's doom are everywhere in the garden.[189] Nampillai reinforces this rather dark reading of the beloved's intent:

> The peahens and nightingales remind her of His way of speaking and His appearance, and thus grieve her. But she thinks, "There is no enmity between them and us such that they should grieve us. Yet there must be some reason why they grieve us so. It must be that the Lord has decided, 'Let us end her life.' He knows that separation is the means to that, but also that separation is not possible unless there was union beforehand. So He joined with me and then parted from me. But when He left me, I did not die. So while I was suffering separation, He decided, 'We will kill her by showing her things that resemble us,' and so He sends things that remind me of Him."[190]

Each following verse reinforces the theme, as she addresses other birds. She is jealous of the nightingales who sing in harmony:

> All this is not really necessary, is it, Nightingale?
> How you and your mate—as if you were one—sing so loudly!

She seems equally angry at Krishna himself, though she may be blaming herself as well:

> That conjuring Govinda is not true to anyone, yet this much is true:
> My life is in his hands. (2)

Later she laments lost union and the suffering that follows upon it, as she cannot recover what is lost:

> He joined with me and consumed me and abandoned me—

Yet still she cannot resist remembering him in every detail:

> Yet His eyes are lovely lotuses and His mouth is an unfading dark jewel,
> That Krishna, my amazing one—

Even the rainbow—he is dark like a cloud and the rainbow is his warrior's bow—and the bees—his sweetness that is sweeter than any honey—torment her:

> You are just like Him, O clustered dark clouds, flashing your curved bow—
> So please don't show me your form—it will be the death of my life. (7)

She begs for silence:

> O bees and beetles, you are so melodious—but
> Your sweet singing is like sticking a spear in a sore, so stop it now.

He had been close enough to consume her, but now he is gone again, and so she is left with nothing but a vivid image:

> Krishna's eyes are like large lotuses blooming in pools of cool water.
> He has consumed my life, then upped and gone. (9)

This foreshadows her own imminent death; indeed, she is like one who has already died, so there is nothing to be done:

> Now we too have upped and gone,
> Become one with Him whose home is heaven—
> O fine cranes, flocking in those pools, what's the use?[191]

But the song ends with a touch of irony, as if her looming death, due to his absence, removes all constraints on the lord's earthly presence. His presence becomes all the more evident as she declines:

> Little by little my lovely body is losing its radiance but still,
> May this bliss spread, climax, and everywhere flourish. (10)

Nanjiyar catches the paradox, and gives her sentiment a moral tone: "Weakened, she begins to die, and yet even so she prays that the Lord's glory may abound. She says, 'No one should suffer what I have suffered,' and so she speaks from the enormity of her affliction. I go, but may the world not suffer by seeing my anguish."[192] Both her word and her departure become gifts to those remaining behind.

In this gloom, 9.6 is all the more striking as a song expressive of the ecstasy of intense union:

> Oh, my heart is melting, overflowing the bounds of my life's breath, and
> My desire grows large—
> So what can this servant do now?

The elusive beloved is once again nearby, right here in the Katkarai temple:

> He dwells in holy Katkarai where the fragrance of kavi flowers perfumes the
>   streets.
> Can I even imagine the wonders of that wondrous one? (1)

Now the saint—in his own voice, hers, both his and hers[193]—cries out a pleasure that floods the present moment. The song gives no clue why this instant
of realization abruptly intervenes. All at once, she gives voice to the overwhelming, intrusive arrival of her divine lover: "By holding onto the Lord she
survives," as she recognizes the unexpected gift of life she has enjoyed: "Even
if the Lord does not unite with her now, He does make her remember the gift
she received when, to her amazement, He had earlier joined with her."[194]

The effect of this takeover is that "she enters a state susceptible to neither
joys nor sorrows."[195] Now fully aware and aware, she addresses directly him
about the state of her own heart:

> In all it thinks, in all it says, my heart breaks down it melts.
> When I sing the excellence of Your deeds, my dear soul burns,

In light of this encounter, what she could possibly do for him in return is a still
deeper mystery:

> O my Lord in southern Katkarai with pools and flowering gardens, but still
> I cannot imagine how to serve You. (9.6.2)

Though her words glow with divine presence, the commentators still read
them in light of the surrounding songs, as words arising amid acute loneliness, desperate conjurings of the beloved. Previously her dire condition was
a matter of life and death, and "she expressed lack of hope regarding this life:
'Now we too have upped and gone and become one with Him whose home
is heaven.'[196] Previously her condition was such that the lord took hold of
the saint by coming and showing his face—or by not coming, in that way
ending her life."[197] Memory has filled the abyss between her and her lord,
remembered intimacies coming alive to create an intense present experience:
"Now this is no longer a matter of mere memories. Rather, an insight from a
past moment arises again here. Thus, she sings of the fine quality of the Lord
who has excellence but leaves that excellence aside and thus humbles himself.
She sings too of His beauty. And so she realizes, 'Now this is experience!
As she meditates on the Lord's good qualities, she melts away.'[198] As those
memories take the form of new words, her song does more than make the
inadequacy of the present situation clear—he was here, now he is not here.
Suddenly memories and words about past union give way to a moment of
realization. Subsequent verses weave together intimacy, surprise, and pleasure, in the face of her lover's abrupt intrusion and sudden, most intimate

presence. Nanjiyar observes that she gets more than she bargained for. She thought her problem was that she "could not imagine how to serve" him, but far more is at stake than that:[199]

> True to character He misled my heart, He entered me,
> He pierced through me, He became my life and consumed it too:

This time, the prosperity of a temple mirrors her own well-being:[200]

> This Lord dwells in southern Katkarai amid flourishing gardens and
> He is dark like a cloud:
> I cannot understand his tricks. (3)

She is astonished; one of these new, unexpected moves is that the beloved, who had once taken within himself all the world and has condescended to live in earthly temples, this time singles her out for the most intimate conquest:

> I cannot understand it:
> All the worlds are inside Him,
> And in the proper way He himself abides within them,[201] and
> My Lord dwells in southern fragrant Katkarai too:
> And yet He still consumes this small person's precious life.
> Such is his grace. (4)

Nampillai notes why this grace is incomprehensible even to those who know something about God: that the lord—enthralled by love—should swallow this small person exceeds all plausibility;[202] this is no judicious and wise love, but an extravagance that speaks vividly of the divine lover, Krishna, the trickster who confounds those he loves:[203]

> As if simply gracious, He entered inside me but then
> All at once He consumed my body, my whole dear life.
> The Lord dwells in southern Katkarai where sacred gardens flourish,
> His body dark and lovely, our Krishna:
> Such are his tricks. (5)

In this holy confusion he arouses her deepest pleasure, as she is emptied out, freed of self:

> My Krishna's tricks are all that is good for me.
> Nothing else is left of my dear life which lovely Krishna consumed.

There is only enough left of her to realize that he has taken all the rest:

> In these straits what's left of me cries out day and night, "My Krishna!"[204]
> And in that way praises His Katkarai. (6)

This surprising deity is for a moment surprisingly reliable, it is his presence inside her that testifies to his presence in the temple:[205]

> What's left of me praises Katkarai, it cries, "Krishna lives there!"
> The disease of my desire climaxes, deep going, melting in a torrent.

Now that Krishna has overwhelmed her, she as it were disappears; all that is left is what he has consumed:

> It seemed He would just rule over me,
> But instead He consumed my life, that amazing one, and
> Just a little is left after He consumed my dear life. (7)

Pillan notes the paradox, that she is entirely consumed but still around to sing of it: "With this desire—I must see Him—I thought of Him and cried out, but then I was depressed. Then, as before, He came as if to draw me into his service, but instead He consumed my life's breath entirely, and yet after that it was as if He had not consumed everything."[206] This most potent song arises from that small inner voice not silenced even when the beloved has suddenly returned and overwhelmed her. Had she simply died, had there been no anguished soul tormented yet saved by remembrance, no such words would have followed, no *Holy Word* sung from within the small remnant of her former self.

Consumed yet still here, she is amazed that anything is left at all. It is as if she exists only as the amazement itself:

> I had not consented, but He came and consumed my life,
> Day after day He came and consumed me altogether.

In this condition, nothing is possible but the service she had long desired:

> Except for serving my Lord in southern Katkarai with its dark rain clouds,
> Is there anything else that my dear life could enjoy? (8)

Periyavacchan Pillai observes that this necessity—nothing but loving service—is based not simply on her proper nature—she was made to serve the beloved—but more directly on her continuing attachment to him, especially in this moment of divine takeover. Given the accidental nature of their bond—a surprise and an act of grace more than a fact of nature—there is nothing she can do but yield to it.[207] And so she finds it is enough to see again his immediate, superlative particularity:

> Whose life has enjoyed what my life has enjoyed?
> His eyes are large blossoming lotuses, His lips red and full,[208]
> He dwells in the temple of southern Katkarai amid dark rain clouds,
> His four shoulders are broad, fine, lovely,
> This ocean of divinity. (9)

He is the "ocean" out of which the many gods arise, yet those gods have never experienced him so deeply.[209]

In this high moment of discovery, she yearns to consume *him*, outdoing his love by her own. But again, she is caught by surprise, for he is always a step ahead of her:

> In my desire I said, "I will swallow You completely when I see You,"
> But He was too quick for me, He completely drank me up,[210]
> My Lord in dark cloud Katkarai.
> How quick of Him. (10)[211]

It might seem then that her anguish is over, the search finished, union gained. But it is still too early, nothing is final. This remarkable song is in turn followed by yet another song of lament. 9.7 hearkens back to 9.5, as if the intervening song was nothing but a dream:[212]

> The saint was very much delighted by this remembrance which had its origin in his experience of not attaining what he desired. Because now there is no longer any direct experience of the Lord, the delight born of remembering too is upended and non-attainment again becomes the main thing. The saint is thoroughly dejected, and he makes his condition known to the Lord by the woman's messenger song. Absorbed in her Lord's beauty, she desires union with Him. Her nature is such that when she does not see Him come, she cannot survive without Him. She stays in her house due to her inability to bear this, and then goes into the garden.[213]

Thinking again of messengers, she appeals to the birds she has long protected, hoping they will make known her condition. She speaks sweetly to the cranes:

> You've hunted in the marshes of our seashore grove and here you happily live,
> O red legged cranes,

So be my messengers to Him who dwells in Tiru Mulikkalam.
Basil flowers brimming with honey adorn His hair, He is our pot-dancer.

In a striking substitution, she is willing then to settle for *their* feet on her head:

So won't you and your consorts then place your feet on my head? (9.7.1)[214]

Perhaps she hopes that he will realize how this humble substitution signals her desperation for him.

Things are no better at this song's end. As if near death, she charges the swans to hold him responsible:

Tell Him it is not right,
O gentle swans seeking food in wide pools,
Enjoying yourselves there.
My body grows weak, my cloth slips down.
Lest my inner self come to an end
Tell Him all this, there in Tiru Mulikkam. (10)

That she had remembered him so vividly in 9.6 seems no protection against this near despair in 9.7. She has not negotiated a better situation, and she realizes all the more acutely what she does not have: she could not find him; he came unexpectedly in a flash of memory and presence; and now he is gone again. Yet as that passing moment, 9.6 is all the more beautiful, intimacy right in the middle of her terrible distress.

The commentators' prior conviction that the *Holy Word* is a sequence of moments in the saint's spiritual journey allows him to read 9.6 not as a new and brief encounter that begins and ends between the surrounding two scenes of absence, but as a remembrance so powerful that it makes the beloved present again. Reading the three songs in sequence, the commentators decide that the passionate, vivid sense of God evident in 9.6—so out of place—is the fruit of her intense longing and desperate remembrance of past moments of union. It is an instant but infinitely powerful counterbalance to her eons of depression. 9.6 as a "real" first-person song, as if in the author's own voice, may then also be reread as a still more interior interlude, the abrupt retrieval of the poet's own voice deep inside her laments; as her voice arose from his, now his arises yet again from hers: as he had become here, she becomes him. The framing songs of lament merely intensify this inner moment, just as in the *Song* beautiful scenes of union abruptly vanish, making unanticipated loneliness all the more poignant. The beloved does not become permanently present, but his momentary visits will be increasingly intense and more than sufficient to counterbal-ance all absences. Yet as we shall see, still she suffers.

INTERLUDE: *Reading, Remembering, Seeing*

Both women vividly recollect the absent beloved, and both draw him back into their presence by the fierce evocation of past moments of intimacy. The *Song* portrays this recollection rather directly. At a loss, she turns to the women, whose questions prompt her to describe him. The imagining is all the more vivid precisely because he is absent. Her words enflame deep longing in the women, even if at first they had approached her merely in curiosity, well inten-tioned but skeptical. She speaks, and they catch on fire. And thereafter, by these same words the reader too gets caught up in her love. In the *Holy Word*, too, her longing and desperation create the conditions for intense remembering and the moment when the beloved is suddenly so very present again. This happens to her, and may also happen to her listeners. By this woman's word, he returns and stands before her by an almost insufferable intimacy; by that woman's word, the women become able to long for the beloved for themselves.

But knowing what to do with all this after the moment has passed requires both imaginative and theological grounds on which to stand while speaking of the beloved. We need to find words that rule out mere absence and mere pres-ence, loves unshadowed by ambiguity, and theories about love and language that drain the vitality of both of them. The gap between what she expects and what does (not) happen is meant to bother us. Twice implicated, we cannot unread what we have been reading so vividly, and so we are caught. Perhaps for a moment we can no longer neatly imagine the separation between the Hindu and the Christian, and can no longer say exactly who is the beloved for whom we are searching. But still, even if the resulting whole may in the end be greater than the sum of its parts, twice over is not necessarily twice as good. We will be better off only if we learn better what it is to suffer the beloved's absence and presence, to search for one who cannot and need not be found, and to speak honest words into that absence. And so it is that Act Two of itself cannot offer any sure and final word. In Entr'acte Two, we must explore how we are to move from such images and passions back a step closer to the more stable theologies by which such traditions live.

ENTR'ACTE TWO
WRITING THEOLOGY AFTER
THE HIDING OF THE BELOVED

FINDING OUR PLACE AGAIN

In Act Two I intensified the work of interreligious reading on a microscale, dwelling on just a few of the more disturbing scenes in the *Song* and *Holy Word*, while passing by others that might have been studied. I made this choice in order to understand more carefully and as it were intimately the core meaning of love in its poetic and dramatic enactment, twice over. I chose to highlight moments of separation, in part because the *Holy Word* does so, and in part because in such hiding we see more clearly what it means to be human before a God who is both near and far, touching us even if from across a seeming abyss. It has been important not to reduce these songs' meaning to a mere list of similarities and differences, as if by tabulation to prove or disprove something about religion or poetry. The practice of meditative reading—slowly, plodding, erring, but still moving forward and back—has at its best entangled us in the images and emotions of two traditions, each in its own way powerfully evoking her loss. At this moment, if we have done well, we are without the comfort of simple solutions, no longer able to draw on just one tradition's devotion with a purity that keeps other loves at a distance. Studying and remembering the *Song* and the *Holy Word* together should make it impossible to revert to a thinking that neatly separates the Hindu and the Christian, this love and that love, God this way and that. If so, in this we will have managed something new, however ephemeral the achievement might be. Like this woman, we will suffer the un-predictable arrivals and departures of a beloved who no longer acts as we were expecting. We will have new memories that aid and vex us in seeking after a God who should not have to be sought after, who now visits the expected places only occasionally, and who returns just when we think this beloved can never be found. Because we do remember, we still have with us our own traditions, but cannot rely exclusively on how they have spoken of God. We find ourselves in the open space of powerful yet discontinuous insights, suspended between two works of poetry, in the gap where no one set of rules applies.

At a loss, we must then find our own new and imperfect words by which to speak of a God who is present and absent, who hides but can be recollected and become present again. Faced with this necessity, we are where we need to be, implicated, obliged to more than we could up to now handle. Our situation is now more difficult and intense than before we had studied these texts together.

And we are better off. Theologically, readers such as myself might still think there are compelling reasons to remain securely and intentionally within only one tradition. Nonetheless, if we have read carefully, in our imagining we now owe a great deal to two traditions, and should be thankful that this is so. What has been gained will be measured by the fruitfulness of the interreligious learning it enables, but before that by the intensity of the difficulty it creates for the religious reader, the confusion following upon deeper reading in several traditions as we strive to imagine and enact together the incomplete stories of these two women, filling them out in our own words. In the face of all this, slow learning is at stake, and conceptual clarity ought not be the sole or first goal. We need also to preserve the wider imaginative and dramatic space won by our readings up to this point.

But still, truth is not deferred endlessly, for it is received over and again in acts of the imagination. It is nurtured, even if hidden in unruly poetic and dramatic forms that never quite add up to doctrinal clarity. Theology reemerges in a certain manner, without any escape from the unsettled situation we worked hard to produce in Act Two. The readings we have undertaken do not rule out further substantive theological reflection entirely focused on Jesus. Indeed, our readings open up those very poetic and dramatic possibilities which a better Christian theology presupposes and which that theology can later on study with a certain reverence, without abandoning the rhythms of the poetic and dramatic.

That is to say, our readings are best seen as exercises in theopoetics and theodramatics such as Balthasar displayed in his serial readings of poetic and dramatic texts over the twelve volumes of his theopoetics and theodramatics. All of this makes difficult but not impossible a return to "theologic." It will be clear that a return to substantive theological discourse is no small task. We must start slow, and on a mundane level our task must for now be considerably more modest than the dramatics of Act Two might seem to promise. Most of us are not this woman in love, bereft of her beloved. We are not inspired. Our words are not on fire. No matter how much we read of poetry or sermons on poetry, we still think and write prose, and need to seek a way to formulate and write about God amid the (un)certainties of our love, now spelled out in prose. For this reason we need to return to Balthasar and tread his path from the theopoetic and theodramatic back to the theologic. I will move in this direction without any polished disquisition on his system and the doctrines arising from it; I will not attempt a neat conclusion to this project by a theoretical melding of his terminology with some new and better theorization of interreligious learning, by which to leave behind the lessons learned in Act Two. In the end, I will stay within the ambit of her problematic, not his. It will be her words—improbable love facing improbable absence—that speak most directly of the beloved, but Balthasar will do us the favor of telling us what comes next.

But if we are serious about keeping all of this together, first we must ask how we are to *write* of this beloved, fully imagined, fully thought, fully loved. It was with this question in mind that, at the end of Entr'acte One, I indicated that before we could return to Balthasar we would first of all have to revisit Jorie Graham, the poet entirely committed to writing down the wanderings of faith. Although her poetry was absent from Act Two, her understanding of language and the ever-dashed hope of human living were implicit everywhere, chastening, deflating, and liberating our readings of the *Song* and the *Holy Word*. All this amounts to the beginnings of a "difficult" theology, with its necessary rough edges. Biblical and Hindu texts now unapologetically jostle one another, linked uncertainly by understated transitions, the tensions between the texts unrelieved, even as our justifications fell far short of more sensible and accessible appeals to the universal experience of love and its disappointments. Graham's immersion in the problem of writing religiously today, when so much has been lost, implicitly guided us in Act Two, and will guide us now as well, as we seek to underwrite theology after theopoetics and theodrama.

WRITING DOWN, WRITING AFTER: MORE ADVICE FROM JORIE GRAHAM

The problem is as follows. Words I write after my observation of the songs and their reception are now also words implicated in two traditions, my own and another, and they are overstressed at the prospect of a nearly endless stream of possible further interpretations. Encountering Jesus, the beloved, is now all the more intense and fragile and inadequate, particularly when we talk about it. The best words are those that communicate only in part, as we notice what is left out and behind by them. In the best words, the invisible and spiritual become all the more elusive, as if in hiding, mimicking the absence of a beloved who is somehow still manifest in those broken words and images. Theologies lose their coherent bounds as we read the traditions together, but even the poetry itself is upset. Hitherto clear (conservative or liberal) paths are shrouded in a lover's fog, and we are with the woman in a perplexity made more acute by the theological expectation that after some hard work, what we are to believe about other religions should become clear. But now we know more, have been awarded a flood of images and events, without any definite point of closure. With Hopkins, we may realize "the impossibility of staying" where we were, as we were—safely on one side or the other of the religious boundary, innocent in our forgetfulness of the other—and yet will not opt for a theology that replaces the uncertainties of the poetry with clear prose conclusions. So we need to be inconclusive, with a certain stubborn passion. And for this, we need to write with a care for the end of our writing.

As Dan Chiasson has observed, Graham is the master of the careful, intense inconclusive. Writing about one of the poems in her volume *Place* (2012), he comments:

> If another poet—Moore or Frost, for example—had written "Sundown," the stream of sensory information would have been broken by a maxim or an adage or a moral: something, anything to represent the kind of counterpressure our intellects make when confronted with a surplus of sensation. Graham's forms of counterpressure are subtler, more provisional, more subject to the pressures they paradoxically contest—and, if what one wants from a poem is paraphrasable content, less satisfying. Her deep distrust of statement makes Graham search for alternate forms of interruption; it is as though this sensibility were too immersed in the current of ongoing sensation to be able to retreat, even for a moment, from it.[1]

A similar commitment to that counterpressure underlies most of what I have written in these pages. To accentuate the issues at stake in a writing constrained by the admittedly underwritten, underexplained Act Two, but without retreating "even for a moment," I draw here on Graham's eighth collection, *Never* (2002), and from it attend to just one more of her poems. Explaining Graham's project, Bin Ramke indicates that "*Never* is about enactment—the taking on and in of the world via perceiving and describing—and being 'pushed forward from behind' by that action, and thus becoming a way of saving the world."[2] By admitting and addressing the problems of the world, Graham also speaks right through them with words riddled by dangers but never entirely defeated.[3] A most striking poem in *Never* is "The Taken-Down God." It recollects Graham's visit to a small Italian church on Holy Saturday, where by custom the corpus of Jesus had been temporarily taken down from the cross, as if to be hidden away in burial. In a 2003 interview with Thomas Gardner, Graham recollects the day the poem came to her: "Yes, I went there, as I had seen the ritual before, because—I don't know—I was feeling very low. I was in the middle of a very sad divorce. . . . I didn't go there intending to write about it, I was just walking through the piazza, feeling a sense of profound exclusion from everything, and saw the little doorway I knew well and thought, Why not, maybe it can help to just go there."[4]

Faced with a pious and sacred scene where ordinarily one watches and prays but does not write, Graham becomes all the more self-conscious of her writing as noisy, intrusive, a not-prayer put down on paper in the presence of the absent and deceased Jesus. Gardner observes that Graham ends up "struggling with the very act of 'writing about,' or 'taking down' the experience.[5] It seems like an inexplicable wrongness—a trespass of the profane on the sacred. She actually seems appalled at the sound her pen makes on paper in the midst of all those forms of worship." The poet is indecisive, wanting to be inside the church near that taken-down Jesus, yet finding that to take it down in her own writing, she must step outside. She sees no possibility of staying; writing in church, in the very presence, seems both forbidden and futile. Needing to write it all down, while at the same time wanting to throw away such writing and either join the scene, no longer a spectator, or to flee it, Graham writes desperately, for an impossible balance between presence and absence, speaking and not saying anything. As Ramke notes, this difficulty, prompted by the specter of the descended body and missing Jesus, gets at the heart of *Never*: "If we take account of the present, beginning with the sensuous body, located in its environment, progressing to the mind which body and place inform, we create a self that can begin to truly see and thus to know this world to which it belongs. A world in danger of erasure is what *Never* celebrates."[6]

I place this poem in counterpoint to "Le Manteau de Pascal," considered in Entr'acte One, for it too evokes a scene where hopes have been great—this time not for a proof of God's existence but for a return of the Jesus who died and then keeps being taken down from the cross, year after year, only to be found there again. As with Pascal's coat, here too a skyward gaze mirrors the frailties of earth, the tattered worn coat now transmuted into this empty cross. If "Le Manteau de Pascal" is about the lost promise of theological certainty—written, sewn in a coat, decaying—and casts the specter of a tattered, empty coat upon the sky, here Graham looks up to the vacant cross and down upon the corpus of Jesus—and as if in a mirror, she is confronted by the remnants—tattered, as if deceased—of her confidence in writing poetry.

And here too, Graham is desperate to see: "I had never felt the hunger to 'see it all' so fiercely before." Yet it is never quite clear what it is that she is hoping to see in these very particular details: "As if there were something in there—something invisible—that only a tracking of the actual details could lead me to. Something only exposure to the actual physical matter, via the act of description—that terrifying act we so take for granted—could get me to." All this is about a faith she cannot count on, "a desire filled with the desire-for-belief, as well, for that Presence." She seeks a kind of inside-outside equanimity, a presence to the scene while yet remaining liminal to it as well: "That feeling of not-needing. I guess it's grace, or 'unknowing'—but at the time I thought of Keats's notion of negative capability. Mostly I kept trying to record and not think, as I felt that thinking—or some activity of the mind—was something I was supposed to be learning to shut down." But, she adds, "it only came more awake." Presence and expectation, which in their disappointment make us think, are not easily replaced by a more stable unknowing, not-needing and not-thinking. Sitting awake without saying something final is not easy, when "the God" is taken-down and written down, yet later put back up, arising. Given that the scene Graham witnessed recurs every year—Jesus dying, taken-down, rising up again—even as different pilgrims come by, it nicely captures the fluidity of this manner of encounter with the God who has gone missing, been taken away, died. Even in the face of death, there is an immediacy to the scene, presence of a desperate sort: now.

But if so, that "now" itself becomes the problem, as Graham is caught up in her writing here and now, at just the wrong time.[7] Indeed, this "now" recurs at least twenty times in the poem, reappearing over and again even in the space of a few lines, as Graham meditates on the ruin of body, of mind, and of the words that come forth in just this (lost, saved) moment:

There: a picture: the ruin of the mind: did you not *make* it?: because you

can, you

really can: you only have to want to: *now*

*

a voice will say "father"—but, no: there is nothing: the
voice will say father meaning by that nothing; *now*

these words will say "you"—but, no: there is nothing:

In this nothing words fail, for she is unable to write off the specter of this dead
man and empty cross:

now

this pen will say raise up the man, pull back
the veil, slide it off to the side, meaning by that dear nothing, *now*

It is the perplexed author who stutters through the interminable moment:

this voice which is called "I" will say to you: *now*:
now: [can you do that?]: *now*: [do you feel it][there in

your face, in your palms]: *now*: [doesn't it still you] [put
birdchatter in][put dusk-wind in olive groves "below"]: *now*:

And so she gives up her effort to account for the church scene, and so her
words—just words, merely written down—stand on their own:

we are done we are alone we are a dialect but it can still be
Spoken . . .

She yearns simply to dwell in this one moment in this one place, so as to see it all
at once, just this once. And so she focuses entirely on the moment, catching every
part of it, as if unfiltered: the dense overlay of sounds heard together in church:
money being slid into the box, a cane tapping the floor, heels clicking on the stone
floor, coming in and going out, whispers, prayers, sniffles, calls, and responses
outside the church, even the soft slide of the cloth across the wooden corpus—
catching all of this, "all laying-low their nets of sound / to catch the absence."
She catches all of this, but in the unwieldy vessel that is a writing that comes
"in from outside" and noisily speaks "explanations of absence as they / group
around." But they do not silence the question arising at the start of the poem:

"The *now*." Why are these words
an insult to

the god? Especially if written down?[8]

It is as if this seizure of the present moment forecloses the possibility of transcending time or retreating into the past or future, as if "the god" is everywhere but in the present moment. There is only this poetic and dramatic "now" even if this account of "the god," not "God," also moves beyond what the material mind can imagine once it has risked everything, letting go of the well-formed ways of writing and speaking known to religious traditions. The postreligious world leaves no structure of faith intact, entirely firm or integral. It is true that some of us continue to trace the symbols of faith and continue to engage in the practices of faith, but Graham helps us too by removing the pretense that God does not "really die" or "really go away." Indeed, it is not for nothing that it is on Holy Saturday that she rudely compels us to ponder the emptied cross where the beloved used to hang. Writing of absence, she makes a difficult present, presence. This delicate balance subsists in the details, in the particular and small ways that small things happen when unencumbered by more enduring answers resonant with great truths that never die.

She pays the price for violating silence by the loud scratch of pen on paper, her noisy and self-conscious writing that wants to turn presence into word, but that also serves as an excuse for not participating, an excuse abetted by her pose as a poet. She asks: "Why was I writing a poem? Why did I need another damned poem? Why did I need to use their very real event? I went outside and started to cry. It was quite a little crisis. I'm not sure I even understand it now. But I couldn't leave. For a while I sat on the very edge of the outside steps—so as not to block access for all those others arriving—thinking, I can recall the details, and still get it from here." Appalled, she suffers "this terrible sensation of exclusion, and of usury, trespass, sacrilege" and "a real revulsion and deep upset."[9]

Disturbed by, drawn into, violating the scene with her pen and paper, Graham is longer sure why she is writing, but still she is compelled to take this risk:

> Thought "if I bring my pen to bear inside something
> will rip." But what?

She evokes a primal urge to survive, as if by writing she will keep her balance in the flow of time:

> We write. We would like to live somewhere. We wish to
>   take down
> what will continue in all events to rise. We wish to not be erased from the
> picture.

Yet even our own disappearing is something we want to take down in words:

> We wish to picture the erasure. The human earth and its appearance.
> The human and its disappearance. What do you think I've been about all this
> > long time,
> half-crazed, pen-in-hand, looking up, looking back down, taking it down,
> taking it *all* down.

Graham here is a blind seer, as if writing down inspired words that have been given to her in a moment of ritual intensity, dangerously near to the bare cross and shrouded body. Or perhaps her words are like incense swirling around the shrouded body:

> Look it is a burning really. See, the smoke
> rises from the altar. And, too, there is the rising that attaches itself to a [veiled] thing:
> what seems to rise off all sides of the lain-down, hand-made [god]. We
>
> > *
>
> would like to say there is *somewhere* from which we are taken to which
> > we will be
> taken. Ruin, in here, grows sweet. The sweetness seems to rise to cover
> everything.

In her dismay, she tries to communicate what's going on around her. She summons "the assistance of the reader . . . as if she can't do it alone—can't bear the situation, can't undertake the act of witness—alone. She uses the word 'here' repeatedly to summon the reader. Finally even pleading with him or her to help her hang Christ back up."[10] Yet even her own audience can barely hear her secret, secretive writing:

> I have written in this manner, rapidly, scratching, hearing them hear
> this constant incompletion as it tries to *be* (softly as possible) over this page.

This writing is inadequate as an alternative to direct participation in the observances of that day, but the poem-to-be is nevertheless her way of remaining engaged, enacting her own ritual of taking-down and—why not?—putting back up the body of Christ: Jorie Graham, poet become priest and theologian.

Getting inside the situation of the woman in the *Song* and the *Holy Word* has now to be refracted in our own richer, less certain writing; we are neither entirely insiders nor outsiders to all we have read. Our writing both traditions together and calling it love is a violation, an intrusion on intimate pieties, twice over. Even if the theologian who is not a poet writes in a style and for a purpose not entirely poetic and dramatic, the disharmonies arising in so very attentive a comparative reading may tear holes in formal expositions of the beloved. After reading back and forth between the two women in love and in absence, even the theologian's prose must become a kind of poetry, tolerant of its own inconsistencies, if it is to say anything. We find a way to observe without flinching the overlapping and conflicting religious desires and participations that arise in these women and, if we are fortunate, in ourselves too. And so Graham, our seer guide, gets us to write and to see how we write and how properly to fail in the writing, conscious of our divided loves and uncertain crossings. Not because we do not care for the taken-down Jesus, but because we care too immediately, too close up.

So what more can properly be said once we know about these women, their aloneness in the night, the mixed and temporary results of their searching, the conjuring of their love? If we wrap more words around either woman's experience, even as the wise teachers and preachers did, we may speak beautifully of their experience, but also risk embalming it from a safe distance, opting for a more controlled realm of sure meanings. The now entangled story of this languishing—both women, and all of us who read—is complex in its poetics and dramatics, and it would be a mistake to theorize or theologize it, as if to tame the images and direct the drama (back) to safer conclusions. For us as for Graham, the task is writing about a Jesus who is taken-down and put aside, put back up later on, gone up and then come down, but always away from us for now. Ours needs then to be a writing scarred with limits and losses, its truth free enough to escape us whenever we think we have caught the words by which to tie it down. And: if it is Jesus who is (not) taken down here, we cannot help but wonder if Krishna is (not) nearby, as it were, hiding here too, on Holy Saturday.

THEOLOGY AFTER POETRY: MORE ADVICE FROM HANS URS VON BALTHASAR

In Entr'acte One we turned to Graham to find our way beyond Balthasar; here, it is from Graham to Balthasar that we return. We listened to him there, albeit drawing conclusions he might have only partially (and uneasily) anticipated, and with his guidance we have opened up theopoetic and theodramatic spaces where traditions live but which they do not smoothly render by definitive words.

Improbably, we are not in an entirely different world than Graham's. Despite the risk that we might overexplain what we are doing and write in a way that kills off the theopoetic and theodramatic, we still have to find our way back into Christian theology, at least part way into that complicated current of great truths precious to this tradition's core self-understanding: Jesus alone is the beloved. It would be most natural and fruitful, I admit, simply to follow the path trod by Bernard, Gilbert, and John, writing in accord with their sermons. We could systematically extract the spiritual or doctrinal theologies they never formalized in those rhetorically charged inquiries. Were I a Srivaishnava Hindu who had studied Act Two and been inspired to write in a modern way about the *Holy Word*, I might likewise write a *new* commentary on the songs from the *Holy Word* considered there—a task which I must leave to readers inside that tradition.

But here I intend more than commentary or historical review, and something other than a systematization of insights tabulated inside a tradition, from its rhetorically rich and diverse commentaries and sermons. I wish, rather, for the theology that follows upon the theopoetic and the theodramatic, truly indebted to my studies of the *Song* and *Holy Word* without being relegated merely to the margins of the great and contested doctrinal issues of our day. So once more I seek guidance from Balthasar: his insights, with their hold on the great central tradition of Catholic theology, can help us begin to digest Act Two, which, despite its extravagances, we (under)wrote for the sake of an incompleteness of the kind Graham too saw as necessary.

Balthasar's exposition of Hopkins's luminous, God-centered vision of reality served well his insistence on the poetic and dramatic energies that are integral to the Christian vision of reality. Yet Hopkins, we saw, was also an unruly, unruled genius who makes it more and not less difficult to talk even in prose about this divine reality, even as disclosed within the material realm. His poems, attentive to that reality in its concreteness and difference, touch ground in a loving attention to detail and by a chastened and liberated linking of words to what is observed, all with an honesty that breaks down and through settled attitudes about that reality. The theopoetic and theodramatic introduce some untoward and inconvenient images and create an unwieldy burden for theology in the narrower, disciplinary sense. Theology's ordinary strictures, though providing a discipline that later on is necessary for doctrinal clarity, have first to be held off, lest they stifle the poetic and dramatic sense of the truly new. Waylaying and delaying theology are ways of saving it, since the theopoetic and theodramatic break open a situation in which we can contemplate concretely and vulnerably the things of God, Jesus in our midst. And then we have something to say.

A real theodrama does not wind down conveniently and in a predictable manner, as if the poetry and the narrative of uncertainty are done with at a certain point. And so it was that in Entr'acte One, reviewing Balthasar's insights in according with Quash's interrogation, I aimed for a Christian theodramatics, truly of and about Jesus as *the* beloved, no longer constrained by unimaginative readings of his story that merely exclude other stories of longing for God. And so it is that we cannot be certain why the beloved is absent, whether he will actually return, and when she will find him again. Fidelity to the truths of faith cannot be confused with shutting down the more compelling dramatic questions; indeed, as we have seen, it is because she is a true believer that her distress is so real and raw. When we theologize, we can at least take a position like that of the medievals, who resisted the temptation to explain away the absence of beloved and reduce the woman's anguish to *her* problem. My contribution has in part been to suggest that Balthasar's vision of the tripartite wholeness of theology—more broadly conceived—opens up more possibilities than he imagined, making room for the imaginative interreligious interplay that is possible on theopoetic and theodramatic grounds.

The challenge is to negotiate properly the transition from the theopoetic and theodramatic back to theology; it is Balthasar who shows us how to leave room within a Christian narrative for uncertain and undigested moments of poetic and dramatic import: the hour of the *Song*'s lovers and the hour of Krishna and the woman who loves him beyond hope. To understand this transition, I turn back to *Theo-Drama*, volume 5, and *Theo-Logic*, volumes 2 and 3.[11] I consider Balthasar's teaching on language, reformulated—uttered and heard differently, anew—in terms of spirit, searching, and silence. These disciplinary guides offer insights into the human condition before God and characterize a certain manner of theology, such as follows upon the exercises at which we labored in Act Two.

SPIRIT

First I turn to *Theo-Logic*, volume 3, the section entitled "Withdrawal as a Precondition of the Gift of the Spirit." Here the possibility and then requirement of a recognition of absence is grounded in the fact of Spirit, since the advent of the Spirit as it were requires, for a time, the absence of the Son. The farewell

discourse in the Gospel according to John, chapters 14 to 17, affirms that the
Son must depart if the Spirit is to come. The tangible and spiritual modes of
the Son's presence are to be distinguished, and attending to this distinction
draws us into the mystery of Jesus, divine and human: "The gap between these
two presences is essential so that the universality latent in the particularity of
Jesus' earthly existence can be made manifest."[12] Jesus bestows the Spirit, so
that all things might be known, but for this to happen, he must then "withdraw
from visibility." We see this in the Resurrection accounts: those who love Jesus
find more than once that they do not recognize him, and cannot hold onto
him. He visits unexpectedly and then disappears, since they are not yet ready
for his new presence in the Spirit. The manifestation of the Spirit requires a
withdrawal by Jesus so "real and irrevocable" that those who love him experience "a kind of death."[13] "It is only by a radical renunciation—not of a thing,
but of one's own self, and in this context this means letting go for a time of the
tangible, visible, experiential Jesus—that we can hope to receive God's highest
gift, the Holy Spirit."[14] It in in this way, I suggest, that we can fill out the words
of Anne Carson where, in her reading Marguerite Porete and Simone Weil, she
notes that "God can only be present in creation under the form of absence,"[15]
since the Spirit is a kind of absent presence. The dramatic implications follow:
until Jesus comes again, we live in-between, by word and sentiment caught up
in heart-rending moments like those the lover suffers in longing for her beloved when he is not to be found.

Later in volume 3 of *Theo-Logic* Balthasar reflects on the incapacity of words
in the face of the (non)presence of Jesus and the (consequent) presence of the
Spirit. The Spirit must always come in-between, timed by no settled schedule. Noticing this divine uncertainty helps us to understand why Jesus wrote
no book, and indeed why Christianity is not a religion of a book. The absent
Jesus will be recognized not in the written word, but in the Spirit. He "wished
to give his disciples the task of handing on his teaching, in part orally and in
part in written form: this living mediation (written and oral) would serve the
propagation of his revelation."[16] What counts as sacred language is by design a
broken eloquence; as divinely inspired, it gets far enough, but then also fails to
say with full adequacy, and so the Spirit inspires words that manage to "present the hidden fullness of the Lord who is present in the Spirit."[17] Even if, as
Origen taught, Christ is very much present in his threefold body—physical,
scriptural, and eucharistic-mystical—it is still the case that in their sublimity
Christ and the Spirit always exceed every such body, for by definition even

these forms "can never fully contain God's inner self-surrender as act."[18] There is nothing "automatic or magical" about modes of divine presence, which depend "on the believing and loving receptivity of the receiving or transmitting subject."[19] Only by the indwelling Spirit, arriving as the Son leaves, do words and acts become able to make the beloved present. Even the words, acts, and sacraments of the Church cannot in any sure and settled manner make Jesus fully and permanently present; for total and permanent presence would also mark a lack of Spirit. Theology does not so securely possess the meaning of Jesus as to leave no room for wondering—in word, in poem, in event—where Christian love ends and other holy loves begin. Wherever the Spirit is, the new cannot be ruled out: while "revelation of God's love in Jesus is 'concluded' with the Cross and Resurrection," nevertheless "the Spirit can interpret it in a new, different, and deeper way until the end of the world," even if "always starting from the testimony given by the Spirit in Scripture." Whatever the manner of these new words spoken or written, "the letter of this testimony . . . is so filled with the Spirit that its 'forward-orientated' interpretation can never come to an end."[20] Progress and completion are not the goals here. Eloquent in expressing Balthasar's point, the *Song* and the *Holy Word* bring into speech what "can never come to an end." This is why we (re)turn to poetry and drama and hear parables of divine love: a woman wanders about her garden, languishing for her beloved. Even if we have heard over and again her sad and lovely words and feel her passion, we still do not know how to call him, by what name. Yet, in that uncertainty, like the neighboring women we can be enflamed by the spirit of this love in absence. This is faith amid unfaith, an ongoing play of disclosure and concealment, the Son going away and the Spirit coming.

Even if the Spirit unquestionably arrives as Jesus withdraws, that Spirit remains elusive, warranting but also resisting an ending. In other gardens too, other poets sing of the absent beloved who necessarily withdraws, that those who love him might be more deeply marked by longing for him. To honor this freedom and follow after the Spirit when the beloved is absent does not require a formal theology of the Spirit's presence in other religions; one might try to work this out, but it is not necessary, and may be harmful if undertaken prematurely or with overconfidence regarding what is to be accomplished. We need not hasten to explain (away) the presence of the Spirit in the *Holy Word* and in the longing of that woman too. Clarity regarding her love is not the point just now. At stake rather is how we, attuned to the interplay of Word and Spirit, become engaged in the poetic and dramatic testimonies evident in these and other religious traditions. This engagement can hardly be denied or deferred if we are serious about a Spirit that "blows where it will," precisely when Jesus seems to be missing, giving no sure sign of residing in one particular, familiar place. The imagination keeps working, even after our best theology has come into play. Even if a reader reasonably enough judges the studies comprising Act Two to be idiosyncratic,[21] their incompleteness is necessary, in order that the Spirit might have time to work.

Even if the Spirit at work in tradition—in Tradition—is the Spirit of the Gospel and of Jesus himself, and even if this Spirit remains faithful to the community as a whole, this does not mean that each of us can do only what is permitted to the whole community. Rather,

> the individual believer could not receive direct illumination from the Spirit concerning a piece of scripture or of tradition without the intervention of the external "teaching office." Ever since the Fathers we know that the *magisterium internum* in the hearts of believers is not bound to the official *magisterium externum*; [yet] the former must not be isolated from the latter. In the mystery of the Church, where everything that concerns our salvation has to be *received*, the *magister interior* speaks to the individual, never in a purely "private" capacity, but with a view to his Christian vocation, which is always related to the Church of today and of all time.[22]

In this way the seer's and the lover's insight—so private, internally driven—is available to all. This is why in both the *Song* and the *Holy Word* the woman keeps on speaking to her neighbors, however uncomprehending they may be. In her love and driven by the Spirit, she is competent to instruct them, even when she has gone astray and wanders where the beloved had been but not where he is. We have invoked her presence twice over, in the *Song* and in the *Holy Word*, in order that we might remember her even in our time and space; as we ponder her words she lives for us too. She languishes for Jesus, the beloved, but not in perfect purity, since the other love, other song, and other woman remain nearby. All of this may be difficult and may seem even dangerous, but it is still the work of the Spirit, who is present when Jesus has gone into hiding, when in memory and desire we wander into presences and absences previously unknown to us, and when we find ourselves speaking to uncomprehending neighbors who do not know this love and cannot understand the necessity of its errors.

SEARCHING

The woman, we know, spoke over and again of her search for the beloved, her Jesus, her Krishna. In the search and its passing successes and failures she gave flesh-and-blood evidence of the crisis that was his departure and her inability to be satisfied by anything but his return. The beloved, intimately close in the past, now seems to be in hiding, as if available only to those ready to seek. But it is not clear whether a proper search is possible. What after all is the meaning of this "search"? To push the question within a Christian theology of the beloved, we turn to Balthasar's meditation, at the end of volume 5 of *Theo-Drama*, on "the creature in God." He first summarizes three points made earlier in the same volume. First, there is "the fullness of life within the Godhead" that contains in itself what is still, among created beings, "permeated by potentiality"; there is always more, not yet realized, beyond any given moment of seeming completeness. Second, the world itself remains a pilgrim, ever stepping beyond itself toward "an ultimate, though unimaginable, state 'with' God," who is the origin but also the goal not yet reached. It is as if all of reality is searching for the beloved. Third, although it is finite and imperfect and needy, the world is never really outside of God, for "this locus, in its finitude, must be always embraced and surpassed by the infinite distinction between the Divine Persons."[23] There is never some other place to which we must go, even in those moments—or eons—when we find ourselves apart from God. To seek God in some definitive sense would require first that we step outside of reality as we experience it.

Balthasar encapsulates this curious dynamic with reference to the "biblical formula" of the two paths, beginning with an "a priori certainty that what is sought is 'beyond' (*via eminentiae*)." We seek out what is not God in order then to pass beyond it, "negating everything finite, definable, and non-divine (*via negativa*) only in order to strive unswervingly toward the object of the search."[24] Like the woman possessed by a love that settles for nothing but God, we wander about seeking the beloved in the wrong places, where he had been in the past; yet we make progress because we can recollect how the beloved had indeed been in those places and still dwells there in our remembering. In the end, though, we must still be ready *not* to find God in those expected places.

It is also the case that God is a beloved who is already on the move, who "suddenly steps forth with the full impact of a spiritual freedom as the one God who has from the very start already found man the seeker and now addresses him with his grace and his demand."[25] The seeker is always first found by God, that the human lover might then come back to the nearby, hidden beloved: "this *quaerere* is less a search than an adversion to the One who awaits man's conversion."[26] To seek God is a matter of "being overpowered, always anew, by the ever-greater God revealing himself in Christ."[27] When the seeker and the beloved finally face one another, there can be nothing but the silence of lovers "struck dumb by the exceeding measure of the gift given."[28] Below, I return to this silence of the dumbfounded.

One cannot seek after God, as if this beloved were in a particular place, here, there, or somewhere else. Balthasar finds that Anselm catches the dynamic well: "Domine, si hic non es, ubi te quaeram absentem? Si autem ubique es, cur non video praesentem?"[29] One does not move from outside of God to inside of God. How the unbounded God is present to limited human beings is best imagined, says Balthasar, by parsing the asymmetries of heaven and earth as spiritual conditions: "There is no distance between heaven and earth—if by earth we mean freedom in its pilgrim state and by heaven we mean freedom's ultimate state, the ratification of its positive fundamental choice by the One it has chosen, namely, God, who can now openly entrust himself to this freedom."[30] To traverse the small, difficult space of this singular freedom, however, we must conceive of God "in dialectical terms," since the most intense presence is what is "beyond all that we can grasp."[31] Because we cannot plumb the depths of God, the deeper we fall into God, the less likely we are ever done with searching. And all of this always retains a poetic and dramatic form, ever resistant to firm conclusions: as we shall mark in Act Three, the *Song* has no definitive ending, and neither does the yearning of the woman in the *Holy Word*:[32] "in God there is eternal life and hence 'eternal surprise,'"[33] and we shall never be done with our astonishment.

When our love has to do with God, it cannot easily escape the prospect of a divided consciousness: "though we live wholly in God and wholly in ourselves, yet it is but one life; but it is twofold and opposite according to our feeling."[34] We cannot become God or live entirely for ourselves apart from God; for us there is only an in-between space where "we find nothing else but the grace of God and the exercise of our love."[35] We plunge into the *now* of God's nearness, but that moment keeps passing us by as well. Searching then is a necessary fiction that helps us to endure the "passing by," in order that we might better be overtaken by the God who hides right here, where we are.

All of this has been imagined and dramatized in the *Song* and in the *Holy Word*, in the lover's story of searching impossibly for a beloved who hides, yet has not gone away. It also comes to life with still greater uncertainty in our reading of both together, where we open up an uncertain space unpredicted by either tradition. In the unfinished drama of our times, we are always stepping away from the certainties of faith, even if we return a moment later, steadfast again until the beloved departs again. When we expect one love to put aside all others but come to see that the intensity of one love does not diminish the intensity of another, then we stand onto admittedly uncharted ground. Thus the interwoven loves that have made up Act Two: religious diversity, dramatized in vivid poetic form, keeps yielding the possibility that we might be surprised yet again by this beloved. He looks for us where we are, while yet keeping his distance, that we might long to search, inside but also outside the familiar scenes of past encounters. This is what it means to say that even today Jesus is the beloved, for whom we have to search.

SILENCE

The restless Spirit comes when Jesus departs, and from that moment Jesus has no settled dwelling place. But the lover still wants to find the beloved. When the Spirit enflames the heart, we are caught in a search both inevitable and impossible. In this situation, the words arising in the desires and absences of this (non)search, necessary and vain, turn out to be more effective than the searching itself. For these words, uttered in desperation, overreach their capacity, say too much and fall short of any useful message. It is in their gaps and failures that their peculiar eloquence makes itself heard.

In volume 2 of *Theo-Logic* Balthasar reflects on the real but always fragile prospects of human words that might be adequate to the reality of the Word, the Son. In a section entitled "The Possibility of Christology," Balthasar dedicates a subsection to the question of "negative theology."[36] The true negative theology of the Bible lies in God's eloquent dismissal of alternatives, the divine negation of all rivals and so too of human deafness to divine wisdom.[37] But this is less polemic and more a matter of the human condition before God. Balthasar quotes Max Picard's *Mensch und die Sprache* to state how language, ever inadequate, overflows when humans venture to speak of God: "In the intact word there is a more that goes beyond the word. This more has to do with the traces of God in the word. The more in the word must also be realized in action. In the action that comes from such a word also resides the plenitude of this more." Even if our speaking seems adequate to the human situation, it always falls short of the living God, for it is still "bound up with the word from which it comes rather than with the event that comes forth from it."[38] The problem is not language itself judged by its essential features, but a speaking that does not know when to stop. We are silent when there is nothing to be said, but more importantly when we have too much to say. Only in the midst of such silences can words speak effectively of the hidden beloved. There is no final filling of silence by words, nor a final abandonment of speech; we have to speak, imperfectly, over and again. This is why in Act Two the woman was most eloquent when her beloved had just departed, when she realizes that he will not return as promised, and when there is no one listening to her plaintive songs. This is why every scene ends with an expectation that there is more to be said, later on.

Balthasar cites Karl Rahner to affirm the possibility that "God will speak, breaking his silence and disclosing his depths to finite spirit."[39] But this divine speech can never be predicted according to a schedule. As Rahner says, it requires waiting, listening: "Absolute being thus appears despite and in its openness to the transcendence of the finite spirit as that reality which . . . freely discloses itself or conceals itself in silence, as the God who may reveal himself through his works, because he is the God who must reveal himself through speech *or* silence."[40] Thus the dilemma of our Act Two, meditations haunted by a beloved who hides particularly from those who love to excess, a beloved who is uncomfortably recollected in two traditions at once—or not. Even amid myriad signs of divine presence, this beloved does not speak; even when it would seem so easy to break the silence, he does not respond to even her lament.[41] Since there is always much more to be said than words can hold, it is fitting that they fall silent: "What speech can grasp of him as Word remains an insignificant portion of the super-word through which God expresses himself. Human silence is a partial aspect of this total word, which in turn harbors in itself the mystery of the divine word-silence."[42]

The New Testament witnesses to a Christ in whom "all the treasures of wisdom and knowledge" are "hidden" (Col. 2.3). This is a Jesus born in obscurity, hiding in full view for thirty years, silent at moments that begged for words, as when he faced Pilate. Almost carelessly, Jesus allowed most of his words to remain unrecorded, as if to ensure that they be forgotten: "He lets his own spoken words fade away, entrusting their later writing down to the Spirit." Even during his public ministry, he "spoke almost more through deeds and gestures of the flesh than through spoken words."[43] And then, after "his return into the silent bosom of the Father," as the age of the Spirit begins, we are forever more confronted, as Ignatius of Antioch puts it, with his "mute Eucharistic presence in the midst of the Church."[44] We have listened to the remarkable silence of God in the songs of the *Holy Word*—where the beloved never speaks—and, though less consistently, the silences of the *Song*'s beloved at just those moments when their union had been most ardent and seemingly settled, just short of a final word that would seal their love irreversibly.

Mystics speak of an annihilation that occurs when union with God is imminent. This annihilation may be thought of as an overintensification of presence that makes ordinary living and self-consciousness impossible; total surrender to God is required, when there is no longer a safe distance to be kept.[45] In the *Exercises* of Ignatius Loyola, for instance, "'negative theology' finally becomes the locus of perfect encounter, not in a dialogical equality of dignity, but in the transformation of the whole creature into an *ecce ancilla* for the all-filling mystery of the ungraspable love of the self-emptying God."[46] This plays out in many times and places, a difficult waiting with no termination. She languishes awake, alone in the night, knowing nothing but his absence. All she can be sure of is that every means of knowing has failed. The theologian who had read our Act Two must heed the silence both women suffer and share, precisely in that overcharged space where traditions meet and at times seem to shadow and obscure one another.

Later Balthasar returns to this timely inadequacy of language, right inside the mystery of what God does:

> God's action in the Biblical sphere is primarily a sovereign doing that man cannot control and of which God bestows knowledge in the measure that he sees fit. This knowledge can never be adequate, because, even supposing man's supreme willingness, he has to believe what God declares and can never survey it from above or retrieve its motives. Consequently, there will always remain within God's interpretive Word a zone of unfathomable silence. Not a silence that withholds explanation, but one that marks the (for man, unguessable) distance between God and creature.[47]

This is the drama of a God who can be unexpectedly other, less and more than we can say and bear. Silence, the not-saying that only seems to be mere waiting, is necessary to our conversation with God. As promising and disappointing as Pascal's coat, every sentence we speak, as soon as it is uttered, is riddled by the suspicion that too little and too much has been said. As Balthasar paraphrases Picard: "Even in human discourse silence presses for speech; nevertheless, a word not based on silence becomes chatter; finally, in God's life speaking and being silent are one."[48] This is Pascal's lost proof, eloquent because it is missing. This is why the day that Jesus is taken down from the cross and for a time hidden from our gaze provokes not only the poet but also the best theologians: difficult poetry, the sacrament of a taken-down God.

—This faltering speech, riddled with silences, is in fact the ordinary speech of the Spirit in the human flesh of each and all: "the seemingly finite content of what [Jesus] says (in whatever form he may speak), and thus the realms of silence that remain in it, are handed over to an ongoing, never to be ended hermeneutic of the Holy Spirit within the history of the Church."[49] What cannot be said properly is all the more communicative, for "the Spirit is capable of taking what seems unspoken within the spoken and of fitting it into always new words that deepen and explain, without, for all that, ever coming to an end, either in time or in eternity."[50] In the Church, too, there is no end to this living word, no final and successful formulation that would at long last put an end to other religions and their other loves, since "the Spirit never arrives at a concluding verbal expression of the whole of Jesus' adequate transposition. Thus, he never exhausts and cancels the *maior dissimilitudo* [the still greater dissimilitude] of God."[51] And so Balthasar recognizes that the act of incarnation—*verbum caro factum est* ("the Word is made flesh")—and our understanding of it become audible only when we are patient in silence: "This fact," his becoming made flesh—"includes the zone of silence and mystery . . . without therefore compromising its facticity."[52] Even the propositions of the great councils "do not in any way lay claim to exhaust the content of the fact," since the faltering of words "does not lie in them but in the object to which they refer."[53] Or as the woman of the *Holy Word* might put it: missing him is due not to the burden of our deeds, but to the fact of his absolute freedom to flee to the hills or herd the cows or ascend into heaven. Faithful theologies are those humbly arising in this zone of silence, in the gap between words never entirely, safely bridged by even the most finely refined analyses.

This silence is central to the interreligious encounter, a dramatic arena home to partly told and still unfinished stories of God and love, incompletely recounted encounters, dialogues without clear beginnings or certain endings, the beloved nearby and gone missing, more than once. Whether the dialogue occurs in conversation or in reading and writing, it eventually falters, silent for intervals of uncertain duration. Balthasar correctly stresses that way of silencing cannot be taken as a strictly negative path, as if all images and words about the Mystery are merely to be discarded. Rather, it is because now we vividly remember God to excess that the problem arises: God is near, expressive, very much present within our experiences—and yet also more than all that, hence distant, absent right in the moment of encounter, ungovernable by any words available to us. The uncertain dynamic of the two women we meet in their moments of union and patient, sad waiting enacts imperfectly but faithfully what cannot be imagined in words intolerant of ambiguity.

If we are serious then about word and its silences, and if we do the hard work of hearing the poetry and contemplating the scenes that fill Act Two, we can see that only a bad theology rushes to pass sure and certain judgments on other people's similarly broken, similarly defective and similarly overflowing words of the beloved. This is not because the beloved is entirely unknown or essentially not to be named, but because this hidden beloved may not play (only) by the rules of the love we already recognize. The beloved, this Jesus, may hide in gardens and on pathways not yet known to us. Here, too, the theologic must keep deferring to the theopoetic and the theodramatic, and so we need not try too hard to undo the eloquent uncertainties of the woman faced with the absence of her beloved. When the beloved goes into hiding, yet leaving myriad signs trailing behind him, then love is all the brighter and more painful, ardent, and arduous, eloquent in its silences.

PATIENT WAITING AS A THEOLOGICAL VIRTUE

After all the wandering experiments of this study in love and the hiding of the beloved, it is important to note that the concerns raised in my Prologue have by no means gone away. The particularities and passions of our love still cannot be denied or explained. It would still be wrong to put the dilemma behind us, and it is still the case that nothing is gained by backing away from the concrete, specific loves that give life to faith and religious living. If we understand this stubborn lover's commitment and are patient with the theopoetic and theodramatic possibilities opened up in patient waiting, then we can also still notice those other holy loves. All of this happens in the particularity, the concrete instance that is also universal. It is by an intense and concrete love that Christian insights into the *Song* arise; one does not languish in love for ideals that cannot be really present or really absent. Nor should a Srivaishnava Hindu retreat to a vague language that dilutes this tradition's intense specificity. We need not abandon our first love or deny what we have read, meditated upon, and not forgotten. This doubling of memories intensifies rather than relativizes the deep yet fragile commitments of our singular, first love. As long as sure confessions of faith and stout theologies do not suffocate the imagination, we are in the difficult right place to be, still admitting that the beloved can go missing and hide from us and may bewilder us by showing up in unexpected places, even near to other lovers in other gardens.

For the Christian, the desired incompletion of our words mirrors the hiddenness of the beloved who is Jesus. In remembering Jesus this way we now find not merely mythic similarities that might be explained (or explained away), but also echoes, whispers, scents of the love story of Krishna and the young woman who was dying of love for him when he did not return. For the Srivaishnava, Krishna too will be absent, even if he too is never entirely gone and forgotten. Such remembrances come to mingle in our imaginations, if we resist the temptation to sort things out neatly, as if Krishna were the same as Jesus, or as if the two of them are merely examples of something more interesting, or as if they are entirely unrelated because a connection between them is forbidden, inconceivable. We may of course sometimes still wish for a more secure garden which the other woman has never visited, wherein the name of no other beloved has been heard; but today there is none, and so we must leave room in love's affirmations for gaps and shadows and secrets. If we are lucky, we will be unable to immunize ourselves against the words—and images and dramatic scenes—by which other traditions have loved God. If we are careful theologians who can still read poetry, hear music, and get drawn into dramas not of our own writing, then we will find ourselves recollecting the precious things of that other religion for which we have no proper conclusive words. The *Holy Word* will everywhere affect our reception of the *Song* and all that follows from it, and our best theology will be mindful of this truth as well. Here we may recall Graham's echo of Hopkins: we hope to be afflicted with *the impossibility of staying just where we are.*

But yes, there is more ordinary theological work still to be done. At this moment and with these memories, the Christian theologian is better placed for the greater theological questions, and that later work can begin again. The deeper matters of Trinitarian and Christological discourse and the great soteriological and ecclesiological questions can thereafter return to center stage, even if they will never more be alone on that stage; the theopoetic and theodramatic do not go away. *His Hiding Place Is Darkness* does not block the return to the great questions; it simply highlights the danger in going back with amnesia to ordinary ways of theology; it pleads for slow learning that sacrifices efficiency for the sake of deeper currents of encounter. In writing of God in more formal doctrinal and systematic terms, theologians must write in the shadow of the images, the poetry, and the drama of a beloved who may still hide even when everything should be most certain, definitively decided. Such theologians write best when chastened by Balthasar's good advice: in the Spirit, searching, silent.[54] The errancy does not end, the work of Spirit always outstrips our best efforts. In this situation, the best theological words are those which are tattered, incomplete, and humble before the silences of the beloved.

And so none of this will add up to a neat ending, any more than the *Song* and *Holy Word* can ever be finally done with the stories they tell. In our brief Act Three we must visit these women once more and let them have the last, incomplete word.

ACT THREE
IN THE END

[13] Thou that dwellest in the gardens,
The friends hearken;
Make me hear thy voice.
[14] Flee away, O my beloved, and be like to the roe,
And to the young hart upon the mountains of aromatical spices!

(*Song* 8.13–14)

¹ These slender shoulders have grown so
    thin.
Alas, without noticing at all how I am
    alone and grown so thin,
The lovely cuckoos still coo, alas, and
The gathered peacocks dance together,
    alas.
The day You go out to herd the lovely
    cows is like a thousand ages, alas, and
Right now with Your lotus eyes You
    pierce me through, alas.
This is no compassion, no compassion at
    all, Krishna.

² This is no compassion, no compassion
    at all, Krishna.
Every time You touch my full breasts
There swells inside me a vast flood of joy
That crests not even in heaven, it
    surrounds and submerges all I
    know—
And yet it ends like a dream.
Desire reaches deep deep inside me—but,
    alas, none of this a soul can bear, oh!
Yet separating from You right now is still
    worse,
When You go out to herd the cows:
It is my ruin.

³ When You go out to herd the cows, it is
    my ruin.
My soul burns with hot sighs, but no one
    helps me.
I still exist, but no longer do I see Your
    ink-dark body in its dance.
When You go out, the day does not pass,
The tears from my slender kayal fish eyes
    never cease.
This is death—to be women of the
    cowherd clan, slaves, entirely bereft.

⁴ I am a slave, entirely bereft, no one
    helps me,
But You don't think at all about this grief,
    Govinda,

You prefer Your herd in its pen, You've
    scorned us for them, and off You go
    to herd them.
And yet I'm still flooded with the
    ambrosia of this ripe fruit.
You've entered deep inside this sinner's
    heart, and still
I keep thinking on the soft deceiving
    words ever rising on Your full red
    lips,
And my soul burns.

⁵ Your words are sweet, I keep thinking
    on them, and my soul burns
When You've gone to herd the cows all
    day, Krishna.
The wind carries the fragrance of musk
    jasmine buds.
Evening returns, wild as an elephant in
    heat,
The fragrant forest jasmine flowers on
    Your jeweled chest make my lovely
    breasts glow.
Give me the ambrosia of Your mouth,
Place Your lovely lotus hands on our
    heads:
We exist only at Your feet.

⁶ We exist only at Your feet, place Your
    hands on our heads.
Your eyes are lovely, deep as the sea.
Many women want to get between us and
    clasp Your lovely feet—
But let that be—
We just cannot bear our womanhood,
Tears never cease to stream from the
    dark corners of our eyes,
Our hearts too cannot stand still.
Your going out to herd the cows repels
    me,
Our life like wax melting away in fire.

⁷ Our life like wax melting away in fire,
Our bright bracelets and cloth slack and
    slipping down,

Tears like pearls trickle from our flower
   eyes, our breasts are pale, shoulders
   frail.
Alas, great jeweled Lord! Your soft red
   lotus feet will hurt
When You go out so joyfully to herd the
   cows,
And won't demons fall upon You there?
   What then?

8 "Won't demons fall upon You there?
   What then? So don't go!"
Thus my dear life cries out.
Now affection and shame mingle inside
   me,
And that mingling hurts, so don't let go
   of my hand.
Show me Your winning lotus eyes,
   mouth, hands, Your yellow cloth.
These are the cowherd women with
   waists so slender they might break,
They please You so very much, these
   good women,
So wander about with them—but do it
   right here.

9 If You wander about right here with
   these good women who please You so,

You will banish entirely Your mental
   anguish and our joy too will be
   amazing—
Even if our womanhood is insufferable.
My Lord, don't go to herd the cows—
Many demons are wandering at Kamsa's
   command, in any form they wish.
If You fall into their hands, calamities
   will befall them and You too—
Mark my word—alas!

10 "Calamities will befall them and You
   too—mark my word—alas!
By Kamsa's command brawny demons
   wander about, disturbing even
   ascetics.
Yet being alone seems so important
   to You, You don't want even Your
   Balarama,
Even with him You won't go about!"
I keep saying this, yet inside me my soul
   burns:
Herding cows pleases You more than
   heaven, but still—
Your lips are so full and red, our smiling
   god of the cowherds.

(*Holy Word* 10.3.1–10)

EVEN AT THE END of the *Song* and the *Holy Word*, there is no sure conclusion, neither permanent union nor final rupture. The theopoetic and theodramatic realities voiced in these verses do not yield the satisfaction of a neatly
accomplished resolution. When the woman and her beloved are together as the
Song closes, she tells him to go away; we do not know if he obeys. When finally
the woman and her beloved are together at the end of the *Holy Word*, he seems
about to leave again; we do not know if he yields to her entreaty and stays. *His
Hiding Place Is Darkness* too must end this way, so that we cannot really summarize what we have accomplished. Both the beloved and our destination will
remain hidden, at times.

FLEE!

Right to the end of the *Song* their love is difficult. As deep as it may be, uncertainties are never entirely banished. Yet we are almost convinced to expect otherwise, since in *Song* 7 and 8 they rejoice in the deep pleasure of their union, as if it will last forever. Near the end she speaks confidently of this love:

> Put me as a seal upon thy heart, as a seal upon thy arm,
> For love is strong as death, jealousy as hard as hell,
> The lamps thereof are fire and flames.
> Many waters cannot quench charity,
> Neither can the floods drown it:
> If a man should give all the substance of his house for love,
> He shall despise it as nothing. (8.6–7)

She wants nothing but to hear his voice:

> Thou that dwellest in the gardens,
> The friends hearken;
> Make me hear thy voice.

But at the *very* end, in the very last verse of the *Song*, she calls to him one last time, unexpectedly urging him to flee:

> Flee away, O my beloved, and be like to the roe,
> And to the young hart upon the mountains of aromatical spices!

What does she mean? Why send him away? Modern scholars suggest that perhaps she is that mountain, and so she is simply calling him closer.[1] Perhaps she implies that they will go off together. If she really is sending him away, though, we should not be entirely surprised. At the end of *Song* 2, she sent him away, even if at the start of *Song* 3, he immediately returned, before disappearing again. The intimate union of *Song* 4 gives way to the fruitless search of *Song* 5. Such reversals are integral to the meaning of the *Song*.[2]

In his 120th and last sermon, John of Ford interrogates her insistence that the beloved should flee. Certainly, she cannot be dismissing him because she is sated, bored, or fickle.[3] "What is it, O fairest of women, what is it that you are saying? Can it really be that you are beginning to grow tired of your beloved and that you are bored with your pleasures? Are you not embarrassed in telling your beloved to flee away?"[4] Perhaps the point is spiritual: if she is truly favored, then after her beloved is gone his Spirit will infuse her words: as he leaves, the Spirit comes, and gives mysterious power to her final instructions.[5] Implicitly, perhaps, the beloved has asked her to bless him at his departure, her own grief notwithstanding: "Was it not the case that Jesus wanted to go away and return to His Father, and His beloved was prepared to hold Him back any way she could—she who could hear not a single word about His departure without having sorrow fill her heart?" She has been holding him back, but he is "eager to depart . . . since He was going where had to go." Still, "He wanted to go with her permission and her blessing."[6] As earlier, it is for her own good that he should leave, and so, in the end, "throwing away her sorrow," she gave "her hands to Jesus as He prepared to go away," offering "the fullness of her hope to the Holy Spirit who had been promised her."[7] She urges him not to linger but to go quickly, since only by his departure will the Spirit come: "So go away, my beloved, or rather flee quickly, for all speed is slow to me as I long so surely for the fulfillment of Your promise."[8]

Still, John thinks that even as she gives this blessing, she is also hinting that he should come back soon, "swift in returning like a gazelle." It is as if she really means, "Be exulted above the heavens, my beloved, but all the same, do not forget to be like the gazelle or the young stag that You were accustomed to be when You were with me."[9] In the meantime, "Be that much closer in spirit, the farther away You are in the body. Be all the swifter to answer my prayers, the more invisible You are to my eyes."[10] She survives with the hope that he will not forget: "When You are illumined with the radiance which You had before the world was made, remember Your handmaid, widowed and poor and lowly. Pour out upon her the consolation of Your Paraclete, along with that radiance of Your magnificence."[11] This moment's departure, however final it may seem as the *Song* ends, is surely but a prelude to still more intimate and intense union.

The beloved's intense, intimate presence makes evident her unworthiness, and reminds her again of the impossibility of this union: "She has had so many kisses and embraces, so many conversations and visits," of the kind "open not to all, but rather to those who love. Is it to be thought extraordinary humility if, after all these things, she feels herself unworthy of them all, and, in the end, says to Him, 'Flee away, O my beloved'?"[12] Yet even if the beloved ascends that fragrant mountain,[13] he should still be disposed quickly to return: "As is only right, be like a gazelle or a young stag, going away according to your custom and coming back again, speeding away in a moment and then, as usual, hastening back."[14]

And so we reach the end of the *Song* and John's reading of its ending.[15] Since love is inherently fragile and uncertain, the unexpected arrivals and abrupt departures of the beloved cannot be avoided, even as the story ends. We do not hear his response, and we do not know whether and when he will return. Perhaps the reader is meant simply to return to the beginning of the *Song*, to hear her opening plea once more:

> Shew me, O thou whom my soul loveth,
> Where thou feedest, where thou liest in the midday,
> Lest I begin to wander after the flocks of thy companions. (*Song* 1.6)

DON'T GO!

Things are still getting worse for this woman. In *Holy Word* 9.9 her suffering had become most acute, anguish heightened by the growing sense that he will not come even if every sign promises his arrival. Her lament punctuates every verse:

> Evening has come, but the dark one does not come.
> Their great bells sounding, the lovely cows gambol near their strong bulls, alas.
> Cruel flutes sound, alas, and buzzing bees circle
> Amidst the bright forest jasmine, malabar jasmine, and musk jasmine flowers, alas.
> The sea resounds, echoing to the sky, alas.
> But what can I say—apart from Him—how can I survive? (9.9.10)

As these vivid, melodious voices fill the air, she is once more acutely aware of her loneliness, bereft of any words that might redeem the moment. But as far as we know, still he does not come that night.

At the beginning of 10.2, Nanjiyar explains that the saint had discerned the lord's presence in the temple at Anantapuram, and imagined spending his life in worship there. But even that temple remains beyond reach: "He reflects on the fact that he is still unable to reach his destination; he still suffers the effects of their previous long separation and is still in this natural state."[16]

Holy Word 10.3 is the last of her songs, and strikingly it is perhaps the first of her songs in which she is face to face with her beloved Krishna.[17] Yet uncertainty, not bliss, fills the scene. It is morning, and now that he spent a night with her, she is terrified he might leave. The poet finds himself having to confront the fact that this is how God is, even when so very close. The beloved is entirely free, like the Krishna who goes out to herd the cows whenever he chooses. As Nanjiyar puts it, the poet is admitting that even now he is still lacking "that highest love by which one is unable to live except by making oneself belong entirely to Him,"[18] and he is afraid: "What can be done if He will not graciously involve Himself in this material thing?"[19] And so the saint—this embodied being, this material thing, flawed yet now comprised entirely of love—speaks one final time in her voice, in a scene where beauty and sorrow once again mix:

> Although she has been fully united with her Lord all night long, so that He had no thought of leaving her at all, now all beings awaken and arise. The cuckoos call out, the peacocks exult, the fresh breeze blows without ceasing, and the calves and cows spread out across the fields. She is afraid that in keeping with past custom He will leave right now. She is in anguish, lest He go forth to pasture the cows.[20]

She experiences terrible anxiety right there in his presence:[21] "Right in front of Him she experiences the dejection she would experience were He to leave. Right in front of Him she experiences that dejection described in 9.5 and 9.9,[22] and she grieves with her whole being."[23] She cries, "This is not right."[24] She wants not merely to delay the inevitable separation, but to secure a lasting, intimate relationship: "I am not satisfied merely with telling You by my own mouth not to go out to pasture the cows. I must tell You what I have been thinking but unable to say: 'Please put Your lotus hands on my head and look me right in the eye. Help me survive.'"[25] Never was their encounter more immediate and direct; never was her pain worse, because she cannot see a way to make it last.[26]

What she previously said to the birds or the wind or her heart, in 10.3 she speaks directly to her beloved, demanding that he take note of her slow, sure decline, a sad state so out of keeping with the lovely setting:

> These slender shoulders have grown so thin.[27]
> Alas, without noticing at all how I am alone and grown so thin,
> The lovely cuckoos still coo, alas, and
> The gathered peacocks dance together, alas.

This time she makes no effort to communicate with these inattentive birds, for now she needs no messengers. Now her longing is due not to a fear that he might not come, but at the prospect that he might leave. She suffers because he is not entirely hers, and seems ready to take the cows to the pasture where, it remains unsaid, the cowherd girls will find him. But she gets no sympathy:

> The day You go out to herd the lovely cows is like a thousand ages, alas, and
> Right now with Your lotus eyes You pierce me through, alas.
> This is no compassion, no compassion at all, Krishna. (1)

This is no compassion, no compassion at all, Krishna.

Absence had signaled his lack of compassion; now presence—uncertain, already over with—is even more cruel.

As the scene unfolds, she keeps insisting that he look directly upon her suffering. In verse 2, she harps again on his lack of compassion, the cruelty of this sporadic intimacy. His presence, his touch, his gestures—all that she desired—now cause her pain, since there is no guarantee that they will last longer than a dream:

> Every time You touch my full breasts
> There swells inside me a vast flood of joy
> That crests not even in heaven, it surrounds and submerges all I know:
> And yet it ends like a dream.

Even direct encounter with this beloved, Periyavacchan Pillai suggests, is merely impermanent, a mirage. He is entirely free, and union occurs as he wishes, until he wants it no more—whether or not her desire has abated:[28]

> Desire reaches deep deep inside me—but, alas, none of this a soul can bear, oh!

This disproportion—his fickleness, her enduring love—is why her fears grow more intense when she considers the otherwise ordinary prospect that a cowherd might go out to herd his cows:

> Yet separating from You right now is still worse,
> When You go out to herd the cows:
> It is my ruin. (2)

She is left behind, alone and worried, with nothing to do to pass the time. She dreads both the uncertainty of what will happen out in the fields and yet too the prospect that he might not return at all:

> When You go out to herd the cows, it is my ruin.
> My soul burns with hot sighs, but no one helps me.
> I still exist,[29] but no longer do I see Your ink-dark body in its dance.
> When You go out, the day does not pass.

The day does not pass; time no longer flows predictably since, as Periyavacchan Pillai indicates, when you are in love, an eon passes in an instant, but when you are apart, an instant seems an eon.[30] All she can do is weep at her fate, born for love yet in the end having nothing at all:

> The tears from my slender kayal fish eyes never cease.
> This is death—to be women of the cowherd clan, slaves, entirely bereft. (3)

I am a slave, entirely bereft, no one helps me,

Nanjiyar reads between the lines and suggests that Krishna must be responding with amusement, a smile, as if to say: "Is there the slightest indication that I am leaving you?"[31] He is playing with her. Even so, she savors his words and the very lips speaking those words, ripe fruit, dripping ambrosia:

But You don't think at all about this grief, Govinda,
You prefer Your herd in its pen, You've scorned us for them, and off You go to
     herd them.
And yet I'm still flooded with the ambrosia of this ripe fruit.

It is as if, Nanjiyar suggests, she struggles to balance the bitter content of his words against the alluring sweetness of his voice:[32]

You've entered deep inside this sinner's heart, and still
I keep thinking on the soft deceiving words ever rising on Your full red lips,
And my soul burns. (4)

As before, everything in nature reminds her of him. Evenings promise reunion, but this evening might reveal only that he is not coming back. So unsure is she that she thinks this way even when he is there with her:

Your words are sweet, I keep thinking on them, and my soul burns
When You've gone to herd the cows all day, Krishna.
The wind carries the fragrance of musk jasmine buds.
Evening returns, wild as an elephant in heat.
The fragrant forest jasmine flowers on Your jeweled chest make my lovely
     breasts glow.

Even as she accosts him, she asks for still more intimate touches of his hands and lips:

Give me the ambrosia of Your mouth.
Place Your lovely lotus hands on our heads:
We exist only at Your feet. (5)

She speaks in the plural—"we" who are at your feet—as if just now she notices right near her those other women who love him too:

We exist only at Your feet, place Your hands on our heads.[33]
Your eyes are lovely, deep as the sea.

As a woman, now with all these other women, she acutely fears losing him:

> Many women want to get between us and clasp Your lovely feet—
> But let that be—
> We just cannot bear our womanhood,
> Tears never cease to stream from the dark corners of our eyes,
> Our hearts too cannot stand still.

No longer alone, she is worse off than when he was merely absent:

> Your going out to herd the cows repels us,
> Our life like wax melting away in fire. (6)

> Our life like wax melting away in fire,
> Our bright bracelets and cloth slack and slipping down,
> Tears like pearls trickle from our flower eyes, our breasts are pale, shoulders frail.

Perhaps realizing that lament accomplishes nothing, abruptly she turns back to him and conjures latent dangers out there among the cows:[34]

> Alas great jeweled Lord! Your soft red lotus feet will hurt
> When You go out so joyfully to herd the cows,
> And won't demons fall upon You there? What then? (7)

> "Won't demons fall upon You there? What then? So don't go!"
> Thus my dear life cries out.

Now she is in turmoil simply for his sake—his risk, not her love—and so she begs him not to let go of her hand:

> Now affection and shame mingle inside me,
> And that mingling hurts, so don't let go of my hand.
> Show me Your winning lotus eyes, mouth, hands, Your yellow cloth.

Perhaps he does, perhaps he does not, meet her request.

But then it occurs to her that those other women, her bothersome rivals, may be her last chance. In her extremity, she wants him to stay even if for that to happen, he chooses them over her. She is ready to give him up to them, as long as he stays nearby, where she can see him:

> These are the cowherd women with waists so slender they might break,
> They please You so very much, these good women,
> So wander about with them—but do it right here. (8)

Conflicted to the extreme, she evinces joy beyond measure and at the same time a sense of her own impending doom, should he stay near her but with them:

> If You wander about right here with these good women who please You so,
> You will banish entirely Your mental anguish and our joy too will be amazing—
> Even if our womanhood is insufferable.[35]

This vision of Krishna with other women is too much for her; rather abruptly she shifts back once more to the specter of the pasture full of hidden dangers, demons lurking in many forms:

> My Lord, don't go to herd the cows—
> Many demons are wandering about at Kamsa's command, in any form they wish.
> If You fall into their hands, calamities will befall them and You too—
> Mark my word—alas! (9)

Those demons, like the women, vex ascetics:

> Calamities will befall them and You too—mark my word—alas!
> By Kamsa's command brawny demons wander about, disturbing even ascetics.
> Yet being alone seems so important to You, You don't want even Your Balarama,
> Even with him You won't go about!

There follows an understated allusion to heaven, perhaps the heavens whence he came, perhaps the moment of their pure happiness together; but in any case, he seems to cast aside such happiness:

> I keep saying this, yet inside me my soul burns:
> Herding cows pleases You more than heaven, but still—

As if in confirmation, Krishna says nothing, and all she can do is focus on his smile:

> Your lips are so full and red, our smiling god of the cowherds. (10)

What does it mean, that he is smiling at her? Is he mocking her or is he indicating his pleasure in her wild love and the renewal of their union? No answer is given. The *Holy Word* continues for seven more songs, climaxing in the saint's final ascent and seeming irreversible union with his lord, but we do not hear her voice again.[36] Perhaps the reader is meant simply to return to the beginning of the *Holy Word*, to hear her story once more:

> O innocent crane with lovely wings, be kind,
> You and your mate with lovely wings, cry "Alas!" and give me your grace.

Be my messengers to the one who rides the bird with fearsome wings—
But if you go and if He should cage you—if that is your lot, what can be done?

But the commentators find still deeper meaning in the song. Nanjiyar, for example,[37] sees it as the exquisite final stage of a surrender already long under way, even in 1.4, where we first met her. And she has grown. In *Holy Word* 2.9,[38] for example, she had asked that she become able to be entirely focused on him, but now she asserts, "Whether I am with Him or not, what I desire is that He prosper." Nampillai, too,[39] recognizes that she is far along the spiritual path; her love is desperate but selfless, since now she does not begrudge those women who might simply hold onto him in a way that her deeper love would not permit. She has learned from her previous failures that relationship with him is a gift, never to be taken for granted. What really frightens her is his freedom to come and go, but this is the freedom all lovers must suffer. Loving God is always a risk.

EPILOGUE
JESUS, THE BELOVED

HIS HIDING PLACE IS DARKNESS has been primarily a series of exercises in the study of the *Song of Songs* and the *Holy Word of Mouth*, potent texts magnified in their possibilities by the insight and grace of their medieval interpreters. In this writing I have sought a delicate balance between a most intense and particular truth—Jesus the beloved—and the unending drama of aesthetic, dramatic, and true apprehensions that draw us perilously near to other such loves—Krishna the beloved. The particularities of faith have been open, disclosed for inquiry, throughout *His Hiding Place Is Darkness*, and I have made no secret of my own Christian faith. But with a certain theological confidence chastened by the discipline of the theopoetic and the theodramatic, I have been mindful not to forget that other woman's love and her hiding, hidden beloved, Krishna.

Even if our understanding of desperate love is all the greater after meditations on the *Song* and the *Holy Word* together, and even if there is no settled ending to love or true thinking, still, as I say in this volume's Prologue, nothing matters more than Jesus, in the distinctiveness of his personhood, as the truth that is beautiful, right here; he is the beloved. This is so, even if to say such a thing is to speak implausibly and with a certain powerlessness, not in triumph. It is to echo the woman's improbable and lonely words, such as never quite name him: he is the beloved—wherever and however he is. But loving Jesus needs to be played out dramatically, and only in this love's garden, in the drawn shadows of our vigils, and in our restless wandering. Chastened by a reading back and forth that is neither neat nor accomplished, but then too by a surfeit of new memories gained in the writing of this book (as well as some thirty years of double readings before this), I have found it necessary to leave it to others and to the Spirit to speak amid the absences of Jesus, spanning gaps of the kind the mind dislikes because they cannot easily be accounted for. Such is the uneven, unkempt ground for a theology willing to stay close to the concrete, particular universality of the beloved, resistant to the urge to be done with searching by inserting an ever-present Jesus who never comes and never goes.

But as everywhere in these pages: even when such faith in Jesus keeps sounding within human hearing, it is a gentle song that does not deafen us to other such words of love, as if there are no other reports of the beloved, or as if one love defeats all others. What (some) theology cannot tolerate, the (engaged) imagination will not forget. The disciplined freedom of the poetic, as in Graham's studiously difficult verse, reminds us that singular insights, written in a singular fashion, still disclose intense and local love, which endures even in its tatters: the proof that works because it is no proof, the god known only in the taking-down. Total devotion to Jesus as the one and only beloved—faithful, true, and sometimes missing, hiding, not coming back, nowhere else—shines better in a world where we need not forget this Krishna about to return to the young woman waiting in the garden. Faith in this beloved, this Jesus, still shines; and yet others too are nearby. Or so we imagine.

We need not decide things too firmly, as if faith needs an end to questing because it cannot suffer poetry and the drama of uncertain love. Better we say more only when we have more to say, in the meantime remaining on edge, holding our breath as we stop our words, love extended beyond its capacity for confident words. Loving God is always a risk.

FOR MEDITATION

Commentary continues, slanting downward.
Ah what am I carrying, what's this load, who's that
                                    out there,
why all this dust? I remember "the oldest of trees."
We drove through it. I "looked." I remember
"all manner of being may swim in my sea."
Slanting upward, tiny bits of rain murmur in my gaze.
Slanting upward, the gaze senses, right *in* the looking—[so
                                    fresh] [after
rain, early spring]—the gaze cannot but sense [since
                                    it's not in the
visual field] [not at all]—cannot but: the slantline down towards
                                    dis-
appearance.[1]

                    .   .   .

        I am soft sift
                In an hourglass—at the wall
            Fast, but mined with a motion, a drift,
            And it crows and it combs to the fall;
        I steady as a water in a well, to the poise, to a pane,
        But roped with, always, all the way down from the tall
                Fells or flanks of the voel, a vein
        Of the gospel proffer, a pressure, a principle, Christ's gift.[2]

NOTES

See "A Note on Editions and Translations," at the beginning of this book, for additional information about the sources cited in these notes.

PROLOGUE

1. Henceforth I will generally refer to these texts as "the *Song*" and "the *Holy Word*."

2. The project is therefore engaged in the texts we have and what they tell us. I do not intend to imply that there is something about "woman" particularly suited to patient waiting and to desperate love, or something about "man" that makes distance and a failure to reciprocate love somehow predictable.

3. On this notion of the larger "Text" composed through comparative reading, see *Beyond Compare*, 203–4.

4. I will say no more about comparative theology in this book, not just because I have recently explained the discipline at length (in *Comparative Theology*), but more importantly because comparative theology is best learned not in what is said about it, but in what it does. All that follows is an act of comparative theology, even if the term itself need not appear again in these pages. I might add that this is the first of my books entirely conceived and carried through to completion at Harvard. Readers familiar with my earlier work can judge for themselves the effects of Harvard on my understanding of theology, comparative work, and faith commitments.

ACT ONE: MISSING HIM

Throughout the book, I have on occasion placed the main passages from the *Song* and *Holy Word* together, without comment, so that the reader can reflect on them together, alone, before and after reading my analyses of them. Not all passages cited from the *Song* and *Holy Word* are included in these "For Meditation" sections.

1. Elie Assis—to be introduced more formally in Entr'acte One—parses these two confrontations by noting that right at the start of the *Song*, we are justifiably puzzled: "The derision of the Daughters seems to be nothing more than tension and jealousy between friends. The background of the tension with the brothers does not appear in the poem itself; we do not know the reason for this attitude by the brothers toward their sister, but the poem does not focus on that, and it should not be loaded with more than there is actually in it." She is at least uncertain in her relationships, since the scene

"reflects the girl's lack of maturity in attempting to create a love relationship, because she cannot take care of herself—because she is busy tending to the vineyards instead of getting ready for a meeting with the man. Her excuses for her self-neglect and her apologetic answer to her friends, only confirm her lack of readiness" (Assis, *Flashes of Fire*, 42–43).

2. Cheryl Exum—likewise to be introduced later on—notes the subtle interplay: "Her question is a double entendre. . . . From elsewhere in the *Song*, we know where the man grazes or feeds: among the lilies and in the gardens, figures for the woman herself. . . . The question, 'Where do you cause to lie down at noon?' also contains a verb without an object, and so suggestively leaves open the question what or whom he causes to lie down" (Exum, *Song of Songs*, 107).

3. "Nearly all translations make the question straightforward and chaste by supplying the flock that the woman neglected to mention. On this level, she is asking her lover where he pastures his flock and where he has his sheep lie down at noon, so that she can visit him in the heat of the day, the time of rest" (ibid.).

4. In Exum's view, these are the words of the women of Jerusalem:

> The badinage here in vv. 7–8 bears some similarities to the verbal play between the woman and the women of Jerusalem in 5.2–6.3. There they ask her where her lover has gone, so that they can help her find him, and she reveals that she knows where he is and what he is doing there: in his garden, grazing. Here she asks where he is, and the answer she receives implies that she knows, which is, in fact, what her double entendre about grazing in v. 7 [verse 6 in the Latin] suggests. (Exum, *Song of Songs*, 108)

But the answer does not really help, since "she is told that if she does not know where her lover spends his time at midday, then she will have to look for him, but the trail will be easy to follow." The implication, Exum adds, is that "she does know and does not need to seek him at all" (ibid.). And so right here, at the beginning of the *Song*, we are puzzled, since "the speech teases the reader with its ambiguities. If v. 8 [7 in the Latin] is the man's speech, we have a guessing game: does she know where he is? does he tell her? (Landy, 171). If 'by the shepherds' tents' is the same place as 'by the flocks of your companions,' then he proposes she join him where she imagined having to look for him. If the phrases refer to two different places, then he may be arranging a rendezvous, a place they can meet while his companions are away elsewhere with their sheep" (Exum, *Song of Songs*, 108). Assis is less optimistic about this exchange between the woman and her beloved. They seem somewhat distant, even so early in the *Song* and even if they are face to face: "The woman is asking him to tell her his whereabouts so that she will not be embarrassed in front of his friends as they graze their flocks, since if he does not tell her, she would be obliged to go looking for him herself." (Assis, *Flashes of Fire*, 45). Instead of promising that he will come to her, he rather coolly gives her an order: take your flock, and go there. He adds:

> If the answer had been positive, we would have expected his words to be of a more intimate nature, expressing affection and anticipation of the meeting. However, the man's answer contains three instances that convey a sense of alienation: "If you do not know," "[you] go on out," "your kids." The stress is on her, expressing separation.

This is especially evident when he says to her, "[you] go on out," instead of a much warmer invitation, such as, "come to me." His words do not express any reference to them as a couple, or any sense that he is looking forward to their meeting. The warmest thing he says to her is "most beautiful of women," but this does not express any intimacy or any reference to them as a couple." (ibid.)

There is a chill in the air; their union has already peaked. While they have been together and can be so again, they also known separation, and the need to find their way back. This dynamic forestalls settled interpretations, and leaves room for uncertainty. And so the place for the imagination is opened.

5. In Sermon 31, he sets the scene.

6. Bernard of Clairvaux, Sermon 31, Mount Melleray translations [henceforth Melleray], 366 (Cistercian Fathers Series [henceforth Cistercian], 125). All translations of Bernard are from the Mount Melleray translation (with occasional slight adaptations), but for reference I give also the page numbers in the Cistercian Fathers Series.

7. Ibid., Melleray, 369 (Cistercian, 127).

8. Ibid.

9. Ibid., Melleray, 371–72 (Cistercian, 129).

10. Ibid., Melleray, 372 (Cistercian, 129).

11. Sermon 32, Melleray, 378 (Cistercian, 135). Bernard further reflects on the ways in which God is diversely present and absent, making himself known partly and in varied ways (125–27). That God speaks so diversely is in part due to the fact of imperfect seeing, in this life. Imperfection and multiplicity go necessarily together.

12. Sermon 31, Melleray, 372 (Cistercian, 129).

13. Sermon 32, Melleray, 378 (Cistercian, 135).

14. Ibid., Melleray, 379 (Cistercian, 135).

15. Ibid., Melleray, 379 (Cistercian, 136).

16. Ibid., Melleray, 381–82 (Cistercian, 137).

17. Sermon 33, Melleray, 391 (Cistercian, 145).

18. Ibid., Melleray, 397 (Cistercian, 151).

19. At the start of Sermon 34, Bernard offers a further explanation. As with Moses or James and John, the disciples of Jesus, her ascent to full knowledge is necessarily slow. Moses first "received another vision far inferior, yet one whereby He might sometime attain to that He desired," while James and John "had to be satisfied with a lower grace, from which the ascent to the higher could occur" (Sermon 34, Melleray, 409; Cistercian, 160). If she seeks her beloved eagerly, desiring immediately to find him, it is not surprising that she is rebuffed. But when she fails, she advances toward him.

20. Ibid., Melleray, 413–14 (Cistercian, 163).

21. Sermon 35, Melleray, 415–16 (Cistercian, 165).

22. Ibid., Melleray, 416 (Cistercian, 165–66).

23. The rest of Sermon 35 is given over to a long meditation on the degradation of the soul that does not know itself or God. Sermons 36 and 37 likewise delve deeper into ignorance and the bondage that comes with it.

24. Sermon 38, Melleray, 449–50 (Cistercian, 190–91). Compare the Srivaishnava

reading of the distress of Shatakopan, the conditions productive of his composition of the *Holy Word*.

25. Ibid., Melleray, 450 (Cistercian, 191). The quote is *Song* 4.7.

26. Ibid., 38, Melleray, 450–51 (Cistercian, 191).

27. And yet, the song does not begin ex nihilo or in a blank space, but presumes knowledge of God. The power of the song requires both the continuity and abruptness of beginning in the middle of things.

28. Periyavacchan Pillai, A 2, 569. On the system of citing the Srivaishnava texts here, see the "Note on Editions and Translations."

29. P. B. Annangarachariar, a twentieth-century commentator deeply immersed in the classical tradition, observes that such imprisonment—for the birds and by extension for her—might signal an advanced state of surrender. Whether he comes or goes, listens or not, such is one's lot. See Annangarachariar, *Tiruvaymoli Dipikai*, 1: 146.

30. Throughout, I translate the Tamil word *alvar*—a general term for the Vaishnava poets that is suggestive of their immersion in the lord—as "saint."

31. Periyavacchan Pillai, A 2, 553.

32. "For her lover" is implicit.

33. Periyavacchan Pillai, A 2, 553.

34. Ibid., A 2, 553–54.

35. Ibid., 556.

36. Ibid., 561–62.

37. In singing this song, he identifies with her entirely (ibid., 562). Nampillai suggests that this is a complete simile: the partial resemblance of the saint and the woman, with respect to love, leads to a portrayal of their total identification with one another.

38. Ibid., 566.

39. "Mates" is in the feminine.

40. For "Narayana" (Nara-ayana) is the "support" of "living beings," that is, the refuge (*ayana*) of all beings (*naras*).

41. Or, "bearing his gracious discus"—which favors those be protects, smites his enemies.

42. Periyavacchan Pillai reports various interpretations of the import of "striped bee," which is generally taken to be indicative of the loveliness of the bee's stripes—though possibly of its circular flight. (A 2, 623).

43. Tirumal, the "holy lord"—or the "lord of Tiru," the goddess Sri.

44. Literally, "how did she pierce the majesty of your feet."

45. Literally, "I have no deeds."

46. "Don't leave" is left incomplete, and could mean, "Don't leave me," such that I die; or, "Don't leave him," or even, "Don't give up" until he loves me in return.

47. Every song's eleventh verse is a first commentary on the preceding ten, an observation and promise that most often gives a practical turn to what has already been said, and this one is no exception:

The lord of the peoples of the seven immeasurable worlds, Krishna:
Shatakopan of lovely Kurukur surrounded by lush fields sang of him

In this ten of the unending *antati* of one thousand, and
Those who sing them beautifully will gain great wealth that reaches high as heaven.

Regarding this and other stylistic features of the *Holy Word*, see Clooney, *Seeing Through Texts*, c. 2. Periyavacchan Pillai reminds us that in the previous song (1.3), Shatakopan had meditated on the extraordinary accessibility of Krishna. Invoking the silent, absent beloved as "Krishna" now—though not in the first ten verses—counters her doubts: he seems absent, but he is still Krishna, physical, vivid, present—so nearby that you can touch him, almost. However tortured her words may be, in her voice the poet's intention may be simply to praise this Krishna who is present even when he is absent (A 2, 658). The reader of course is neither the poet nor the woman. The point of learning Shatakopan's verses in the woman's voice is not to repeat her experience, but to discover how close he is, even when her lament is most acute. This woman suffers, sings sad and beautiful works, and we profit. This we know from ordinary life, Periyavacchan Pillai observes (A 2, 659): a father toils, but the son inherits the wealth. Readers are not meant to strive to be her, but gratefully to learn from the songs of her love and sorrow. Annangarachariar rather directly states the point of this verse: "Simply learning the words of this song suffices for reaching the Holy Place," Narayana's heaven (1: 176).

ENTR'ACTE ONE: LOVE IN-BETWEEN

1. *His Hiding Place Is Darkness* therefore has a narrow focus. To understand what it is about, it is important to notice what it is *not*. It is not a full study of the *Song* or the *Holy Word*, nor a study of their reception in tradition. Much has been written on commentary in the Christian Middle Ages and there is much more to write—regarding the tradition of Bernard, Gilbert, and John, for instance—but I do not intend to make a formal contribution to our understanding of medieval exegesis. Much more needs to be written on the content and styles of traditional Hindu commentaries, but although I have studied this material for more than three decades, I leave much of that detail to other occasions and even to other scholars. It is not my main goal to contribute directly to the important field of comparative Christian-Hindu exegetical studies. Nor is this primarily a contribution to our understanding of gender and the divine, or the cultural politics of how we represent male and female. I do not take the fact of the prominence of the woman in each set of songs—for it is she is the one who suffers the absence of him—as saying something essential about women or, worse still, about "woman." The wider issues implied here are real, but tasks for another time, and in many cases better suited to the talents of other scholars. This book is reserved for a smaller, simpler, and rarer project: reflection on the possibility of knowing and loving God in the particular, even amid a plurality of intense, vivid loves, even in an skeptical age where radical religious commitment, received and cultivated in its specificity, seems nearly impossible to justify as intellectually defensible.

2. The numbering of the verses varies in the Hebrew, the Greek Septuagint, and Latin Vulgate. Except where otherwise noted, I use the numbering found in the Vulgate.

3. To situate the *Song* as a Hebrew text, I have relied on Exum and Assis. But in what follows I learn also and primarily from the Latin text, in part due to my linguis-

tic limitations and in part because my medieval commentators—to be introduced in a moment—are likewise reading the Latin. My reasoning—and the reader can decide whether it convinces—is that the most basic issues about the *Song* and its meaning, for this theological study, are quite adequately dealt with by attention of several of the best contemporary commentaries on the Hebrew text of the *Song*. In lieu of comparably first-rate commentaries on the Latin of the *Song* as a whole, it has seemed reasonable to draw on the wisdom offered by Exum and Assis, to avoid overextending their insights to the Latin text, and then listen also to the medieval Christian readers as they uncover the riches of the Latin text. See also Griffiths's justification of his use of the Latin of the *Song* in his Christian theological commentary.

4. Assis, *Flashes of Fire*, 24.

5. I have added 3.1–5, to highlight it as an intrinsic sequel to 2.8–17.

6. Here I am *not* dealing directly with the end of Assis's unit.

7. These titles taken from Assis, *Flashes of Fire*, 21, but a more inclusive list is on page 24. I have slightly modified his titles for the sections. The five sections I focus on reflect what Assis identifies as the climaxes, respectively, of the five rendezvous scenes in the *Song*: 1.1–8, 1.9–2.17, 3.1–5.1, 5.2–6.3, and 6.4–8.14.

8. The fact of a complete commentary accomplished by three connected monks is a key reason why I have chosen to use the commentaries of Bernard, Gilbert, and John.

9. On the layers of meaning in the medieval readings of the *Song*, see Turner, *Eros and Allegory*, especially chap. 5, "The Logic of Typology."

10. Halflants writes the introduction to volume 1 of the Cistercian Fathers Series translation of Bernard's sermons on the *Song*. Scholarship on Bernard is vast, but my intention in the studies that comprise Act Two is simply to listen to how he reads particular scenes in the *Song*, as imaginative explication and more constrained theology come together in his sermons on this poetry. Similarly, Gilbert and John offer us guidance on disclosing the spiritual meanings of the *Song* in its Christian context. If Christ is the beloved who comes and goes—on the vast scale of human history, in the Church, and in the life of every devout Christian—how do these readers save and dramatize that uncertainty?

11. Halflants, ix.

12. "Surely in some way similar." The Latin is from Bernard's Sermon 31 on the *Song*.

13. Halflants, xi–xii.

14. Ibid. xvii.

15. In his brief introduction to Gilbert's sermons, Lawrence Braceland stresses the continuity between Bernard and Gilbert.

16. Jean Vuong-dinh-Lam's doctoral thesis, "Doctrine spirituelle de Gilbert de Hoyland," xxix.

17. Pointed out in "Le monastère."

18. Dutton, "Learned Monk," 161–63. Dutton is drawing on Gilbert's letter to the "teacher-scholar" Adam.

19. Costello, *Sky-Blue*, xiii.

20. Ibid., xv.

21. Ibid.

22. Ibid., xvi.

23. See also Costello and Holdsworth, *Gathering of Friends*.

24. *Theo-Logic*, 1: 8.

25. Ibid., 21.

26. That is, seven volumes in the English translation; the number of volumes in the German differs.

27. *Theo-Drama*, 1: 16; and quoted in Quash, "Theo-Drama," 155; and in Quash, *Theology and the Drama of History*, 38.

28. *Theo-Drama*, 1: 16.

29. Ibid.

30. Ibid., 16–17.

31. Ibid., 17.

32. The "restless heart."

33. Balthasar, *Explorations in Theology*, 80, as cited in Quash, *Theology and the Drama of History*, 184.

34. Quash, "Theo-Drama," 155. Quash highlights four major problems:

> The problems bequeathed by the Balthasarian model have the power utterly to disable a theodramatics' value as a heuristic for theological thought about history. It is worth summarizing those problems here. They include, i. the evacuation of time of much of its significance as the carrier of divine revelation and as the medium for human encounter with life-giving and death-dealing questions—therefore of time as an *ethical* and what I have called an *existential* space. They also include, ii. The habitual neglect of awkward or resistant material, and especially of particulars that do not seem assimilable to a unified vision of history and theology in their interrelation. More specifically, iii. There is the subjugation of one *class* of "particulars," namely persons, to institutions or what are identified as historical movements (the subjugation of subjects to structures) and ultimately to what is thought to be the will of God in such institutions and movements. This indicates the final problem iv., the presumption to have a God's eye view of what is and is not significant in the world. (Quash, *Theology and the Drama of History*, 196–97)

On the particular challenges raised by attempting religious reflection on the novel, Quash most interestingly asks, "What would have happened had [Balthasar] engaged in as serious and sustained a way with the modern novel, for example, in which the complex embeddedness of human characters in their interrelations and in the midst of all the exigencies of time finds a uniquely involved and layered literary expression?" (Quash, "Hans Urs von Balthasar's 'Theatre of the World,'" 30).

35. Quash, "Hans Urs von Balthasar's 'Theatre of the World,'" 30. And, "This is a vital statement of what Balthasar understands his concern with dramatic theory to be aiming at: not a concern with the static, with formal or timeless coherences or relations. Not for him a treatise on the divine perfections that suppresses the fact that God's life is a 'super-action'. God's is the dynamism of a love utterly possessed because utterly donated, and most manifestly so on the Cross" (Quash, "Theo-Drama," 155). The quote is from *Theo-Drama*, 1: 16.

36. Quash has rightly characterized the *Theo-Drama* as capturing the *indeterminacy* typifying human life, the *dynamic staging of particulars* staged successively, and the *essentially and irreducibly social nature* of human reality. Superlatives do not adequately express the eternal, but only the comparative, the opening into the "ever-greater" (Quash, *Theology and the Drama of History*, 183).

37. In the *Glory of the Lord*, vol. 3, in a section chapter entitled "Sacramental Poetry." For reasons that will become evident, I use Hopkins, even if one might also fruitfully use Balthasar's study of John of the Cross, in the same volume, as an example here.

38. *Glory of the Lord*, 3: 398.

39. Ibid., 391.

40. Ibid., 392.

41. Ibid.

42. Ibid., 394.

43. Ibid., 393–94.

44. Ibid., 394.

45. Ibid.

46. Ibid.

47. Ibid., 396. But it is surely too much for Balthasar to say that this knowledge of God in Christ "presupposes" a dogmatic knowledge; for even in the life of the Church as a whole, dogma follows upon that knowledge, ever dependent on it. This is all the more true in the lives of individuals.

48. *Glory of the Lord*, 3: 396–97.

49. Ibid., 399.

50. Quash, *Theology and the Drama of History*, 194.

51. Ward, "Hopkins, Scotus, and von Balthasar," 67.

52. Ibid.

53. Ibid., 68.

54. Ibid., 69.

55. Ibid., 71.

56. Ibid., 72.

57. Ibid., 73.

58. Ibid.

59. Ibid., 73–74, citing Hopkins. See also Hopkins, *Journals and Papers*, 289; my emphasis.

60. Ward, "Hopkins, Scotus, and von Balthasar," 74, citing Hopkins. Balthasar is perfectly right in seeing the sacramental specificity necessary to Hopkins's apprehension of beauty—and even, as Ward stresses, the grounding of Hopkins's worldview in the individuality and sacramental power of the person of Mary, mother of Jesus. But Balthasar may hold on to all of this too tightly, not allowing it to breathe or speak for itself.

61. *Glory of the Lord*, 3: 398; emphasis mine.

62. Ibid., 399.

63. Quash, *Theology and the Drama of History*, 201.

64. Ibid., 206, citing Rowan Williams.

65. Ibid., 209.

66. Here is the full list of the songs in the voice of the young woman, or her mother or friend: 1.4, the young woman sends messengers; 2.1, she sends messengers; 2.4 (mother says), this young woman wastes away in love; 4.2, she is confused and cries out, says her mother; 4.4, she sees everything as the Lord's, says her mother; 4.6, her mother asks, who can cure this young woman of her disease? 5.3, she says, I care nothing for the rebuke of my neighbors; 5.4, she says, I am awake for an endless night, and he does not come; 5.5, she says, women, do not blame me, I saw him at Tirukurunkuti; 5.6, she is possessed by the lord and speaks as him; 5.9, she says, I seek the lord who lives in Tiruvallaval; 6.1, she sends a third message; 6.2, Krishna, stop playing the fool; 6.5, she worships him at Tolaivillimangalam, cares for nothing else; 6.6, she is lovesick for him; 6.7, she yearns only to go to Kolur; 6.8, the young woman sends a fourth message; 7.2, the young woman desires only the lord of Srirangam; 7.3, friends, I am infatuated, I care only for the lord of Tiruppereyil; 7.7, I am infatuated with him, women—what can I do? 7.10, will I ever reach Tiruvaranvilai? 8.2, my friend, I cannot explain even to you; 8.6, his city is Tirukkatittanam; 8.9, she is lost, to the lord of Tiruppuliyur; 9.5, she begs the birds to understand her predicament; 9.6, (she) remembers vividly how the lord came to him; 9.7, she voices to the birds her lament over the lord of Tirumulikkalam; 9.9, she laments, it is evening, but he does not come; 10.3, she laments Krishna's lack of concern for her as he goes to herd the cows.

67. Messengers: 1.4, 2.1, 6.1, 6.8; Birds: 9.5, 9.7.

68. 5.9, 6.5, 6.7, etc.

69. 5.3, 5.5, 7.3, 8.2.

70. 5.4.

71. 9.9.

72. 6.2.

73. 5.6.

74. 10.3.

75. By tradition, Nampillai's text was put into writing by his disciple Vatukku Tiruviti Pillai (1217–1312). One might then more properly speak of Vatakku Tiruviti Pillai's commentary and insights, but I defer to the tradition of taking this very large commentary to be the teaching of Nampillai. The first commentators whose work has come down to us is Tirukurukai Piran Pillan (born 1161), who sets the tradition on the course of reading the songs as the spiritual journey of the saint; in a mix of summary and word by word explanation. On the commentators, see K. K. A. Venkatachari, *Manipravāla Literature* and *Srivaisnavism*.

76. These commentators depend heavily on the notion of experience (*anubhava*) and the saint's drawing his intense experience into his words. By studying the songs closely, with the (speaking and writing) teachers, we come to participate in that experience. They are sensitive to the role of psychology in the narratives they expound, both of a song like this, and of the *Holy Word* as a whole. They explore the psychology of sending messengers, the dynamics of communicating through likely intermediaries who are nonetheless—as birds, as unreliable—dubious, and of her sending these particular mes-

sengers. They savor her choice of messengers, and her naïveté, agitation, being-like-Sita. There is little scholarship on these teachers-commentators in English, but see Carman and Narayanan, *Tamil Veda*; Raman, *Self-Surrender*; and Clooney, *Seeing Through Texts*. Old but still instructive is the collection of anecdotes drawn from the commentaries in Govindacharya.

77. The songs give no clue that they chart the saint's spiritual journey. By themselves, they are simply lined up in a series, one hundred songs of eleven verses each, without any indication that the order is important or that there is a forward movement in the whole of the *Holy Word*. These commentators too develop a rich story line around the myriad images, teasing out the implied dialogue, and highlighting events only partially described in the verses; they read them as expressive of the desolations and consolations endemic to the saint's longing for God. By reading the songs as this developing story, they channel for us the imaginative and dramatic resources of the verses, now imaginatively and dramatically conceived as a manner of spiritual progress. Nanjiyar dramatizes separation's purpose in this way: "In order to bring to birth in the saint that healthy state of devotion suitable to participating in the lord, He deepens a little the saint's desire to experience Him, just as physician will forbid a sick person to eat anything. Filled with desire, the saint cannot endure this separation, because he exists only as entirely belonging to the lord. If he should unite with the lord in experiencing this participation, there will be born in him that desire which a young woman has [for her lover]. Such union alone is his enjoyment, and he can no longer endure separation." To give voice to this unendurable absence, the saint takes on the persona of the young woman: "So the saint compares himself to a young woman who suffers greatly because after union with her beloved she is separated from him and cannot bear it. . . . By voicing her words makes he known to the lord his own condition." And so the woman comes to center stage: "She is sorely grieved that her lord has parted from her after his union with her. Because he does not return, she thinks, 'He won't come, simply because he sees and counts our faults. So we must point out to him how he is renowned for tolerating sins.' . . . As messengers to her lord, she sends birds living in the garden [and the wind and her heart], not seeing that they will not understand what she is saying" (Nanjiyar, 2: 553–54).

78. 1.4 can be usefully read in light of its literary background in poetry that is *not* religious, for instance, this *cankam*-era poem from perhaps four centuries earlier:

> O great rain clouds pregnant
> with child, approaching
> with winds mixed with the roaring voice
> of thunder, who frighten snakes
> on the slopes of long mountains:
> you have a character strong enough
> to shake the glorious Himalayas.
> What is this?
> Have you no pity for poor women
> separated from their men? (*Kuruntokai*, 158, as translated by Pillai and Ludden, 79)

This old *cankam* poem is evocative of the plight of the woman awaiting her "man" who does not return before the rains come. Like the *Song*, it is bereft of any directly religious symbolism. Later Tamil religious poets recognized that the mood and affect of such songs, their existential situation, could illumine the human condition as oriented to and related to God. They made this connection not by replacing the old poetry with explanations of it, or by correcting its worldview, but more simply and powerfully by reimagining its possibilities in new poetry, such as we see in song 1.4 of the whole. Their shift into the voice of the woman enables commentators, later on, to read the songs with a sense of poetic and religious drama, the imagined life experience of the saint whose suffering the absence of God is itself an experience of loving God.

79. 1.1–3.

80. Nampillai, 2: 156–57. The quotation is from the *Brhadaranyaka Upanishad* 2.4.5, which more fully reads, "One must see, must hear, must think, must meditate."

81. The most recent volume at the time of this writing, *Place*, was released in May 2012.

82. Brian Henry defends the "memorability" of Graham's "long lines"—lines that are too long, disregarding the patterns of ordinary breathing and so too of reading—as a strategy for implicating the reader: "Their memorability resides not just in the various enactments—physical, philosophical, spiritual, visual—in them, but in the reader's experience of sifting through, struggling with, succumbing to—experiencing—the poems." As Henry puts it, Graham privileges enactment over mimesis, in this way confirming Wallace Stevens's adage, "To read a poem should be an experience, like experiencing an act" (Henry, "Exquisite Disjunctions," 284). Henry also rightly detects inner connections: "Graham's ability to make her 'small devices' and 'habits' more than superficial changes in technique affirms the coexistence of stylistic development and inner change in her poems." Honoring her overly long lines that also spill over down the *right* side of the page, Henry finds a link therein to her sense of self, as she herself confesses: "the taking on, only apparently arbitrary, of stylistic devices—the inhabiting of them until they become the garment of one's spirit life, the method by which one touches the world, the means by which one can be touched oneself, and changed. The changes I made in my 'technique' are changes that occurred in my life: I became the person I couldn't have otherwise been by these small devices, habits" (ibid., 286, citing Graham, in Wright, *Quarter Notes*, 44).

83. Jorie Graham, first interview with Thomas Gardner, 1987; included in Gardner, *Regions of Unlikeness*, 217.

84. *Breaking of Style*, 91. Vendler is commenting on one of Graham's poems, "The Turning," which at the time of Vendler's essay was unpublished (87), but was published later in *The Errancy*.

85. Ibid., 92.

86. Vendler, "Jorie Graham: The Moment of Excess," in Gardner, *Jorie Graham: Essays on the Poetry*, 57.

87. *Breaking of Style*, 91–92.

88. Brian Henry, "Exquisite Disjunctions," in Gardner, *Jorie Graham*, 109.

89. Ibid., 112.

90. Ibid.

91. "Jorie Graham's Incandescence," Gardner interview with Graham in *Regions of Unlikeness*, 227.

92. Ibid., 205.

93. Ibid., 202.

94. Several themes recur throughout the collection. For instance, there are six guardian angel poems; these nearby but spiritual beings observe close up realities of which they are not a part. "The angels are expert in the implications of various human responses to finitude; they see through our attempts at making order, our writerly gestures. Each of them looks down on the wreckage or exhaustion of our attempts to order the world, while also calling attention to something new and fragile, beginning there again" (208). And then there are the "dawn/aubade" poems: "The most fully developed attempt to actively wake and blossom in this way, full of 'shy first-glancings,' is a set of aubades—dawn poems. They are vulnerable poems, live to all of the implications of speaking and making sense that the rest of the book declares at issue or in play. They are poems that, quite literally, awake, stirring before the glance asserts itself, poems in which only the skeleton of the dream of reason, charged and incomplete, is there to come to grips with mystery" (Gardner, *Regions of Unlikeness*, 211). At such moments of awakening, we are aware, yet not yet armored about the ambiguities of the day.

95. Ibid., 206.

96. Spiegelman, "Repetition and Singularity," 164.

97. Karagueuzian, *No Image There*, 144–45. Despite being an errancy, a wandering quest that is replete with error, a futile project like "seek[ing] to hold the wind" within "a net," as the book's epigraph from Thomas Wyatt suggests, Graham's project of looking is justified in this volume (*The Errancy*). Yet this wandering eye with its vain quest is essential: as Graham puts it, "you do understand, don't you, by looking?" The project of a carefully fractured narrative matches my exercise, in Act Two, of reading with reverence and care the *Song* and but also, by reading them together, putting them under undue stress.

98. James Longenbach details Graham's artfulness, with reference to the same poem: "Having forced herself not to indulge in fantasies of interiority or escape, Graham nonetheless reaches for those fantasies—the proof of God's existence hidden in the fold of Pascal's coat." Whatever she achieves in her writing, she remains acutely aware of such fantasies, resisting the comfort of right system. In poems that "offer sophisticated meditations on identity, language and culture" and that "are deeply moving because they turn against their own best discoveries, refusing to settle for the consolation of what is merely right" (review of *The Errancy*, 42). This is an errancy, a wandering that is necessarily also error and as futile as seeking to hold the wind within a net (as the book's epigraph from Thomas Wyatt suggests). Yet Graham's project of looking is justified in this volume (*The Errancy*). The project of a carefully fractured narrative that discloses in part by way of its failure to add up to the coherent matches the exercise enacted particularly in Act Two of this book, reading the *Song* and with reverence and care but also, by reading them together, putting them under an undue stress that could be their ruin.

99. Graham melds two days' entries. The first part (up to "But I shall study them further") is from July 11, 144–45 in Hopkins 1959, and the reference to leaving the Church is from July 17, ibid., 146.

100. See Ward, as cited above, 28.

101. Emphasis is mine.

102. In Carson, *Decreation*, 155–83.

103. Porete, as cited by Carson, 173.

104. Ibid., 176, citing Porete.

105. Ibid., 179.

106. Fragment 2, beginning, with Carson's added word, ". . . [come] here to me from Krete . . ." As Carson summarizes the sixteen lines, action is held off until the very last word, the command "Pour." Sappho has, in Carson's words, depicted the whole of creation as "waiting for an action that is already perpetually *here*. . . . Sappho renders a set of conditions that at the beginning depend on Aphrodite's absence but by the end include her presence. Sappho imitates the distance of God in a sort of suspended solution—and there we see Divine Being as a dazzling drop that suddenly, impossibly, saturates the world" (ibid., 179).

107. Ibid.

108. In *The Breaking of Style*, her lectures on Hopkins, Seamus Heaney, and Graham, Helen Vendler notes that "poets are not primarily original thinkers; they, like other intellectuals, generally think with (and against) the available intellectual categories of their epoch." While philosophers "invent the thought of their epoch," poets invent "the style of their epoch, which corresponds to, and records, the feelings felt in their epoch" (7). In this way, she catches the difficult intersection of thinking, experiencing, and writing where we find ourselves when we read the *Song* and *Holy Word*, read them together, and begin to write on that very narrow ground.

109. Ibid., 94–95.

110. When the *Song* was received into the medieval and monastic world of Bernard and his heirs, the reading of it presumed and cultivated a coherent Christian world that did not anticipate or serious alternative narratives. Unbelievers, sinners, and Jews—in scripture and outside it—are noted as representing alternative narratives, but they are reduced to types useful in furthering a spiritual Christian reading of the *Song*. In like manner, the *Holy Word* and the Srivaishnava commentarial reception and explication of it similarly adds up to an exceedingly compact and dense Hindu discourse that pays only minimal attention even to the Tamil literary models presumed by the woman's songs in *Holy Word*. By Srivaishnava tradition, the whole of the *Holy Word* is but a single love story, in which there are no subplots, entertainments, or even more abstract considerations of God, self, and love. Stories of Shiva and other deities, and of the Buddhists and other contemporary competing groups stand as anecdotes remembered in order to highlight and illumine the glories of Narayana within the tradition. The gods and heterodox teachers stand as types for paths not to be taken. On the closed worlds of spiritual, see Clooney, *Beyond Compare*, c. 2.

ACT TWO: SPIRITUAL EXERCISES IN TIMES OF ABSENCE

1. In Exum's translation of the Hebrew we have: "turn, my love, be like a gazelle or young deer upon the cleft mountains" (Exum, *Song of Songs*, 120). "Turn!" here is not merely "turn toward me," but contains something of "turn away," even "flee." Exum notes that the woman herself may be the mountain to which he is to hasten, and if so, "she is inviting him to spend the night with her" (ibid., 132). Or she might be "telling him to 'turn' in the morning," that is, to leave for a while, "after having been with her all night." Or is it rather, "to 'turn' in the evening, and stay with her all night?" (132–33). Exum prefers this latter possibility. Only when evening comes, it will be time again for him to come back to her. This is a crucial moment since "*Song* 2:8–17 ends as the *Song* ends, with the woman seemingly sending her lover away and calling him to her in the same breath." With this one word—Turn!—the woman is at once "sending the man away and calling him to her" (133). Yet this "paradoxical sending away and calling for(th) is a prelude to the lovers' union, a union that throughout the *Song* is simultaneously assured and deferred, and, on a figurative level, enjoyed . . ." (133). Exum deals with the opening scene, sleepless suffering in the night, rather briefly: "The woman speaks in the present, telling the women of Jerusalem and us, the poem's ultimate audience, about something that happened in the past. Often at night, she says, she lay in bed longing for her lover. On this particular night she decided to go out looking for him in the city streets" (133). Assis makes more of the shift in mood from 2.17 to 3.1. At the end of his analysis of the prior unit, *Song* 1.9–2.17, Assis imaginatively recasts the drama encoded in this pair of verses by suggesting that she is both the victim of their separation and the provocateur of a greater passion. Just now, he "arrives at the woman's house and wants to rendezvous with her. . . . He invites her to come outside," since He wants to hear her voice and to see her." Yet she balks, "rejects him and sends him back to where He came from." Assis speculates that this is not out of a diminishment of her love, but due rather to "external factors that may jeopardize their love and prevent it from blooming. This sabotage is possible, says the woman, because the relationship between them is still unripe." And so we are left expecting more: "She does not send him away forever, but only until the circumstances mature and enable them to meet when their love can become complete" (Assis, *Flashes of Fire*, 92–93). He leaves, yet she is expecting him to return. When he does not come back, she suffers a loneliness all the sharper because it is unexplained. Paul Griffiths puts it succinctly: "Then she urges him to 'turn back,' showing as she does that he has gone away, as he does again and again in the *Song*. Presence and intimacy are always shadowed by absence and loss, and the former almost always directly turns into the latter" (Griffiths, *Song of Songs*, 73).

2. *Revertere*; see also 6.12, at which this word occurs four times.

3. Sermon 73, Melleray, 362 (Cistercian, 75).

4. Ibid.

5. Ibid., Melleray, 365 (Cistercian, 78).

6. Sermon 74, Melleray, 377 (Cistercian, 88).

7. Ibid., Melleray, 373 (Cistercian, 85).

8. Ibid., Melleray, 374 (Cistercian, 86).

9. Ibid.

10. Ibid.

11. Ibid.

12. The truth of what God intends lies at the deeper level, yet so great a mystery is somehow disclosed, imperfectly, in frail human words. Scripture "speaks of the wisdom hidden in the mystery, but does so in our own words." (ibid., Melleray, 374 [Cistercian, 86]) Human speech serves its purpose, for this word, "even as it enlightens our human minds," also "roots our affections on God, and imparts to us the incomprehensible and invisible things of God by means of figures drawn from the likeness of things familiar to us, like precious draughts in vessels of cheap earthenware." Ibid.

13. Ibid., Melleray, 375 (Cistercian, 87).

14. Ibid., Melleray, 377 (Cistercian, 88).

15. Ibid., Melleray, 375 (Cistercian, 87).

16. Ibid., Melleray, 377–78 (Cistercian, 89). During his absence, however, what is *not* happening deserves special emphasis: "When, therefore, the Divine Bridegroom visits my interior, as He often does, He gives no sign to indicate His entrance, whether by voice, by vision, or by the sound of His footsteps. For it is not to any movements on His part, nor to any activity of my own senses that I am indebted for the knowledge that He has come into my soul. I have been made conscious of His presence from the motion of my heart" (ibid., Melleray, 380 [Cistercian, 91]).

17. Sermon 75, Melleray, 387 (Cistercian, 98–99). The timing is important: night is the time for sleep, dreaming, remembering, and intimate union, and thus for her all the more difficult: "She cannot rest even when she is asleep. The poem describes again and again her disappointment at not finding the man, and thus the feeling of the enormity of her desire is intensified." Nor is it a one time occurrence: "And yet she is not describing a thought or a passing dream, but rather a repeated experience. 'Every night' suggests she has experienced this feeling many times. This fact strengthens the argument that this does not refer to an experience that happened in reality but is rather an event within the woman's inner world" (Assis, *Flashes of Fire*, 97–98).

18. Sermon 75, Melleray, 397 (Cistercian, 105–6).

19. Sermon 1, 43.

20. Ibid., 44.

21. "Her cries, though changing so suddenly, do not break the link as long as they echo her changed affections" (ibid.).

22. Ibid., 45.

23. Ibid., 46.

24. Ibid., 44.

25. Ibid., 46.

26. Sermon 3, 65.

27. Ibid., 67–68.

28. In the cosmic geography, the lord's abiding on the Milk Ocean, intermediate between heaven and earth, signifies that he is nearby, in theory able to come to the aid of those depending on him.

29. Tirukurukai Piran Pillan (henceforth Pillan) is indeed the first commentator

whose work comes down to us. See Carman and Narayanan. The cited text is from his introduction to song 5.4.

30. Nanjiyar, 5: 149.

31. Ibid.

32. Nampillai, 5: 154.

33. Nanjiyar, 5: 152. Nampillai: "She cannot pass the time by listening to what people say . . . and there is nothing that can serve as the object of her eye, and so she cannot pass the time by looking at things" (5: 155).

34. Nampillai, 5: 155. He also cites Periyalvar, another Vaisnava poet-saint, who had evoked the *Mahabharata* battlefield scene where Krishna raised his discus to hide the sun, so that the warrior Jayadra, thinking the sun had set, would let his guard down and become vulnerable to the ensuing mortal wound: There, in front of the kings who stood in Jayadra's defense hour after hour, as hours passed, the armed warrior (5: 150), Devaki's young son, by his discus hid the sun, so that the warrior Arjuna with his weapon could roll Jayadra's head in battle—before everyone (*Periyalvar Tirumoli* 4.1.8; 346). It would be all the more poignant that even this cosmic night may be simply the work of Krishna, who is hiding the sun from her. She is also like Sita, who in her captivity was tempted to hang herself by the one resource she had left, her own hair (5: 150–51, in reference to *Ramayana*, the episode "Sundara kanda," 28.18). So too, she thinks again of her lord's promise to be a protector, and how it raises expectations about how he will, or should, protect her: "Thus seeking death in this way, she remembers how he said, 'Because we are the protector of all, we came to lie on the Milk Ocean, to protect all. We are committed to protecting you.'" That this does not happen in the expected sequence causes her confusion: "Even if he is protector of all, even if he is committed to protecting us, we are confused because it does not happen in the expected sequence. Will not protection, meant for people just like us, come to be for me too?" (Nampillai, 5: 151).

35. Nampillai, 5: 151.

36. Ibid.

37. Ibid.

38. *Vishnu Purana* 5.3.8. *Kavi* is the color of young lotus leaves, and indicative of the renunciant.

39. See 1.4, considered in this book's Act One, where she sends her heart as a messenger.

40. Here Rama is invoked as Kakuttan, "descendant of Kakutstha."

41. Or, "What is the condition?"

42. As above, Krishna might also be using it as he did in the *Mahabharata*, to hide the sun and in that way trick a warrior who had been promised that he would never be killed after sunset. Hiding the sun, Krishna tricked him into coming out of his shelter, to face death.

43. Nampillai (5: 179) refers to Sita's questions to Hanuman, regarding when Rama is to come, in the *Ramayana*, "Sundara Kanda," 39.30, and also to the well-known promise of the lord (in the *Varaha Purana*) to the Earth Goddess, that he will always come and protect those devoted to him, even if they are trapped in the netherworld.

44. That is, the wind blowing in the Tamil month of Tai, mid-January to mid-February.

45. Nampillai, 5: 189.

46. At the start of the next song, 5.5, we hear that there has been no clear resolution: "The young woman has thus been terribly depressed throughout the night. But she eases her distress a bit as dawn breaks, able to revive a little by remembering the beauty and other qualities of her master as she had experienced them in the past. But now she begins to suffer again due to the distress of not being able to see him in the present moment" (Nanjiyar, 5: 196). She argues, Nanjiyar goes on to recount, with the local women who are used to settling for less, and cannot understand why she is so upset. In response, she takes us this new song, "*Women, how can you be angry with me? After I saw our master who lives in lovely Tirukurunkuti, My heart has united with his conch, his discus, his lotus-eyes, His incomparable full red lips*" (5.5.1).

47. The words are potent, and the song is liberative even for those who simply hear it, for they are nourished by the intense devotion of the saint, the woman. Nampillai captures the power of the song: "Those who hear even one verse composed by those immersed in the topic of the lord will not fail, immediately upon their separation from material nature, to reach their destination." In desolate solitude she sings words that save those who, though not desolate, sing as she did; we cannot really imitate her, but we can receive in her words the fruit of her suffering.

48. Periyavacchan Pillai, 5: 193.

49. Exum highlights the language of immediacy that intensifies the search and yet too, in the purity of this spare, reduced language, also creates by word what is fruitlessly sought in time and space:

> The poetic preoccupation with conjuring—the drive to overcome absence with presence through language—becomes particularly intense in 3.1–4, where desire is channeled into one overriding concern, seeking and finding the loved one. This is conveyed through an ordered pattern of repetition in which a few key phrases take on particular weight with each repetition and variation. Thus, words of searching and finding appear four times in 3.2–4, as does "him whom my soul loves," and thus the word "seek" had already been used twice in verse 1, and now twice again in verse 2, a seeking that takes place in her room, and now the search in the city. Every extraneous detail is sacrificed to the intensely repetitive sequence as the narrative "strains relentlessly onward towards the resolution of the search." (Exum 134, *Song of Songs*, citing Munro, *Spikenard and Saffron*, 134)

The tense interplay between the expectation of external resolution—by way of search—and the unyielding assertion of desire as already constructive of reality—in the poetry—aptly combine to intensify the drama, as well as this book's own theopoetic and theodramatic possibilities.

50. Here too Assis (*Flashes of Fire*, 96–98) detects a deeper psychological pattern: her decision to rise and search for her beloved may be simply a moment of inner vision, akin to a dream. Exum also considers whether the passage is a dream sequence, but concludes that the question is not pertinent, since "whether something represents 'reality'

or 'fantasy' is a curious kind of distinction to press when it comes to a lyric poem whose artistic hallmark is the blurring of boundaries between wishing for, desiring, anticipating, and experiencing sexual gratification" (Exum, *Song of Songs*, 136). As internal as this may be, however, her suffering is real.

51. See Assis, *Flashes of Fire*, 98.

52. Sermon 76, Melleray, 401 (Cistercian, 110).

53. Ibid., Melleray, 402 (Cistercian, 110).

54. Ibid.

55. Ibid., Melleray, 402 (Cistercian, 111).

56. Ibid., Melleray, 402–3 (Cistercian, 111).

57. Ibid., Melleray, 403 (Cistercian, 111).

58. Ibid., Melleray, 406 (Cistercian, 114).

59. Ibid., Melleray, 407 (Cistercian, 114–15).

60. Ibid., Melleray, 407 (Cistercian, 115).

61. Ibid.

62. Bernard returns then to the issue of the watchmen as guides, closing the sermon with reflection on their responsibilities.

63. Sermon 79, Melleray, 435 (Cistercian, 137).

64. Ibid.

65. Ibid.

66. Ibid., Melleray, 436 (Cistercian, 137–38).

67. Ibid., Melleray, 436 (Cistercian, 138).

68. Ibid.

69. Ibid.

70. Sermon 79, Melleray, 436 (Cistercian, 138).

71. Assis, *Flashes of Fire*, 98–99.

72. Sermon 79, Melleray, 436 (Cistercian, 138).

73. Ibid.

74. Ibid., Melleray, 438 (Cistercian, 139).

75. Sermon 84, Melleray, 495 (Cistercian, 188).

76. Assis observes: "In verses 4 and 5 there is a resolution, for she finds him and brings her to her mother's house. Her failure had been repeated, since she failed in her bed, she failed in her search in the city, and the silence of the watchmen is a third failure." And even when she finds him, there is a note of apprehension, evident in her clinging to him: "The woman again finishes the poem with a reservation and with a feeling of trepidation that the man does not feel towards her the same type of love that she feels towards him, and again she fears that because of the intensity of her feelings she is likely to scare him away and to spoil their love. Therefore she adjures the Daughters of Jerusalem not to arouse the process of love before its time is ripe (3.5)" (Assis, *Flashes of Fire*, 100). But Assis thinks that even this is not entirely satisfying:

The poem (3.1–5) ends with a retreat, with an adjuration of the Daughters of Jerusalem not to arouse love until it is ready. What does this retreat stem from? The man's absence in this poem in comparison to the parallel poem in Unit 2 explains why the woman feels that she needs to be careful and not excite love prematurely. The great enthusiasm of the woman, in contrast to her feeling that the man is not sending her signals on the same wavelength as she is sending them to him, is also expressed in her words, "I held him . . . and would not let him go." This does not suggest intimacy; on the contrary, it suggests the woman's apprehension that the man is not as interested as she is to come to her mother's house, which reflects her feelings towards the man's attitude. Therefore it is only natural that after the woman has expressed her desire in such strong terms she feels that this desire is likely to intimidate her beloved and cause him to withdraw. (Assis, *Flashes of Fire*, 102)

Hence the need for the opening of a space between them. Her words and those secret words of the watchmen are driven by desire, by knowledge of the beloved. Such words open into the knowledge that is never finished. She knows only in part what her beloved is up to. Too little knowledge or too much would undercut the urgency of her seeking. Some weakness and some ignorance—signs of the human condition—comprise unnecessary and impossible search for God, but are also characteristic of the spiritual life. If the drama enacts a theological problem—seeking a beloved who necessarily can never be fully seen—still it yields in return a fuller, richer theology grounded in this necessary failure. Of this we shall have some inklings in Entr'acte Two.

77. Sermon 3, 65.

78. Ibid., 68. Gilbert admits that in the past he has found himself similarly "diminished by half," caught in between: "For I did not wholly depart from you. Though in yearning I am swept toward you, I am kept from your presence. Whatever solace I have in my yearning is wholly hidden and swallowed up by the ordeal of waiting. How is it all solace is not hidden as long as you hide your face from me?" (ibid., 66). Those who desire most deeply and cannot forget their beloved are those who suffer most: "From me consolation is hidden, because to me this union had been granted." Since it now has been withdrawn, "desolation presses upon me as long as I happen to be separated from you" (ibid., 67).

79. Ibid., 65.

80. Ibid., 68–69.

81. Ibid., 69.

82. Ibid.

83. Gilbert does not appeal to the narrative of the Ascension as does Bernard, nor does he characterize the city as a dangerous place where God is not.

84. Sermon 3, 71.

85. Sermon 4, 74.

86. Ibid.

87. Ibid., 76.

88. Ibid., 81–82.

89. Ibid., 82.

90. Ibid.

91. Ibid., 83. In Sermon 5, after a sharp critique of false and dishonest searches—charged to Jews, to pagans—Gilbert ponders how she searches in both streets and

squares, the broad way and the narrow, and the ways of "strictness" and of "dispensation." The application to the monks' lives and interior journeys is direct. Like Bernard, Gilbert adds some comments on his own experience, times when he finds himself suddenly shifted from the broad squares back to the narrow streets (91–92). But in the end, all searches are in vain if the name of Christ is not the center, the object of the search (94–95).

92. Like Bernard, Gilbert too (in Sermon 6) judges the watchmen to be graced with the vision she is seeking, and she rightly trusts their experience. Yet they respond in a secret language, and what transpires remains concealed: "Soft, I think, are the whispers exchanged between the bride and the watchmen and pleasant their conference, if it can be called a conference, for no answer on their part is mentioned here. If any there be, it is very secret, a secret which she judges must be wrapped in deep silence" (Sermon 6, 104). Their words propel her toward the goal, and yet she must pass them if she is to find her beloved: "She was swept on by the impulse of fervent love and therefore admits that she passed on, as if surpassing in avidity and desire anything that words could convey" (Sermon 7, 109). Between human longing and the discovery of the beloved, there is a wide gap, since "between the image and the reality can be found nothing intermediate, which would be superior to the one and inferior to other" (Sermon 8, 123).

93. In the previous song, 5.8.

94. Nanjiyar, 5: 371.

95. Nampillai points to the mythic story of three men, named One, Two and Three, who are near to the most desirable "White Island" (*Svetadvipa*), but unable to reach it, even when they hear the bustle of activities on the island. See Clooney, "Nammalvar's Glorious Tiruvallaval," 264.

96. Nanjiyar, 5: 371.

97. Nampillai (5: 374) adds a reminiscence of his teacher Nanjiyar, who once was trapped across a river from a festival he could not reach because the river was in flood. Yet he could hear and smell and even see the festival, and his desire grew all the greater. So too, she is very near to what she desires—and cannot reach it.

98. Periyavacchan Pillai, 5: 372.

99. See Nanjiyar, 5: 371.

100. The serpent, the lord's gentle abode, is fierce against his enemies.

101. Periyavacchan Pillai, 5: 393; Nampillai (5: 396) sees this material flourishing as a sign of spiritual benefits.

102. Nampillai, 5: 396.

103. Ibid., 399.

104. Nanjiyar (ibid., 400) and the later commentators detect in this reference to their fine mouths her hope to put their quarrel and her languor behind them, restoring their old, good relationship.

105. I have repeated in the last line the question appearing only in the first line.

106. Periyavacchan Pillai notes several interpretations of this line: she worships by placing flowers there; she worships the feet only as covered by flowers; the feet that are worshipped are all the more beautiful because of the flowers upon them (5: 404).

107. I have added "the flowers at his feet" from the first line.

108. As Nampillai notes (5: 406), worship "without end" normally proceeds by rites practiced in accord with a teacher's instruction; by contrast, her unending offering is fueled by nothing but her desire.

109. The commentators observe that their brows are fair because they are accustomed to touching the dust in offering obeisance at his feet.

110. I have repeated the question from the first line.

111. I have repeated "join our hands in worship" from the second line.

112. Nanjiyar (5: 408) and also the later commentators.

113. "Names" appears only in the fourth line.

114. That is, the deeds are due to the grace, not the reverse (Periyavacchan Pillai, 5: 411).

115. In the eleventh verse, Shatakopan seems to disappear inside her, for now he too sings only the thousand names:

"At the feet of our lord who has a thousand names, in safe southern Kurukur,
Shatakopan with clarity has composed a thousand names,
And of them these ten are about Tiruvallaval, the southern, protected city."

Such words—hers, his—are for listeners who themselves come to praise the beloved by her words, uttered when lovers are apart. She does not reach him here, but those words save the world:

"Whoever recites them will prosper even in this birth" (5.9.11).

The word is what matters; it is this word of the *Holy Word*, inclusive of the woman and her beloved, the other women and his temple, that readers receive down the generations. Like the divine descents (*avatara*) of old, these words save people even in the midst of a troubled world in which the beloved is always just beyond reach (Periyavacchan Pillai, 5: 414). But even such words come to fail, as we shall see, until the only solution left lies within.

116. On 7.1, see Clooney, "Divine Absence," 227–55; and Clooney, "For Your Own Good," 169–85.

117. The commentators, uncomfortable with the idea that the saint has already reached the lord at this point in the *Holy Word*, read this line as a promise of future union.

118. Nanjiyar, 7: 94.

119. Nampillai, 7: 97.

120. Periyavacchan Pillai notes how at the end of 7.2, this woman was temporarily consoled by hearing of the divine beauty, energized in her longing to see him and in uttering the divine name, Narayana. But as 7.3 begins, he notes, she has been dragged down again by her failure to reach him, and so decides to seek him at another nearby temple (Periyavacchan Pillai, 7: 102). The song unfolds as her argument with the women, who seem reluctant to let her go, much less go with her: such behavior is not proper for a woman such as her. Periyavacchan Pillai adds another reason: his absence is for her well-being, lest she be destroyed by too overwhelming a divine presence (K 7, 102–3). But the divine scheme fails, and she is worse off than before; all she can understand is

that he is gone. Ordinary wisdom, divine or human, cannot save the infatuated person, even when the subject is God. Both sin and love are dangerous: "Just as one is not able to save by scriptural instruction those who are immersed in things, even by teachers (that is, by the women) one is not able to save those immersed in the lord. Here the alvar thus manifests her extreme inclination [toward the lord]" (7: 103).

121. Nanjiyar, 7: 101.

122. Periyavacchan Pillai, 7: 102.

123. Nanjiyar dramatizes the scene: Her mother and friend and other relations ask her, "What's wrong with you?" She answers, "My mind is captivated by him in whose ears are slender crocodile jewels, and I cannot endure except by going to Tirupereyil where he dwells. Go there with me." They stop her, saying, "This does not fit with our women's nature and related considerations." Shattered, she replies, "Even if you do not grant this, I will not give up the idea of going there." Nanjiyar goes on to compare the moment to a king's decision to leave his wife for a time, under the pretext of going hunting, to intensify in her the experience of separation—and therefore the desire for union (7: 101).

124. Nampillai notes (7: 112) a parallel here: he rules and reigns in Tiruppereyil, just as he has conquered and rules her. One might add, though, that he rules her without dwelling with in her. Such is the difference, and such is her anguish.

125. Nampillai (7: 104) explains more philosophically, perhaps scientifically, the suffering she and her beloved suffer when their intimacy is interrupted and their very existence threatened: "When there is separation after a time of intimate union, both suffer destruction. It is like when two elements mix entirely together and blend into a single liquid, and the two entities become one. Were there separation after that, it ends in destroying both. In this instance, it had looked as if the lord would have them live as one, but suddenly they were separated again. She sinks into separation, utterly alone, without even a trace left of their union." Nampillai also develops an analogy between this woman and Sita, who had suffered separation from Rama after times of intimate and prolonged union. For both of them, each moment of intimacy prompts greater desire, which in turn causes great anguish, until even momentary separation is ended and desire satisfied by more intimate union (7: 104). But unlike Sita, this woman seems to have fewer moments of intimacy on which to draw.

126. Guessing what her heart sees but she cannot, she cherishes images of her beloved:

> My heart is captive to His berry red lips.
> Bending low before His ravishing long hair,
> Seeing His conch and discus and rejoicing,
> Now it's done with everything but His lotus eyes:
> Festivals never cease, month and day, in southern Tiruppereyil where resides our
>   Lord.
> Before Him, friend, my heart has lost both reserve and modesty. (7.3.3)

Nampillai catches nicely the drastic nature of the moment in which she glimpses her beloved: "I have lost my self; my mother and my friend have lost me; my heart has lost its reserve and modesty" Nampillai, (7: 123). The song continues: "My dear heart has gone off after my lost good color, and ended up staying there. So now when I grieve, in whom can I confide?" Her self-defense is simply that she is irretrievably lost in her beloved—so why add to the temple din by scolding words? The verse concludes:

> Roaring like the thundering ocean
> The Vedas resound throughout southern Tiruppereyil where He lives,
> Resounding conch in His hand.
> In that marvelous one I am immersed.
> So women, what's the use of getting angry at me? (7.3.4)

127. On these standard myths about the young Krishna in battle with demons, see Narayanan, *The Way and the Goal.*

128. Periyavacchan Pillai sees this as a case of *uruvelippatu*, the meditative construction of a nearly visible and palpable object of prolonged meditation (7: 133). See also Clooney, "*Uruvelippatu.*"

129. I have repeated the question from the first line here.

130. In the next verse, exultant, she suddenly boasts and asks her friend to confront those ever-skeptical women, for now her love has grown larger than everything else:

> All of them saw how it was between me and the Lord dark like the sea,
> And together they spread gossip.
> If you will speak of my love, friend,
> Just say how it has become greater than the solid earth and seven seas, the lofty sky.
> He resides there in Tiruppereyil surrounded by clear streams.
> Just say that I'm going there, there I will reach. (7.3.8)

Even if her desire to go to the temple remains strong, in this instance intention approximates reaching the goal.

131. As we saw in the previous note, verse 8 similarly expresses her determination.

132. What is the benefit of this powerful yet ambivalent song so focused on her searching, while yet showing it to be superfluous? Once again, the eleventh verse is a step distant from the drama:

> Age after age, in various forms and names and deeds, He protects the earth.
> He is in color like the deep sea, this unfailing one, and of Him
> Shatakopan of lovely Kurukur has sung a thousand incomparable linked verses.
> Those who praise Him by this ten about Tiruppereyil—
> The lord whose lovely hand holds the discus—
> Plunge deep into his service. (7.3.11)

The song's drama seems to have evaporated, and it is merely "about Tiruppereyil," and her plight is not mentioned. It is not that he has failed to come; he has ever come in many forms and by many names, and of him, in her voice, Shatakopan sings, catching at once the manifold and the absence. Now it is the song that matters, her word sustenance for those who make it their own; in singing it they draw near to the beloved and serve him. Though not directly sharing her experience, listeners are drawn into her world. At the start of the next song (7.4), Nanjiyar suggests that her failure to reach her beloved's dwelling places opens the way to his showing her more of himself, in that way alleviating her suffering. And so now the poet-saint himself is in a new situation: "Even amidst waves of depression that are impossible to stop, the saint abandons everything outside himself but not himself. Yet because he is unable to see him, he is exceedingly depressed." To assuage the grief that arises when he cannot see his beloved, the lord shows him the array of divine deeds, and in this way the saint is consoled (Periyavacchan Pillai, 7: 152).

133. Exum highlights the striking reversal of the happy scene in *Song* 3: "In each of the woman's narratives, her report of her lover's speech is followed by an account of seeking and finding. She seeks him in the city streets, and in both accounts she reports, 'I sought him but did not find him'" (Exum, *Song of Songs*, 188). This second time, too, the woman appeals to the watchmen, though with a different outcome. Exum adds that a refrain, "'I am my lover's and my lover is mine, the one grazing among the lilies,' appears before the search in 2.8–3.5, where it provides a note of assurance at the conclusion of the first of the two episodes the woman narrates. In 5.2–6.3 it comes at the end of the search, bring the entire unit to closure now that the lovers are reunited" (188). The reunion will be different this time; for in 6.3, it is by the power of speech that he is made present, not by any sudden arrival on his part. Assis too highlights her lack of action this time: here "the woman does not initiate anything, she dreams rather that it is her beloved who comes to look for her, and even when He calls her by highly affectionate names, she does not respond to his entreaties to come out to him" (*Flashes of Fire*, 161). Worn down, she turns within, for despite her exhaustion, her love still burns: "Her desire has been fulfilled and now she is tired and does not feel her old, insuppressible craving. Her love is internal; she is quiet and introverted and she feels neither desire nor physical attraction toward her beloved." This second time around, his sudden presence contrasts with her lethargy: "The expression of her desire is the result of the words and actions of her beloved, which arouse her, but she is not internally driven. The woman's lack of passion is also expressed in her dream in the fact that, in the end, she does not find her beloved" (162). Accordingly, a new encounter will not happen, for it seems that "she has no desire for another meeting with her beloved" (161–62). He also notes: "In this poem in which the man had wanted to meet the woman, and his wish has not been fulfilled, and the woman sought the man, but did not find him, in this poem of missed opportunities, it is appropriate to end with the woman's love for the man even though she did not find him" (156–57). But we might see it the other way around: this game of presence and absence, eagerness and delay, is a way of catching hold of their vital, unpredictable love.

134. Sermon 42, 504.

135. Ibid.

136. Ibid.

137. Gilbert also interprets her sleep as utter simplicity of focus: "The task then is to be asleep to all else, but awake to this particular voice; it is only at his invitation that she can arise, to open to him. . . . Let it be futile, nay frightening, for you to arise uninvited, when you are sleeping a sweet sleep until the Beloved says to you, 'Open to me.' . . . Arise

only at the voice of your Beloved" (ibid., 512). And so, awake in love, she sleeps to all but the beloved.

138. That she cannot find him does not surprise Gilbert, to whom Gospel precedents are well known. Yet he does not hesitate to ask Jesus why he so quickly departs: "Perhaps, in this way, do you draw out her yearnings to greater keenness and warmer desire by withdrawing your presence? Obviously it is so. All the disappointments of love add more fuel to love itself, and as they deceive her they raise love to its peak" (Sermon 44, 530).

139. Sermon 43, 516.

140. Ibid., 517.

141. Ibid., 518. When she finally acts, it is still only in response to his initiative: "The bride's heart would not be thrilled, she would not rise, would not open to her Beloved, unless previously he had thrust in the hidden hand of his inspiration. Hidden is the cause of the first call, concealed its reason and not yet wide open is the entrance. But the entrance is widened when the soul cooperates with the bridegroom who predisposes, and so makes an effort, arises and opens" (ibid., 521).

142. Ibid., 523.

143. Sermon 44, 530; the imbedded quotation is Ecclesiastes 7.24–25.

144. Since she cannot make him stay, her condition worsens in a dire manner: "He had gone beyond me, gone beyond my powers, gone through me. So he went through her, as one without strength to contain him and stand fast. A sword is the word of God; a sword is Jesus; he passes through the soul without delay or difficulty. The soul faints, when the mind dissolving cannot sustain his passion. Fiery is this sword. Hence, 'as wax melts before the face of fire,' so the soul enkindled melts before his face" (Sermon 44, 530).

145. Sermon 45, 539–40.

146. John of Ford takes up *Song* 6.4 (otherwise not treated in this book) in his Sermon 48, where he offers a series of interpretations: she should cast down her eyes, in order to learn to see the spiritual and no longer material Christ (19); by this discipline, she is purified in heart, made ready to see him "here and now" (25); she is being tested, since her beloved hopes that she will demur, continuing to gaze upon him (27).

147. Sermon 45, 540.

148. Ibid.

149. Ibid., 541.

150. Gilbert offers this summation: "Observe four points here, either in her or about her: searching and longing, precepts and prayers: the searches of meditation, the longings of desire, the precepts of teachers, and the prayers of the faithful" (Sermon 45, 543). These elements—searching, longing, precept, and prayer—add up to the wholeness of her search, whether it succeeds or fails.

151. Study 2.3. An earlier version of this analysis appears in Clooney, in "By the Power of Her Word."

152. For the second question, see below.

153. Exum highlights the woman's new strategy. Here, in 5.8–6.3, she uses both gaze and words effectively, combining "narration (storytelling), the report of sequenced actions, which distinguished the woman's earlier speech in 2.8–3.5, and figuration, static

description of the loved one cast in densely metaphoric language, which dominated the man's speech in 4.1–5.1." Search itself turns out to be superfluous, as she finds him not in the streets, but "through describing him, conjuring him up by depicting him from head to foot in simile and metaphor, as He had conjured her up in his speech (cf. esp. 4.1–5)." By her words, he appears, there "in his garden, with her, in an image of sexual intimacy" (187). The interplay of questions and descriptions is vivid and dramatic: "This dialogue between the woman and the women of Jerusalem seems to take place in the present, creating the impression that we are overhearing it." Exum finds their exchange somewhat casual: "First they ask her what is so special about her lover, and she responds with a metaphoric description of him hardly helpful to anyone trying to pick him out in a crowd" (*Song of Songs*, 201–2). Even the repetition of each question by the women serves a purpose: "Repetition lends the women's questions a kind of singsong quality. Each time they ask their question, they address the woman as 'most beautiful of women,' and then repeat the question with a kind of explanatory embellishment that hearkens back to her 'story' and specifically to her adjuration in v. 8" (202). Assis detects a darker mood. The women are not merely seeking information regarding the beloved's appearance. Somewhat aggressively, they are asking what, if anything, "makes her beloved more special than other men. There might even be a derisive undertone to this question posed by the Daughters of Jerusalem. The woman is asked to explain her personal preference in choosing him over any other" (166). He adds: "The question posed by the Daughters has a sarcastic edge and is meant to tease the woman," and "the woman's answer is not straight but evasive. . . . The Daughters ask the woman in a mildly mocking tone what is so special about her beloved that she has adjured them thus. The woman answers by giving them a description of the special appearance of her beloved" (178–79). She "answers this convincingly in her metaphorical descriptions of her beloved" (ibid.), but the real point has to do with the source of her description: "This descriptive poem does not concern what the woman sees, but rather what she remembers" (178).

154. For the description, see the meditation at the beginning of this section. Regarding it, Exum notes that "what she singles out as setting him apart from other men is his body, every bit of which is desirable. This is the answer of a lover fascinated by her partner's physical attributes, which she describes metaphorically not so much in terms of things he resembles but rather in terms of what he means to her" (202). And yet there is a certain distance evident in her words. She describes him now, not because she sees him anew, but because, prompted by their questions, she remembers him anew. She constructs and describes him "part by part, to conjure him up through the evocative power of language." Indeed, "all the bodily descriptions in the *Song* are poetic acts of conjuring that bring the lovers' bodies into view, for their mutual pleasure within the world of the poem"—and also for "the pleasure of the poem's audience, our pleasure in the text and in the poetic representation of the body" (203). And so the women help her "by asking a question that prompts her to invoke his presence through praising his physical charms (5.9–16). Having conjured him up, she needs no further help in order to find him" (202). In fact, they will soon—in *Song* 6—be together again, though the cir-

cumstances leading up to their reunion do not figure precisely in the poetry. Here too, Assis reads the situation less optimistically: "In her distress, when she cannot explain the man's absence, she insists on saying that although the beloved is absent, the relationship between them is still strong, and in order to prove it, she has no choice but to refer to their past relations" (180). Confused by how the women are questioning his absence, all she can do is "recall the act of love from the past, and her inner certainty about the mutual love between them" (181), and so she discovers him in her remembrance of past encounters.

155. Sermon 46, 552–53.

156. Ibid., 554.

157. See *Song* 8.6.

158. Sermon 46, 554.

159. Ibid.

160. See Exum and Assis on this point, in note 153.

161. Sermon 47, 561.

162. Ibid., 561–62.

163. See, for example, 1.12–2.7.

164. Sermon 47, 565–66.

165. Ibid., 554. This of course is the point of messenger songs in the *Holy Word*, beginning with 1.4.

166. Sermon 46, 555.

167. Exum: "Next they ask her where he is, which suggests that they know that she knows, and her answer reveals that she does indeed know: he has gone down to his garden, where spices abound, to graze and pluck lilies" (201–2).

168. As Exum suggests: "It sounds as if they are volunteering to help her search for him . . . by offering to seek him with her. But like their question in 5.9, the question here is rhetorical. They have, in fact, helped her to seek her love, first by asking a question (5.9) that gave her opportunity to find him by praise, and now by asking a question that gives her the opportunity to reveal her success" (209–10). The implication is that the woman seems to have found her beloved, or at least knows where he is: "My delightful man has gone down into his garden to a seedbed of spices to graze in the gardens to gather lilies" (*Song* 6.2). Exum notes the inconsistency of asking for their help in finding him, while yet seeming to know where he is.

169. In his first sermon, John recaps the dynamics of the beloved's absence, the tension between what she has found and what still lies beyond her grasp. She had been in close embrace with her beloved (e.g., at *Song* 2.6), in "the full realization of her desires" (Sermon 1, 78). But so intense a union must be momentary, since "spiritual delights, once tasted cause unease, and though they satisfy at the time, in the long run they afflict. Kisses once enjoyed are anxiously sought again, and the more richly the abundance of her spouse satisfied the bride's desires in the past, the more bitterly are those favors mourned when they are over. The beloved is sought and not found; He is called and does not answer" (ibid.). This drama is inevitable, and the woman "consoles herself as best she can with the bare memory of her beloved" (ibid.). He deliberately delays his return,

testing her for the sake of her greater love, for "what graver trial" can be there "for a soul seeking God, than to be held back from finding Him? As there is no joy like the joy He gives, so, if it may be said, is there no sorrow like the sorrow He gives" (Sermon 1, 79).

170. In his second sermon, John addresses the women's first pair of questions, on the beloved's appearance: "What manner of one is thy beloved of the beloved, O thou most beautiful among women? What manner of one is thy beloved of the beloved that thou hast so adjured us?" (*Song* 5.9). He interprets them as did Gilbert. Enthused by her languor, the women are eager to know more. They realize that she is sending them to meet the lord, even to see his glory (Sermon 2, 91–92). In turn, their eagerness prompts her to make him still more vividly present: "They bring Him sweetly to mind, and by bringing Him sweetly to mind they subtly make the bride conscious of his presence. They were sent to seek and yet, in asking the bride about his appearance, they have already begun to seek Him" (Sermon 2, 92). Her eloquence is born from her troubles, not despite them. She speaks from a turbulent interplay of presence, absence, and memory, as John notes in highlighting the importance of "lovely": "Now the sweetness of his presence and in the pain of his absence make Him lovely to his bride. Especially when He is absent, she longs for Him to be present and never stops turning over in her mind how sweet is his lovely presence and what it has meant to her." Conversely, "the more painful his absence, the more desirable his presence; the more lasting his memory, the more self-abasing the recollection of it, the more passionate the expectation of his coming" (Sermon 38, 110). Intensely recollecting past moments of union, she speaks so intimately that her mood infuses the women too, who become drunk on her word: "He has led me into his wine cellar, and there I have drunk as much as sates my thirst. I have come out from it, and as yet that is a place where I cannot bring you. What I can do, is let you feel the wine upon my breath, making you aware, by its scent, of the sweetness I have swallowed" (ibid.). At this point, they too are captivated by the same tastes: "The sweetness you then taste will draw you too to a fuller and more ardent longing for that sweetness in its fullness" (Sermon 42, 152). In return, the women decipher her experience, since "from their long companionship with the bride" they understand "the 'turnings aside' and 'journeys' that the spouse makes," and in the end are entirely taken up with her words.

171. Sermon 40, 124.

172. Ibid., 129.

173. "When you speak to us of your beloved, we can understand in the language of angels" (ibid., 130).

174. Ibid., 131.

175. Galatians 4.19.

176. Sermon 40, 132.

177. Sermon 43, 158; the quote is from Psalm 18.11, with my emphasis.

178. Ibid., 158.

179. Ibid., 159–60.

180. Ibid., 160. For John, the upheaval is painful, but also a mark of tenderness: "I feel the state of sweetness disappearing after a little while; for he can stay with me no

longer, because I am flesh; at these times, I reflect that Jesus has bidden me farewell, because seeking him and desiring to cleave to him, I faint away, I tire and my strength melts" (ibid., 160). The beloved is near, but whenever human strength—love taxing the limits of the flesh—wanes, he returns "to somewhere that he knows" (ibid., 162). Accordingly, while experiencing real absence and presence, John says that he can understand the patterns of those arrivals and departures, what are theologically his ascent and the return in the Spirit.

181. Sermon 46, 200. By John's reading, there is a gap between her closing words in *Song* 6.2, "I to my beloved, and my beloved to me who feedeth among the lilies," and his sudden, unanticipated words in *Song* 6.3–4, "Thou art beautiful, O my love, sweet and comely as Jerusalem, terrible as an army set in array. Turn away thy eyes from me, for they have made me flee away." She has run out of words, the women have no more to say, and suddenly he is there, speaking of her terrible beauty. John struggles to make sense of this command—that she not look at him—in Sermon 48, where he reads it to mean that she is to look more closely and deeply, without clinging to what she first sees.

182. Ibid.

183. 9.4, the prior song, in the poet's own voice and not that of the woman, seems far more hopeful about the possibility of union:

My eyes have seen, they are full with exhilaration,

My old deeds and their attachments destroyed:

That his servants might enjoy ambrosia

I have uttered this garland of words,

I am the servant of the lord of the world's immortals. (9.4.9)

But here too, the commentators do not take this seeing to be the direct vision the saint yearns for, after which there could be no further lament. The series of anguished songs that follow make it necessary to read such verses more soberly, in their view.

184. Nanjiyar, 9: 132.

185. Ibid.

186. Ibid.

187. Ibid.

188. Ibid.

189. Ibid.

190. Nampillai, 9: 134.

191. That is, we are already as if dead—so why torture us with your happy songs?

192. Nanjiyar, 9: 161.

193. But I will use "she" throughout, even if "she" is the "he" of the poet's own voice erupting between the songs in the voice of the woman.

194. Nanjiyar, 9: 167. He refers specifically to 8.7.1:

I begged unceasingly for many days,

"Amaze me, put me beneath your radiant feet."

And then that dwarf favored me and He himself entered me,

And now He rules over my mind as his own,

Gazing at me.

195. Nanjiyar, 9: 167.

196. 9.5.10.

197. Nampillai, 9: 168.

198. Ibid., 168–69. As elsewhere, "melting away" can be from sorrow or, as here, from intense joy.

199. Ibid., 177.

200. Ibid.

201. "In the proper way": the commentators say that he properly maintains the necessary order of things, the world's dependence on him, in harmony with other such divine acts.

202. Nampillai, 9: 182. More literally, "not simply in accord with prior knowledge of my proper form; if what were desired were in accord with knowledge of that proper form, then it would go only so far as that proper form. By contrast, this infatuation is beyond all bounds."

203. See Nampillai, 9: 185.

204. Nampillai discusses at some length whether this situation is anguished or joyful, and prefers the latter option (9: 187–88).

205. Nampillai cites the *Ramayana*, "Sundara kanda," 33.17, as another case in which a town, Ayodhya, is praised due to its association with the divine person (9: 188).

206. Ibid.

207. Periyavacchan Pillai, 9: 191.

208. Literally, "like ripe fruit."

209. Nanjiyar, 9: 193.

210. Nanjiyar points out that now he drinks rather than eats her; for by showing her his beauty, he has melted her (9: 195).

211. Nampillai detects an echo of an earlier verse expressive of her absolute dependence on the lord alone:

"My rice for eating, my water for drinking, my betel for chewing—
Kannan, my lord!"
Her eyes flowing tears, she keeps crying,
When she searches for His city,
Abundant in His excellence in all the earth,
Tiru Kolur is surely the city my young doe will enter. (*Holy Word* 6.7.1)

Now, though, everything is reversed. Those words might as well be his, for he can survive only if he consumes her, eating her and drinking her entirely (Nampillai, 9: 197). As always, the eleventh verse speaks to the purpose and power of the first ten. The violence of Krishna in killing the evil king Kamsa parallels these mighty verses that wipe away the confusions of rebirth:

The lord killed cruel Kamsa, and about Him
Shatakopan of southern Kurukur with its firm walls
Sang these ten verses from his thousand so lovely in form.
By them birth ends, the mirage vanishes: take note. (9.6.11)

She cannot by herself find and hold her beloved in any permanent way, but her words allow listeners to banish life's ambiguities, right now.

212. Yet the tradition does recognize the importance of 9.6. In commenting later on 10.7, and beginning to summarize the whole of the *Holy Word*, Nampillai quotes 9.6 six times, far more than any other song.

213. Nanjiyar, 9: 200.

214. The modern commentator Annangarachariar finds here a hint of a deeper meaning to her words: the cranes are in fact the great teachers of the tradition, discriminating in their hunting, able to find the subtle details. To be at their feet, those feet on her head, is her way of venerating their role in her journey to the lord (Annangarachariar, 9: 82).

ENTR'ACTE TWO: WRITING THEOLOGY AFTER THE HIDING OF THE BELOVED

1. Chiasson, "Actual Hawk, the Real Tree," 64.

2. Ramke, "Celebrating a World in Danger."

3. Patrick Byrne ("Jorie Graham") notes the volume's "new ways of viewing and understanding today's natural world," observing how "Graham perceives the landscape with a sense of immediacy and urgency," and how as a writer "she promotes an interactive involvement with the environment through encounters in which the poet's structural technique and sensuous language reveal an individual in the act of contemplating the beauty or the disfigurement of the world she discovers around her." In her "ongoing commentary" Graham describes her emotional reactions even while crafting an response to those reactions that moves beyond them without betraying them. The poems are "deliberately detailed, though sometimes difficult, meditations" that speak to nature's power and its contemporary endangerment. Her "magnificent images . . . often seek to unite the earth and sky, to merge elements with one another, or blur the distinctions separating the physical from the abstract." In *Never*—Byrne uses the poem entitled "Afterwards" as his example—Graham "displays a desire to combine the visual and the lyrical," a seamless lyrical surface that continually blends the senses—sight, sound, smell, touch, and taste." This surface becomes firm and complex enough that readers can pierce it and "reflect and contemplate upon what they observe in order to recognize the depths that lie beneath the surface." Byrne also quotes Helen Vender, *Music of What Happens*: "Graham's subject is the depth to which the human gaze can penetrate, the opening in reality into which the poet can enter. Under the clothed, she seeks out the naked; over the soil, the air; inside the integument, a kernel; through the cover of the grass, the snake; from the bowels of the earth, the interred saint" (455). Vendler finds in Graham a spirit that *His Hiding Place Is Darkness* also intends: "Against writers who press against the opacity and resistance of the material world, she suggests its profundity and penetrability—though there seems to be no stopping place for that penetration" (ibid.).

4. Gardner, "Jorie Graham."

5. See the discussion on this in Entr'acte One.

6. Ramke, "Celebrating a World in Danger."

7. Graham's intense focus on the "now" follows upon a similar dwelling "here," a few lines earlier:

> Weren't we here? Wasn't I
> *in* here? And you here too? We have "written"—can't you feel it
> in your hands [this pen for instance, this scratchy weightlessness] or in your
> eyes [the incense filling up this church] or mind ["at the summit of the tiny
> hilltop town"]—haven't our eyes the empty cross before them now: here:

We are reminded also of the vividly remembered "here" and "now" of *Holy Word* 9.6, God entirely *present*.

8. I have italicized the word "now" in these lines.

9. Gardner, "Jorie Graham," 53.

10. Ibid.

11. Recall that volume 1 of *Theo-Logic* was written before the twelve volumes of the poetics and dramatics.

12. *Theo-Logic*, 3: 297.

13. Ibid., 298–99.

14. Ibid., 299.

15. Carson, *Decreation*, 177.

16. *Theo-Logic*, 3: 321.

17. Ibid. Carson (as already cited in Entr'acte One) observed, "God's absence is something tricky, perhaps impossible, to tell. This writer will have to invoke a God who arrives bringing her own absence with her—a God whose Farness is the more Near. It is an impossible motion possible only in writing" (*Decreation*, 179).

18. *Theo-Logic*, 3: 322.

19. Ibid.

20. Ibid., 325–26.

21. As they surely are, since no one has ever before read these songs and sermons and commentaries together.

22. *Theo-Logic*, 3: 328. *Magisterium internum, magisterium externum*, and *magister interior*: the internal teaching authority, the external teaching authority, and the interior teacher.

23. *Theo-Drama*, 5: 394–95.

24. *Theo-Logic*, 2: 97.

25. Ibid., 95.

26. Ibid., 103.

27. Ibid., 104.

28. Ibid., 107.

29. *Theo-Drama*, 5: 395: "Lord, if you are not here, where can I seek you, absent? But if you are everywhere, why do I not see you present?" (my translation of the Latin).

30. Ibid., 395.

31. Ibid., 396.

32. But this interplay of repose and getting lost tells us something about God, too.

The divine Persons (and here Balthasar alludes to Ruysbroeck) are in eternal embrace but without ever losing their mutual otherness (ibid., 399), as if, we might say, they are always seeking and always finding one another, searching and finding the search to be unnecessary. For the sake of this sacred instability, they must also be imagined as somehow stepping apart from one another even if only to return.

33. Ibid., 400. Balthasar also quotes, on page 401, Adrienne von Speyr, "Our discoveries will take us from one degree of astonishment to another. . . . There is adoration, the soul's complete openness before God, and in love we allow God to fill and fulfill us" (ibid.; the von Speyr quote, writes Balthasar, is from her *Objecktive Mystik*, 75–77).

34. Ruysbroeck, as quoted by Balthasar (*Theo-Drama*, 5: 400).

35. Ibid., likewise quoting Ruysbroeck.

36. See Nichols, *Say It Is Pentecost*, 77–80.

37. I cannot avoid disagreeing with Balthasar in this matter, over what to me seems a lack of imagination when it is most needed. His judgment on other religions is swift, without hesitation, as if knowing more about them, even modestly commensurate with his vast knowledge of Christian tradition, could make no difference regarding the outcome. With unseemly haste he distances Christian negative theology from other traditions of faltering word and growing silence. Their negative theologies are merely a failure really to find God in the world. Whatever of substance happens in the religions, even today it seems, is no more than what happened in Neoplatonism, where "total conceptual ungraspability unites with unrelinquishable, ever-circling seeking, which can occasionally arrive at a momentary 'contact' and 'finding'" (*Theo-Logic*, 2: 91). In Mahayana Buddhism, Balthasar goes on to say, there is the further extreme of Nirvana, "beyond every finite, conceptually graspable existent" (ibid.), a Nothing that shows all else to be unreal. The resultant nothing (*sunyata*) "is profound enough to encompass even God, the 'object' of mystical union and the object of faith." Indeed, this is the emptiness out of which even God arises (ibid., 93). Zen Buddhism's search for the unknowable ground becomes a recognition that the present moment is the truth and the end of all searching (ibid., 93–94). But all this is merely the negation into which nonbiblical thought falls, and indeed the "primary negative theology [that is] the strongest bastion against Christianity" (ibid., 95). In another sweeping generalization alien to texts such as the *Holy Word*, Balthasar concludes that in the East "the search for the living God becomes a *technique* for finding something that is beyond all searching" (ibid., 94; my emphasis), man's extrabiblical search for God, the search of man who, weary of a seeking that never arrives at its goal, takes refuge either in a system (even Zen is such) or in a resigned agnosticism, which goes on negating even after it has already given up the quest. Christianity instead assumes "both the original affirmation that sustains all negation and its equally original eminence, which reaches beyond all negations" (ibid., 99). My point in these pages is that Balthasar's deep appreciation of the negative theology, silence, and the inadequacy of our words for God can also open us to these other traditions of silence, and without a positing of a *noumenon* beyond all words, and so on, that would be similarly objectionable to Srivaishnavas. There is much work to be done before judgments can be handed down.

38. *Theo-Logic*, 2: 115; Picard, 143.

39. *Theo-Logic*, 2: 116, citing Rahner, *Hörer des Wortes*, 115.

40. *Theo-Logic*, 2: 116; Rahner, 117.

41. Balthasar's evocation of Rahner also mirrors Graham's insight into writing that is a silencing, as the writing she manifests in her poetic line. Graham explains: "Also, lines of breath-length, say, lines that contain up to five stresses, sometimes feel to me like measures that make that silence feel safe. A silence that will stay at bay for as long as it takes to get the thing said. Writing in lines that are longer than that, because they are really unsayable or ungraspable in one breath unit for the most part (and since our desire is to grasp them in one breath unit) causes us to read the line very quickly. And the minute you have that kind of a rush in the line (emphasized perhaps by the absence of commas and other interpretive elements) what you have is a very different relationship with silence: one that makes it aggressive—or at least oceanic—something that won't stay at bay. You have *fear* in the rush that can perhaps cause you to hear the *fearful* in what is rushed against" (1987 interview, in Gardner, *Regions of Unlikeness*, 225). Such too, I would add, is the "rush" that comes when poems such as the *Song* and the *Holy Word*, different in many ways yet strikingly similar in some, are read together in a way that shatters our stable lines and takes away our breath.

42. *Theo-Logic*, 2: 118.

43. Ibid.

44. Ignatius of Antioch, quoted in ibid.

45. See *Beyond Compare*, c. 4.

46. *Theo-Logic*, 2:, 122.

47. Ibid., 277.

48. Ibid.

49. Ibid., 280.

50. Ibid.

51. Ibid. See also *Theo-Logic*, "Withdrawal as a Precondition of the Gift of the Spirit," 3: 297–301, on the necessary gap between the earthly Jesus in his tangible form and his "pneumatic mode of being" in the coming of the Spirit: "It is only by a radical renunciation—not of a thing, but of one's own self, and in this context this means a renunciation of the possession of the tangible, visible, experiential Jesus—that we can hope to receive God's highest gift, the Holy Spirit" (299), and, "The Fathers interpret the sacramental act of death, documented in the Gospel, as an attitude that governs a person's entire Christian existence: it is a 'dying with Christ' and a hidden life with him in God (cf. Colossians 3.3)" (301).

52. Ibid., 281.

53. Ibid.

54. Whether the theologian who would engage religious diversity in a systematic theological fashion *must* be one who has engaged in the theopoetic and theodramatic, and done so also across religious borders, can remain for now an open question. On the one hand, it may be asking too much of one person in one lifetime to do all these things. On the other, the theologian who in the twenty-first century has not gone to those other

places may have nothing of import to say on what such ventures are supposed to mean. Conversely, those who have gone deeply, to excess, into the interreligious theopoetic realm may not have the erudition and precision to write up the necessary new insights into the established fields of Christology, Trinity, ecclesiology, and so on. For now, theologians may take Entr'acte Two, and indeed this entire project, as what traditional Indian scholars call a *paribhasha*, a set of rules stated at the beginning of a treatise that govern all subsequent inquiries in that treatise.

ACT THREE: IN THE END

1. Exum notes that many commentators find nothing awkward here, since the "mountains of spices" may be the woman herself. If so, she would then be entreating him to come to her. But Exum herself insists that we still are faced with "the seeking latent in finding and the finding latent in seeking, the separation prerequisite to union" (Exum, *Song of Songs*, 262–63).

2. According to Exum, this is what "the *Song* leads us to expect to happen, over and over. The effect of 8.14 is to assure us that the *Song* will never end, that the lovers will evermore be engaged in love's game of seeking and finding" (ibid., 262–63). There is no resolution; love proceeds as an ongoing story of coming and going. Or as the Blochs put it, "The *Song* thus ends with the motif of the lovers parting at dawn, as in the aubade of later traditions—an ending that looks forward in anticipation to another meeting" (Bloch and Bloch, *Song of Songs*, 221). According to Assis, "the most reasonable interpretation is that the woman indeed sends the man away" (Assis, *Flashes of Fire*, 259). It is simply another instance of the recurrent pattern: "But she is not sending him away because she does not desire him; she is only sending him away for a while, for a limited period of time. Her words indeed suggest that she regards herself as connected to him, but that she is nevertheless sending him away. She says to him, 'Flee, *my beloved*'" (ibid., 260). This uncertainty is necessary: "Ending the story with the uniting of the man and the woman would have left the reader complacent and unmoved because his expectations of a happy ending to the story would have been fulfilled." Instead, the poet seeks "to show that the story has not ended at this juncture, that the development of the love between the man and the woman has not reached its final ending" (ibid.).

3. See John of Ford, Sermon 120, 241–43.

4. Sermon 120, 240.

5. Sermon 120, 243. To make sense of the beloved's departure at the *Song*'s end, John detects a hint that she intends to follow him: "We cannot doubt that these are the words of the bride bidding farewell to her spouse, as he departs to some more hidden land and as she follows after him" (Sermon 120, 243).

6. Ibid., 243–44.

7. Ibid., 244.

8. Ibid., 245.

9. Ibid., 246.

10. Ibid.

11. Sermon 120, 247.

12. Ibid.

13. Here John takes the mountain to be the holy ones already immersed in divine love.

14. Sermon 120, 248.

15. Since only a brief concluding prayer remains after his reading of 8.14.

16. Nanjiyar, 10: 67.

17. See 6.2, where she seems to be arguing with Krishna face to face:

I am afraid before those lightning-waisted women garbed in Your grace,

Marvelous one who burnt that king's fort in Lanka,

But I know Your games:

So what have I to do with all that?

Give me back my ball and ankle bracelet and go away. (6.2.1)

18. Nanjiyar, 10: 67.

19. Literally, in this material nature (*prakrti*). It seems that in Nanjiyar's conception, the saint is thinking of his embodied self, "this material thing that I am."

20. Nanjiyar, 10: 67.

21. Her condition is not peculiarly hers, since "she is experiencing that painful love experienced by all those who love him."

22. Regarding 9.5, see Act Two.

23. Her whole being: her *prakrti*, as a flesh-and-blood being.

24. Nanjiyar, 10: 67.

25. Ibid.

26. And after the intervening songs, 9.10, 10.1, and 10.2, where the poet, in his own voice, praises the lord's presence in the Tirukannapuram, Mohur, and Anantapuram.

27. "Slender": literally, "bamboo."

28. Periyavacchan Pillai, 10: 82.

29. Periyavacchan Pillai explains this liminal state succinctly: "She keeps on existing. Because of the exceptional object of her attention, she is unable to die, yet unable to survive. She is unable to die because she loves; she cannot survive, since she cannot bear it" (10: 86).

30. Ibid.

31. Nanjiyar, 10: 89. "Slightest indication": *sambhavana*, suggestion, possibility.

32. Ibid.

33. I have carried "hands" over from the previous verse.

34. Thus echoing the old stories of demons sent to kill the young Krishna.

35. That is, to rejoice in his being with the other women, she needs to deny her own womanhood. Nampillai compares her to Surpanakha, the demoness who failed to seduce Rama in the epic, and was mutilated, her ears and nose cut off (10: 113).

36. Here too the eleventh verse is seemingly removed from the emotional tumult preceding it. The first lines recollect where this lovely deity is to be found, right here where the saint lives:

His lips are so full and red, our god of the cowherds who are at His feet

There in bright cool Kurukur, amidst conches along the Porunal river,

And there bright Shatakopan sang these thousand verses,
This garland of verses sung by women grieving at separation from Him,
Lest He go out to herd the cows.

It may be that just as the poet expresses in her voice what he cannot say directly, now she surrenders even her own voice and joins the chorus to sing with them what she cannot bear to sing alone: You are here, so stay here, with any and all of those who love you, even if I am just one of them. There is perhaps a certain irony in the seemingly flat words that close this eleventh verse:

"These verses have the same result as all the rest they sang."

Perhaps all that was said, lamented, prayed earlier in the *Holy Word* finds recapitulation in this song, in her utter self-abnegation: love me all the more, by loving them. Perhaps this song will be just as good as the earlier ones by which the cowherd women expressed their yearning for him, that is to say, ineffective: nothing will change, and he will still come and go as he pleases.

37. Nanjiyar, 10: 67–68.

38. For example,

Conqueror of the seven bulls,
Lofty radiant light reducing lovely Lanka to ashes,
Don't trust me.
Bring me to Your golden feet quickly,
And never let me go anywhere else. (2.9.10)

39. I paraphrase here Nampillai's words, 10: 69–72.

EPILOGUE: JESUS, THE BELOVED

1. Opening lines of "Kyoto" by Jorie Graham, *Never*, 62.

2. Gerard Manley Hopkins, "Wreck of the Deutschland," section 4, *Poetical Works*, 120.

BIBLIOGRAPHY

Annangarachariar, P. B. *Tiruvaymoli Dipikai.* Vols. 1–3 as one volume. Vols. 4–10. Sriran-gam: Sri Vaisnava Sri Publishing, 1951–52. Repr., Kanchipuram: Granthamala Office, 1998.

Assis, Eliyahu. *Flashes of Fire: A Literary Analysis of the Song of Songs.* New York: T&T Clark, 2009.

Baker, Timothy C. "Praying to an Absent God: The Poetic Revealings of Simone Weil." *Culture, Theory, & Critique* 47.2 (2006): 133–47.

Balthasar, Hans Urs von. *Explorations in Theology.* Vol. 1. Translated by A. V. Littledale with Alexander Dru. San Francisco: Ignatius Press, 1989.

———. *The Glory of the Lord: A Theological Aesthetics.* 7 vols. Translated by Erasmo Leiva-Merikakis. Edited by Joseph Fessio and John Riches. San Francisco: Ignatius Press, 1982–89.

———. *Theo-Drama: Theological Dramatic Theory.* 5 vols. Translated by Graham Har-rison. San Francisco: Ignatius Press, 1988–98.

———. *Theo-Logic: Theological Literary Theory.* 3 vols. Translated by Adrian J. Walker. San Francisco: Ignatius Press, 2000–2005.

Bernard of Clairvaux. *On the Song of Songs.* 4 vols. Translated by Killan Walsh. Intro-duced by M. Corneille Halflants. Kalamazoo, MI: Cistercian Publications, 1971–80.

———. *Sermones in Cantica Canticorum.* Innsbruck, Austria: Academica Wagneriana, 1888.

———. *Sermones super Cantica Canticorum.* 2 vols. Rome: Editiones Cistercienses, 1957–58.

———. *St. Bernard's Sermons on the Canticle of Canticles.* 2 vols. Translated from the original Latin by a priest of Mount Melleray. Dublin: Browne and Nolan, 1920.

———. *Sermons on the Song of Songs.* 4 vols. Translated by Killian Walsh and Irene M. Edmonds. Cistercian Fathers Series. Kalamazoo, MI: Cistercian Publications, 1971, 1976, 1979, 1980.

Bloch, Ariel, and Chana Bloch. *The Song of Songs: A New Translation with an Introduc-tion and Commentary.* New York: Random House, 1995.

Byrne, Edward. "Jorie Graham: *Never.*" Review of *Never*, by Jorie Graham. *Valparaiso Poetry Review* 5.2 (2004). Available at www.valpo.edu/vpr/coverv5n2.html (accessed May 24, 2013).

Carson, Anne. *Decreation: Opera, Essays, Poetry.* New York: Alfred A. Knopf, 2005.

Carman, John, and Vasudha Narayanan. *The Tamil Veda: Pillan's Interpretation of the Tiruvaymoli.* Chicago: University of Chicago Press, 1989.

Chiasson, Dan. "The Actual Hawk, the Real Tree." Review of *Place*, by Jorie Graham. *New York Review of Books*, September 27, 2012.

Clines, David J. A. *Interested Parties: The Ideology of Writers and Readers of the Hebrew Bible.* Sheffield, England: Sheffield Academic Press, 1995.

Clooney, Francis X. *Beyond Compare: St. Francis de Sales and Śrī Vedānta Deśika on Loving Surrender to God.* Washington, DC: Georgetown University Press, 2008.

———. "By the Power of Her Word: Absence, Memory, and Speech in the *Song of Songs* and a Hindu Mystical Text." *Exchange* 41 (2012): 213–44.

———. *Comparative Theology: Deep Learning Across Religious Borders.* Malden, MA: Wiley-Blackwell, 2010.

———. "Divine Absence and the Purification of Desire: A Hindu Saint's Experience of a God Who Keeps His Distance." In *Knowing the Unknowable: Science and Religions on God and the Universe*, edited by John Bowker, 227–55. London: I. B. Tauris, 2009.

———. *Divine Mother, Blessed Mother: Hindu Goddesses and the Virgin Mary.* New York: Oxford University Press, 2005.

———. "For Your Own Good: Suffering and Evil in God's Plan According to One Hindu Theologian." In *Deliver Us From Evil*, edited by M. David Eckel and Bradley L. Herling, 169–85. New York: Continuum Publishing, 2008.

———. "Nammalvar's Glorious Tiruvallaval: An Exploration in the Methods and Goals of Srivaisnava Commentary." *Journal of the American Oriental Society* 111.2 (1991): 260–76.

———. *Seeing Through Texts: Doing Theology Among the Śrīvaiṣṇavas of South India.* Albany: State University of New York Press, 1996.

———. "*Uruvelippatu*: A Tamil Practice of Visualization and Its Significance in Srivaisnavism." Dr. V. Raghavan birth centenary commemoration volume. *Journal of Oriental Research* (2010): 81–82, 209–24.

Costello, Hilary. *Sky-Blue Is the Sapphire Crimson the Rose: Stillpoint of Desire in John of Forde.* Cistercian Fathers Series. Kalamazoo, MI: Cistercian Publications, 2006.

Costello, Hilary, and Christopher Holdsworth, eds. *A Gathering of Friends: The Learning and Spirituality of John of Forde.* Kalamazoo, MI: Cistercian Publications, 1996.

Dutton, Marsha L. "The Learned Monk of Gilbert of Hoyland: Sweet Wisdom in the Cells of Doctrine." In *Praise No Less Than Charity: Studies in Honor of M. Chrysogonus Waddell, Monk of Gethsemani*, edited by E. Rozanne Elder, 161–74. Cistercian Studies Series 193. Kalamazoo, MI: Cistercian Publications, 2002.

Exum, J. Cheryl. *Song of Songs: A Commentary.* Louisville, KY: Westminster John Knox Press, 2005.

Gardner, Thomas. "Jorie Graham: The Art of Poetry No. 85." *Paris Review* 165 (Spring 2003): 53–97.

———. *Jorie Graham: Essays on the Poetry.* Madison: University of Wisconsin Press, 2005.

———. *Regions of Unlikeness: Explaining Contemporary Poetry.* Lincoln: University of Nebraska Press, 1999.

Gilbert of Hoyland. *Sermones in Canticum Salomonis.* In Patrologia Latina, edited by J.-P. Migne, 184: 11–298. Paris, 1854.

———. *Sermons on the Song of Songs.* Vols. 1–3. Translated and introduced by Lawrence C. Braceland. Cistercian Fathers Series. Kalamazoo, MI: Cistercian Publications, 1978–79.

Govindacharya, Alkondavilli. *The Divine Wisdom of the Dravida Saints.* Madras: C. N. Press, 1902.

Graham, Jorie. *The Errancy.* Hopewell, NJ: Ecco Press, 1997.

———. *Never.* New York: Ecco/HarperCollins, 2002.

Griffiths, Paul J. *Song of Songs.* Grand Rapids, MI: Brazos Press, 2011.

Henry, Brian. "Exquisite Disjunctions, Exquisite Arrangements: Jorie Graham's 'Strangeness of Strategy.'" *Antioch Review* 56.3 (1998): 281–93.

Hopkins, Gerard Manley. *The Journals and Papers of Gerard Manley Hopkins.* Edited by Humphrey House and completed by Graham Storey. New York: Oxford University Press, 1959.

———. *The Poetical Works of Gerard Manley Hopkins.* Edited by Norman H. Mackenzie. New York: Oxford University Press, 1989.

John of Ford. *Sermons on the Final Verses of the Song of Songs.* Vols. 1–7. Translated by Wendy Mary Beckett. Cistercian Fathers Series. Kalamazoo, MI: Cistercian Publications, 1977–84.

———. *Sermones Super Extremam Partem Cantici Canticorum.* Edited by Edmund Mikkers and Hilary Costello. Corpus Christianorum Continuatio Mediaevalis. Volumes 17 (Sermons 1–69) and 18 (Sermons 70–120). Tournai, Belgium: Typographi Brepols, 1970.

Karagueuzian, Catherine Sona. *No Image There and the Gaze Remains.* New York: Routledge, 2005.

Landy, Francis. *Paradoxes of Paradise: Identity and Difference in the Song of Songs.* Sheffield, England: Almond Press, 1983.

Longenbach, James. "The Errancy." Review of *The Errancy*, by Jorie Graham. *The Nation*, July 21, 1997.

Ludden, David E., and M. Shanmugam Pillai, trans. *Kuruntokai: An Anthology of Classical Tamil Love Poetry.* Madurai: Koodal Publishers, 1976.

Mariaselvam, Abraham. *The Song of Songs and Ancient Tamil Love Poems: Poetry and Symbolism.* Rome: Editrice Pontificio Istituto Biblico, 1988.

Munro, Jill M. *Spikenard and Saffron: A Study in the Poetic Language of the Song of Songs.* Sheffield, England: Sheffield Academic Press, 2005.

Narayanan, Vasudha. *The Way and the Goal: Expressions of Devotion in the Early Sri Vaisnava Tradition.* Washington, DC: Institute for Vaishnava Studies, 1987.

Nichols, Aidan. *Say It Is Pentecost: A Guide Through Balthasar's Logic.* Washington, DC: Catholic University of America Press, 2001.

Paulsell, Stephanie. Commentary on the *Song of Songs.* In *Lamentations and the Song of Songs*, edited by by Harvey Cox and Stephanie Paulsell, 169–283. Louisville, KY: Westminster John Knox Press, 2012.

Periyalvar. *Periyalvar Tirumoli*. Kanchipuram: Srivaishnava Sampradaya Sanjivini Sabha, 1995 [1909].

Picard, Max. *Der Mensch und Das Wort*. Erlenbach-Zurich: Im Eugen Rentsch Verlag, 1955.

Quash, Ben. "Hans Urs von Balthasar's 'Theatre of the World': The Aesthetics of a Dramatics." In *Theological Aesthetics After von Balthasar*, edited by Oleg V. Bychkov and James Fodor, 19–31. Burlington, VT: Ashgate Publishing, 2008.

———. "The Theo-Drama." *The Cambridge Companion to Hans Urs von Balthasar*, edited by David Moss and Edward T. Oakes, 143–57. New York: Cambridge University Press, 2004.

———. *Theology and the Drama of History*. New York: Cambridge University Press, 2005.

Rahner, Karl. *Hörer des Wortes*. Munich: Kösel, 1963.

Raman, Srilata. *Self-Surrender (Prapatti) to God in Śrīvaiṣṇavism: Tamil Cats and Sanskrit Monkeys*. New York: Routledge, 2007.

Ramke, Bin. "Celebrating a World in Danger." Review of *Never*, by Jorie Graham. *Boston Review* 27.5 (2002). Available at http://bostonreview.net/BR27.5/ramke.html (accessed May 24, 2013).

Shatakopan. *Bhagavat Vishayam*. Edited by S. Krishnaswami Ayyangar. Trichy: Sri Nivasam Accukkutam, 1975–87.

Spiegelman, Willard. "Repetition and Singularity." *Kenyon Review* 25.2 (2003): 149–68.

Turner, Denys. *Eros and Allegory: Medieval Exegesis of the Song of Songs*. Kalamazoo, MI: Cistercian Publications, 1995.

Vendler, Helen. *The Breaking of Style: Hopkins, Heaney, Graham*. Cambridge, MA: Harvard University Press, 1995.

———. *The Music of What Happens: Poems, Poets, Critics*. Cambridge, MA: Harvard University Press, 1988.

Venkatachari, K. K. A. *The Maṇipravāḷa Literature of the Śrīvaiṣṇava Ācāryas: 12th to 15th Century A.D.* Bombay: Ananthacharya Indological Research Institute, 1978.

———. *Śrīvaiṣṇavism: An Insight*. Mumbai: Ananthacharya Indological Research Insitute, 2006.

Vuong-dinh-Lam, Jean. "Doctrine spirituelle de Gilbert de Hoyland." Ph.D. diss., Theologica Pontificii Athenaei, Rome, 1963.

———. "Le monastère: Foyer de vie spirituelle." *Collectanea Ordinis Cisterciensium Reformatorum* 26 (1964): 5–21.

Ward, Bernadette Waterman. "Hopkins, Scotus, and von Balthasar: Philosophical Theology in Poetry." In *Thelogical Aesthetics After von Balthasar*, edited by Oleg V. Bychkov and James Fodor, 67–77. Burlington, VT: Ashgate Publishing, 2008.

Wright, Charles. *Quarter Notes: Improvisations and Interviews*. Ann Arbor: Unversity of Michigan Press, 1995.

INDEX

Absence: causing desolation, 93–94; as
drama of inner disturbance, 54; evoking longing, 31–32, 55, 62–63, 116–17;
and nearness, 5, 61, 80, 159n49,
170n180; necessity of, for presence, 44,
95, 115–116, 132, 165n132; necessity
of, as spiritual practice, 7, 9, 53–55,
62, 70, 75, 145n19, 152n77, 169n169;
sharpens desire, 55, 85, 109;
Assis, Elie, 18, and in the notes
throughout, on the verses of the *Song*

Balthasar, Hans Urs von, 22–31, 47,
105–6, 113–25; and Gerard Manley
Hopkins, 26–31, 114–15; and Jesus,
115–25; theology of, 23, 175n37;
Works: *Glory of the Lord*, 23–24; *Theo-
Drama*, 24–25, 119–21; *Theo-Logic*,
23, 115–25; on Balthasar: Quash, Ben,
25, 30, 115, 149–50nn34–36; Ward,
Bernadette Waterman, 28–30, 42,
150n60
Beloved: consumed by, 99–100; desire
for, 6, 70, 80, 85; rebuffed by, 8; return
of, 52–53, 132; sent away, 52, 55, 131,
156n1; 177n2; union with, 32, 83, 85,
97, 132, 169n169; visit from, 6, 102–3;
withdrawal by, 9, 67;
Bernard of Clairvaux, 19–22, and
throughout, on the verses of the *Song*
Bride, 22, 55, 71 85, 92–93, 162n92,
167n141, 169n169, 170n170, 177n5;

and bridegroom, 6–8, 52–56, 71, 85,
92, 157n16, 167n141; and spouse,
7–8, 52, 55, 67, 72, 83, 93, 169n169,
170n170, 177n5

Carson, Anne, 43–44, 117, 155n106,
174n17

Dependence, 10, 33–34, 74, 172n201,
172n211
Desire, 5–10, 18, 31–33, 46–47, 53–63,
69–76, 85–87, 91–95, 100–3, 113–18,
134–35, 152n77, 156n1, 159n49,
160n76, 162nn92, 97, 163n108,
164n125, 166n133, 167n150, 169n169,
177n2; and languor, 91–93, 162n104,
170n170
Devotion, 9, 13, 31, 68, 70–77, 93, 98,
104, 141, 152n77, 159n47
Drama, 6, 8, 14, 16, 22–34, 44–47, 54–55,
58, 63, 68, 70, 87, 104–6, 111–23,
126–27, 140–41, 152nn77, 78, 156n1,
160n76, 165n132

Enjoyment, 20, 33, 55–56, 66, 93–95, 98,
152n77, 156n1, 169n169
Exum, Cheryl, 18, and in the notes
throughout, on the verses of the *Song*

Gilbert of Hoyland, 19–22, and throughout, on the verses of the *Song*
God, 5–8, 20–36, 39–40, 44; in absence

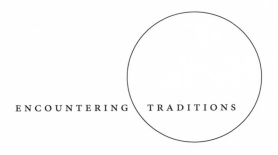

ENCOUNTERING TRADITIONS

Rapid globalization and portents of a post-secular age drive unprecedented encounters within and between traditions. Encountering Traditions seeks to capture this wave of creativity and offers authors a venue to speak unapologetically from any one of the Abrahamic scriptural traditions and beyond. Potential authors are invited to explore topics that would interest a broad readership as well as specialists. Series editors welcome studies that highlight the dynamism of encounters between traditions—religious as well as secular, mainstream as well as marginal ones. Authors who draw on a rich heritage of scholarly disciplines in order to clarify and illustrate their observations will enjoy priority, as will proposals that offer attention both to tradition and to social and historical context. Encountering Traditions seeks to show the multiple ways that the energies of faith and reason, texts and history enhance our life worlds through creative scholarship.

MUHAMMAD IQBAL, *The Reconstruction of Religious Thought in Islam*